MAPPING EXILE AND RETURN

MAPPING EXILE AND RETURN

PALESTINIAN DISPOSSESSION AND A POLITICAL THEOLOGY FOR A SHARED FUTURE

ALAIN EPP WEAVER

Fortress Press
Minneapolis

MAPPING EXILE AND RETURN

Palestinian Dispossession and a Political Theology for a Shared Future

Scripture quotations are from the New Revised Standard Version Bible, copyright © 1989 by the Division of Christian Education of the National Council of the Churches of Christ in the USA. Used by permission. All rights reserved.

Cover image: Olive Branches and Israeli Separation Barrier © Thinkstock
Cover design: Rob Dewey

Library of Congress Cataloging-in-Publication Data

Print ISBN: 978-1-4514-7012-3

eBook ISBN: 978-1-4514-7968-3

The paper used in this publication meets the minimum requirements of American National Standard for Information Sciences — Permanence of Paper for Printed Library Materials, ANSI Z329.48-1984.

Manufactured in the U.S.A.

This book was produced using PressBooks.com, and PDF rendering was done by PrinceXML.

For Sonia K.

They scattered us on the wind to every corner of the earth, but they did not eradicate us.

———FR. (ABUNA) MANUEL MUSALLAM,
JENIN CAMP, SEPTEMBER 8, 1993

CONTENTS

Praise for *Mapping Exile and Return*

"Like many modern technological advances, maps have significant origination in military needs dating back to the early years of Euro-Christian colonialism and conquest. Yet maps are entirely artificial devices, mere representations of any actual terrain—and always created from particular perspectives to serve particular needs and all too often creating rigid but nevertheless artificial boundaries and borders. Alain Epp Weaver reminds us that maps have also come especially to serve a powerful political service to modern states, including the state of Israel in its claim to Palestinian lands. The power of this volume, however, is that Epp Weaver traces for us the use of mapping technologies as acts of resistance on the part of Palestinians, created from the perspective of exile. The result is a creative call for re-imagining the modernist notions of states, borders, and boundaries."

—**Tink Tinker**, Clifford Baldridge Professor of American Indian Cultures and Religious Traditions, Iliff School of Theology

"Although Epp Weaver's proposals will be resisted by those on both sides of the Israeli-Palestinian conflict, *Mapping Exile and Return* will revitalize discussions about what it means for the people of God to live as exiles (as in ancient Israel) or as aliens and strangers (for the apostolic community), and whether there are implications and applications for especially Christian witness amidst the Middle Eastern *Realpolitik* of our present time. The pages of this volume may even chart a viable political vision for the future—those who take up and read may be so inspired and will have new occasion to discern."

—**Amos Yong**, J. Rodman Williams Professor of Theology, Regent University

"In a field already saturated with textbooks, monographs and excellent research it is refreshing to encounter a highly original and novel perspective of the endless and hopeless story of Palestine. The theological cartography of the land in the land introduces the reader to the subterranean forces that shape the conflict on the land. Through theoretical probing of interpreting the past and envisaging the future, the book also offers a focused view on how its new paradigm is at work in one particular and illuminative case study. This is a hugely important scholarly intervention that would greatly assist those who are interested in, and care for, Palestine."

—**Ilan Pappé**, Professor of History and Director of the European Center for Palestine Studies, University of Exeter

"With theological sensitivity Alain Epp Weaver unveils authentic Jewish sources beyond ideological Zionist readings of the purported binary of exile/ return. Here a minority Christian voice enlists minority Jewish voices to open that polarity to reveal a 'shared future,' a future foreclosed by the current use of that polarity. Epp Weaver's study suggests new ways of living together in west Asia, imaginatively mining the psyche and resilience of Palestinians and Israeli Jews alike to replace violent binaries with fresh hope."

—**David Burrell, C.S.C.**, Hesburgh Chair of Theology and Philosophy emeritus, University of Notre Dame

"The right of Palestinian refugees to return to their homes is in many ways the central issue of the Israeli–Palestinian conflict. Epp Weaver takes on this topic from the novel perspective of political theology. Examining a wide variety of cartographic imaginings of return demonstrates the vitality of practical thinking on this issue. It highlights the diversity and creativity of Palestinian Christian thinking on—and mapping of—return. This nuanced and moving book will be valuable to scholars and activists concerned with refugee rights, and to all of those interested in theological conceptions of place, rights, and liberation."

—**Amahl Bishara**, Assistant Professor of Anthropology, Tufts University

Acknowledgements

This study has its roots in the West Bank village of Zababdeh, a small, predominantly Christian town south of Jenin to which my spouse and I were sent by the Mennonite Central Committee in 1992 to teach English at the Latin (Roman Catholic) Patriarchate School for three years. That initial assignment led to a total of eleven years of work with Palestinian Christians and Palestinian refugees and has stimulated an enduring fascination with how Palestinian Christians (and Middle Eastern Christians more broadly) actively participate in and engage the wider society and with how they theologically interpret their contexts.

Scores of Palestinian Christian and Muslim neighbors, friends, and acquaintances patiently helped me learn to speak colloquial Palestinian Arabic (albeit not, as the proverb would have it, "like the nightingale"), to read Modern Standard Arabic (haltingly), and to understand (incompletely) the world around me. I owe a particular debt of gratitude to Msgr. Manuel Musallam, who in 1992 served as Zababdeh's priest and school headmaster (and whom I will always think of simply as "Abuna"), and to Radwan and Maysoon Isa'yed, our landlords in the village: visits with them over Arabic coffee and sage-flavored tea taught me more about Palestinians generally and Palestinian Christians particularly than I would ever learn from reading.

I have greatly profited from the critiques, affirmations, and insights of numerous persons while completing this book. Special thanks go to Kathryn Tanner, Dwight Hopkins, Malika Zeghal, Dipesh Chakrabarty, Jean Bethke Elshtain, Susan Schreiner, David Reinhart, Jon Pahl, Larisa Reznik, Antonia Daymond, and Michael Sohn. Any abiding flaws in my argument should of course be attributed to me.

The love of family has sustained me over years of research and writing. My parents-in-law, J. Denny and Mary Weaver, have affirmed my research. Anthony and Dianne Epp, my parents, have been a constant source of love and solace. I have reveled in the opportunity to discuss some of the ideas in this book with my children, Samuel Rafiq and Katherine Noor, as they have become young adults. Most of all, I am grateful to my wife, Sonia. She inspires me by her example of steadfast determination (what Palestinians call *sumud*) and has enthusiastically urged me throughout this long-gestating project. I have been privileged to experience the vicissitudes of parenting and of life together with

Sonia in good times and in bad. Without her sense of adventure, I would have never left the United States for the Middle East and this study would have never come to be. It is fitting, therefore, that the book be dedicated to her.

Note on Transliteration

Rather than burden the text with extensive diacritical markings when reproducing Arabic nouns and names of places and persons, I have instead opted for simple, straightforward transliterations. Where possible, I have used common English spellings of Arabic words. *Hamza* is indicated by ', while *'ayn* is marked by '.

Introduction

And so I come to the place itself,
but the place is not
its dust and stones and open space.

— Taha Muhammad Ali[1]

In one of his best-known works, "The Place Itself," the shopkeeper and poet Taha Muhammad Ali explores the tensions embodied in conceptions and practices of memory, homecoming, and return. As Ali stands amidst the ruins of Saffuriya, the village from which he was expelled in 1948 at the age of eleven, he recognizes that the physical topology of the present-day site no longer corresponds with the Saffuriya of his memory. Today, like so many other internally displaced Palestinians from the lower Galilee, Ali lives in Nazareth, less than ten kilometers away from the remains of his natal and ancestral home.[2] This proximity, however, is only physical: the people who turned the "open space" into the "place" of Saffuriya—Taha's best friend Qasim; his early adolescent object of adoration, Amira, with the "ease" of her braid; peasants in their fields—are nowhere to be found. The village of his memory, a pastoral landscape of persons, animals, herbs, and fruit and nut trees, has, like hundreds of other Palestinian towns and villages, been erased from the map, leaving only traces on the landscape in the form of crumbling ruins, trees spared the axe and the chainsaw, and clumps of prickly-pear cactus.

Ali's bewildered plea of "where?" drives a plaintive litany running through the poem. Where "are the red-tailed birds/and the almonds' green?" Ali asks. Where are the "hyssop and thyme?" The "rites and feasts of the olives?" These questions drive home the realization that a restorationist return of the past to the present is out of the question. The remembered village has been snatched away, just as, at the end of Ali's poem, a speckled hen is grabbed by a kite diving from the heavens. Saffuriya may be gone forever, but the poet can, like the tragicomic figure of the peasant woman yelling at the kite in the poem, curse the Israeli Jewish subject responsible for Saffuriya's destruction, with the hope that the Israeli erasure/digestion of the Palestinian landscape will not be

1

completely successful and will at least cause a serious case of heartburn or constipation: "You, there, in the distance: I hope you can't digest it!"[3]

PALESTINIAN THEOLOGICAL AUTOBIOGRAPHIES OF EXILE

Ali's reflections at the ruins of Saffuriya poetically map Ali's exile from "the place itself," while also ruminating on what appears to be the impossibility of return—at least the impossibility of return understood as the reclamation of prelapsarian village life, the reconstitution of individual and communal existence as it was prior to what Palestinians term the *nakba*, or catastrophe, of 1948, the events of which left hundreds of thousands of Palestinians refugees and hundreds of villages in ruins.[4] "They scattered us on the wind to every corner of the earth," proclaims the Latin (Roman Catholic) priest Manuel Musallam, reflecting not only on the forced dispersion of Palestinians during the *nakba* but over the ensuing six decades as well. Yet, despite this involuntary exile, Musallam continues, "they did not eradicate us."[5]

Assertion of endurance and presence in the midst of exile has marked Palestinian responses to the *nakba*. Not only does the language of exile and return permeate Palestinian poetry, political speeches, memory books, and websites dedicated to specific villages destroyed in 1948, exile is the location from which Palestinians imagine and remember home.[6] This exilic imagination also shapes a particular form of Palestinian Christian theological reflection one could call "theological autobiography of exile." Across the ecumenical spectrum, Palestinian Christian theologians narrate the exiles they and their families have endured, with such narratives providing the framework for their theological interpretation of Scripture and Zionism and for their theological visions of the future. The stylistic similarities among these theological autobiographies reflect growing ecumenical cooperation across confessional lines within Palestinian Christianity over the past two decades, a cooperation driven in large part by the pressing need to present a united political front to the Israeli state and toward the global Christian community.[7] The rhetorical parallelism between Palestinian Christian and Palestinian Muslim accounts of exile, meanwhile, reveals that Palestinian Christian identity participates in a broader construction of Palestinian identity marked by exile and dispossession.[8]

These autobiographical narratives of exile, meanwhile, issue in differing understandings of what return, as a counterpoint to exile, might mean. For some Palestinian Christian theologians, as for the Palestinian Muslim poet Ali, return represents an impossible dream: the "place itself" is gone. For others, however, the state of exile provokes political activism for the sake of return.

Among Palestinian Christian theologians, the Anglican priest Audeh Rantisi is most pointed in naming return an impossibility. Rantisi offers perhaps the most vivid example of a theological autobiography of exile in his narration of the forced trek he and his family undertook from their centuries-old home in Lydda to Ramallah, a trek Rantisi named "the Lydda death march":

> By now the heat had reached 100 degrees. The scene was chaotic. Women in black *abbahs* and heavily embroidered Palestinian dresses hysterically clutched their infants as they stumbled forward to avoid the expected spray of machine-gun fire. . . . Atop the gate sat soldiers with machine guns, firing over our heads and shouting at us to hurry through the gate. I did not know it at the time, but our death march had begun. Behind us, forever, was our home, our family business, our clothing, and our food, along with those possessions we were never able to replace. . . . The one thing I do remember my father taking with him was the key to the front door of our home.[9]

Decades later, Rantisi wrote that the pain of the expulsion "sears" his memory, branding him for life as a refugee.[10] The contrast between the rooted, respected life the Rantisis enjoyed in Lydda, where they had lived since the fourth century ce, and the family's new lot as refugees hit Audeh hard: "In Lydda my family lived in a large house, with sixteen centuries of tradition, our olive oil soapmaking business, and positive self-esteem. In Ramallah we lived in a tiny tent, with no local roots, no way of making a living, and a constant sense of worthlessness."[11] For Rantisi, as for many Palestinian refugees, this formative event of being uprooted from his natal town fueled dreams of home and hatred of the Zionist soldiers who had carried out the expulsion orders.[12] For some refugees, like the young George Habash, another Lydda native whom Rantisi met on the death march and who later founded the Popular Front for the Liberation of Palestine (PFLP), such dreams of return eventually translated into military action. For Rantisi, in contrast, anger and bitterness eventually gave way to a pained recognition that "[w]e whom Israel evicted in 1948 can never return to our homes."[13] After the Israeli conquest of the West Bank in 1967, Rantisi eagerly took the opportunity to join other Ramallah-based refugees in visiting former homes in Lydda. "As the bus drew up in front of the house, I saw a young boy playing in the yard. I got off the bus and went over to him. 'How long have you lived in this house?' I asked. 'I was born here,' he replied. 'Me too,' I said."[14] Rantisi continued to identify with his ancestral house, but the life it represented, Rantisi underscored, was irrevocably lost. Rantisi might affirm the theoretical right of Palestinian refugees to return to their homes, but such an affirmation for Rantisi is coupled with the grim recognition that return is unlikely at best—and, more realistically, impossible.

In contrast, the Palestinian Quaker theologian and activist Jean Zaru weds a theological autobiography of exile to a commitment to refugee return. Zaru stresses that the "narrative of my life and of that of my Palestinian family is a narrative of exclusion": this does not differentiate her or her family from other Palestinians, but simply makes her family's story representative of a shared experience of exile.[15] While Zaru and her immediate family were not displaced from their home in Ramallah, all of her maternal grandmother's relatives joined Rantisi and Habash on the "death march" from Lydda to Ramallah. Zaru's father and older brother organized relief convoys from Ramallah to bring emergency water and food supplies to Lydda's fleeing refugees, and the Zaru family hosted over 150 refugees within their home and gardens for weeks after the expulsion, with the Quaker Meetinghouse welcoming scores more. After 1948, meanwhile, the Zaru family in Ramallah was now separated from its Nazareth branch by new political borders.[16]

The Palestinian sense of being an "uprooted people," Zaru argues, stems from the fundamental reality of the "deliberate displacement of the Palestinians by Israel as a matter of policy."[17] This policy of "deliberate displacement," argues Zaru, expressed itself most potently in the Israeli expulsions of hundreds of thousands of Palestinians in 1948, but has continued since then in numerous other forms: from land confiscation (inside Israel and also, since 1967, in the Occupied Territories) to the revocation of residency permits to the construction of physical and legal barriers separating Palestinian from Palestinian.[18] So, for example, Israel deported Zaru's brother-in-law, a former mayor of Ramallah, to Jordan in 1968: six years later Israeli authorities prevented his return home to attend his mother's funeral.[19] Or, to take a more quotidian example, the bureaucratic battles Zaru, like all other Palestinians, must wage in order to obtain travel permits, including permits to visit Jerusalem, only ten kilometers from Ramallah, leave her feeling "like a stranger in my own country."[20]

For Zaru, the political diagnosis is straightforward: "Israel is doing all it can to dispossess us. It considers Christians and Muslims who live in occupied Palestine as resident aliens. We are not recognized as native, nor as an indigenous people having the right to live where we were born."[21] Confronted by such an exclusionary regime, Palestinians will "always begin with the loss of our land and our rights," including the refugees' demand of "their right of return to their towns and villages."[22]

PALESTINIAN REFUGEE RETURN AS A MIRROR OF ZIONIST RETURN?

Zaru's stress on the Palestinians' daily experience of living in Israel and the Occupied Territories as "resident aliens," and on the right of uprooted and dispossessed Palestinian refugees and internally displaced persons to return to their homes and properties, points to the key questions with which this study will grapple. Palestinians have encountered the Zionist return to the land as a cartographic regime of erasure that works to remove all Palestinian traces from the landscape and the map. Palestinians have been "abolished from the map," in the words of Palestinian cartographer Salman Abu-Sitta.[23] Zionism, as an Orientalist discourse and practice, produced an "imaginative geography," a cartographic conceptualization of Palestine as a land without a people for a people without a land.[24] As Julie Peteet observes, "The spatial strategy of the Zionist enterprise was to reduce the indigenous population by installing them elsewhere."[25] Zionism understood as a political project of establishing and maintaining a polity in historical Palestine with a Jewish demographic majority is, in the terminology coined by Israeli geographer Oren Yiftachel, ethnocratic. As an ethnocracy, the Israeli state established by the Zionist movement "facilitates and promotes" the "expansion and control" of a dominant nation over contested territory and resources.[26] Within the Israeli ethnocratic regime, Palestinians are resident aliens to be controlled through legal, geographical, and architectural practices of separation.[27]

Ethnocratic regimes rely on strategies of partition and separation in order to maintain territorial control. Prior to 1948, Zionists of the left imagined possibilities of the "voluntary transfer" of the Palestinian Arab population from the land, while a Revisionist Zionist like Ze'ev Jabotinsky articulated an "iron wall" strategy of creating a well-defended fortress within the land.[28] Between 1948 and early 1950, visions of "transfer" became a reality, as hundreds of thousands of Palestinians, nearly two-thirds of the Palestinian population, became refugees or internally displaced persons, with some of them forcibly expelled from their towns and villages and with others fleeing in face of advancing Israeli troops. Between 1948 and 1967, the Israeli state expropriated millions of dunams of refugee property through the Absentee Property Law of 1950 and other legal mechanisms while tightly circumscribing the movement of the Palestinian Arabs who had remained in the new State of Israel through the enforcement of British Mandate–era emergency military regulations.[29]

Israel's conquest of East Jerusalem, the West Bank, and the Gaza Strip in 1967 presented a challenge to Zionism understood in demographic terms, as a project of securing a decisive Jewish demographic majority within a circumscribed territory: Israel's sovereign control now incorporated a large

Palestinian Arab population.[30] Annexing the territories was out of the question, because extending citizenship to the Palestinians in the Occupied Territories would undermine the Zionist character of the State of Israel. The spatial strategies Israel has pursued since 1967 have consistently resulted in Palestinians being refugees in their own land. The Israeli state's consistent strategy for how to handle these new territories has followed the dictum first laid out in the Allon Plan of the late 1960s: "maximum territory for Israel with a minimum number of Arabs."[31] As Israeli geographer Eyal Weizman explains, "The logic of partition of the Occupied Territories has always swung between selective presence and absence, addressing two contradictory Israeli strategies: territorial (attempting to annex as much empty land as possible); and demographic (attempting to exclude the areas most heavily populated by Palestinians)."[32] Precisely this logic of selective presence and absence, of attempting to control a maximum amount of land while incorporating a minimum number of Palestinians, has guided Zionist mapping practices from the movement's inception up to the present. The Israeli state, Palestinian sociologist Sari Hanafi asserts, has pursued a spatial strategy in the Occupied Territories of "spacio-cide": the transformation, through the expansion of settlement blocks and the construction of bypass roads, walls, fences, and checkpoints, of "the Palestinian territories into noncontiguous enclaves."[33]

Political theorist Adi Ophir has described Israel's spatial strategy as "inclusive exclusion": the exclusion of the alien matter represented by Palestinians into camps bounded by legal and physical barriers but nevertheless included within the scope of Israeli sovereign control.[34] Ophir's analysis dovetails with James Ron's description of how the Israeli state apparatus (including the military government in the Occupied Territories) works to expand the Israeli frontier through the construction of settlements and checkpoint and road networks, expansion that in turn creates ghettoized spaces.[35] The rhetorical embrace in principle of a two-state solution to the conflict by Israeli politicians of the center-left as well as the center-right, from Ehud Barak to Ariel Sharon to Binyamin Netanyahu, does not conflict with Israel's spatial strategy but rather represents its apotheosis: through the peace process, Israel seeks Palestinian acceptance of the ghettoized spaces to which they have been confined as the extent of the proposed Palestinian state.[36] Not surprisingly, many Palestinians have begun to determine that new geographic realities have erased the territorial basis of a tenable two-state solution to the Palestinian-Israeli conflict.[37]

The Zionist cartography of the Israeli ethnocratic regime thus substituted the heterogeneous Palestinian landscape with the imagined smooth, homogeneous space of the Israeli nation-state. As Peteet underscores, "An Israeli state in Palestine replaced a culturally, linguistically, and religiously diverse space with an *ostensibly* undifferentiated and utopian world."[38] The word "ostensibly" suggests that while the triumph of the Zionist designification of the Palestinian landscape has been overwhelming, the erasure of Palestinian presence is not complete. Israeli historian Gabriel Piterberg emphasizes that although "the physical and discursive 'Zionization' of Palestine was on the whole successful," it simultaneously gave "birth to what is embodied in the discourse" of the *nakba* as "an indomitable countermemory to Israeli Independence, an attempt to resist erasure."[39] Confronted by Zionist cartographic practices of exclusion which reduce them to at best the status of resident aliens, Palestinians have vigorously entered into the realm of cartographic production in order to inscribe themselves on the map, waging a battle "over the right to a remembered presence, and with that presence, the right to possess and reclaim a collective historical reality" and to chart possible modalities of return.[40]

The insistence of Zaru, then, on the Palestinian refugee right of return echoes broader Palestinian refugee efforts to return their presence to the landscape. In this study, I analyze how Palestinian Christian theologians and church leaders like Zaru map exile and return, asking what futures are embedded within and proposed by their theopolitical cartographies. Specifically, I ask if Palestinian refugee return, as championed by a theologian like Zaru or projected cartographically in various forms of Palestinian refugee memory production, must inevitably mirror Zionist return to the land understood as return to an empty space onto which the project of the nation-state can unfold, a form of return necessarily imbricated with the expulsion and exclusion of others. Or, as I will explore throughout this book, might there be a form of return to the land that maps complex spaces in which difference is welcomed and disrupts and transcends the rigid boundaries of nationalist ideologies? If so, how might such a cartography of return be shaped by a political theology of exile?

Developing and defending such an understanding of return, I argue, requires careful theological analysis of exile and its interplay with return. To be sure, one can trace a long history of Christian appropriation of the language of diaspora and exile to describe the church's embodied political witness in the world. The risen Christ's missionary dispersal of his disciples throughout the world (Matthew 26) underscores that the *place* of the *ekklesia* is not fixed and static. Rather, the place of God's people as a chosen race and a holy nation (1 Peter 2) is a *diasporized*, or *exilic*, place: because God is sovereign over all of creation and history, all times and places become potential homelands for the Christian, even as anticipation for the consummation of God's redemptive work means that Christians maintain an exilic vigil wherever they reside. This early Christian understanding of the diasporic vocation and location of the church is memorably captured in the *Epistle to Diognetus*: "Christians are distinguished from the rest of men neither by country nor by language nor by customs. For nowhere do they dwell in cities of their own; they do not use any strange form of speech or practice a singular mode of life. . . . They live in fatherlands of their own, but as aliens. They share all things as citizens, and suffer all things as strangers. Every foreign land is their fatherland, and every fatherland a foreign land."[41] In this early Christian ecclesiology, Christians live as resident aliens of all lands, yet, sharing all things with their fellow citizens, they seek the *shalom* of the cities of their dispersion (Jer. 29:7). Nearly two millennia later, Stanley Hauerwas and William Willimon reaffirm the status of Christians as resident aliens within the countries in which they reside, with exile understood not primarily in terms of punishment or estrangement but rather as a missionary location.[42]

One could, of course, supplement this truncated history of exile as an ecclesiological and missiological trope with scores of other examples from church history. However, this abbreviated account of how exile and diaspora have been used to name the church's location is sufficient to underscore the historical connections between ecclesiologies of exile, on the one hand, and the spiritualization of biblical land promises, on the other. As W. D. Davies argued in his magisterial study of early Christian understandings of land, the early church understood Jesus Christ in his death and resurrection to have broken not only the bonds of death but also the "bonds of the land," in the process shattering "the geographic dimension of the religion of his fathers." Scripture and the early church, Davies insists, saw the holiness of the land and the promises of the land to the people Israel as being taken up and fulfilled in Jesus. With the risen Christ now accompanying his people as Lord throughout the world, all land becomes holy for Christians, even as they are freed from binding attachment to any particular territory.[43] To be a resident alien, within this theological perspective, is to follow the risen Christ into mission in the world, to resist becoming permanently settled in any specific place in the sense of becoming accommodated to the myriad ways that economic and political structures prevent people from dwelling securely in the lands in which they live.

While contemporary theologians like Hauerwas and John Howard Yoder turn to exile as a trope for describing the church's calling, their critics counter that they do not offer resources for thinking about how to live faithfully in the land. For Palestinian refugees—as for the millions of other refugees and internally displaced persons around the world—exile does not name a missionary vocation to be embraced but is rather a political condition of hardship and estrangement to be resisted and combated. As inheritors of a theological tradition that has spiritualized land promises, what theological resources do Palestinian Christians—attached to particular trees, rocks, homes, fields, and villages—have for articulating a positive vision for return? Over the course of this study, I will show how the view from exile can shape projects of return to and of life in the land. While return is often conceptualized as wedded to the political form of the nation-state, I argue for a theological cartography of land and return in which exile and return function as potentially interpenetrating, instead of irreducibly opposed, realities. Such a cartography, I contend, will be a cartography of palimpsests rather than a mapping of smooth, undifferentiated space, a cartography that abjures the "overcomplex and clearly unsustainable practices and technologies that any designed territorial 'solution' for separation inexorably requires" and that instead transcends the politics of partition.[44] Furthermore, by articulating a theology of return to the land through an analysis of Palestinian Christian cartographies of exile and return, I will simultaneously gesture toward the possibility of a Zionist return to the land not wedded to the prior conceptualization of the land as a smooth, homogeneous, empty space onto which the project of the nation might unfold.

The theological cartography of exile and return that I will advance and defend is explicitly Christian, rooted in Christian confession. That said, the vision of reconciled Palestinian-Israeli Jewish existence in the land is a public proposal in the sense that it invites persons from other theological, religious, or philosophical commitments to put forward reasons rooted in their own specific thought traditions for a cartography of palimpsests, for a politics of overlapping and interpenetrating landed existence. My constructive proposal, moreover, unapologetically builds on writings by Palestinian Christians, a distinctly minority population within both Israel and the Occupied Territories. While some might question whether proposals originating within a minority community like the Palestinian Christian community can gain traction within the broader Palestinian Muslim and Israeli Jewish societies, I would counter that one should not be surprised, indeed one should expect, to find creative proposals for reconciliation and shared, communal life emanating from minority groups, as such groups arguably have the most to gain from peaceful resolution to intercommunal conflict.

With the research question animating this investigation now stated, some observations about my own social location are in order. In this study I do not purport to occupy an objective position hovering above the Palestinian–Israeli Jewish conflict. Rather, I concur with Daniel Monk's assessment that "[a]nyone who lives this struggle knows that to stand apart is already to be implicated, and that to presume a transcendental standpoint toward the culture of this conflict is to 'speak the language of a false escape.'"[45] Having lived among Palestinian refugees and worshiped with Palestinian Christians for over a decade, I deeply sympathize with the Palestinian refugee desire to return to the towns and villages from which they and their families were uprooted. I trust that the ensuing chapters will prove that these sympathies do not prevent me from critically engaging the forms of Palestinian refugee memory production I will be examining here. Having been inspired by the work of Israeli Jewish friends who organize and act on behalf of Palestinian refugee rights, I also hope that the coming pages will demonstrate that commitment to a just resolution of the Palestinian–Israeli conflict is not "pro-Palestinian" in some unnuanced fashion, but instead part of a vision for Israeli Jewish–Palestinian reconciliation in the land, a vision for a day in which both peoples might live securely under vine and fig tree.

Furthermore, I am keenly aware of my own location within political and theological maps of power and privilege. A descendant of European immigrants who settled on land claimed by Pawnee and Cheyenne nations, I have inherited my own history of cartographic erasure: my critiques of Zionist mappings must thus proceed with confessional humility, with due recognition that I write not from a place of superior judgment but from a location of being implicated in histories of cartographic dispossession. Moreover, as a Western Christian I am an heir to a history of anti-Judaism. This legacy impels me to join in the task of pushing beyond theologies of repudiation and to grapple with the theological challenge of affirming God's enduring covenant with the Jewish people while simultaneously confessing that God's promises to the people Israel have been fulfilled in Jesus Christ. This dual commitment means that I will not reject Jewish claims to the land of Israel on the basis that God's covenant with the Jewish people has been broken, even as I critique the Zionist project of actualizing this claim through return to the land for having been tied to a political vision of landedness that required the dispossession and cartographic erasure of the land's inhabitants, a political vision which, I will argue in chapter 2 below, is incompatible with the trajectory of the scriptural witness regarding how God's people are to live in the land.

CARTOGRAPHY, PLACE, EXILE

Several key words have surfaced over the preceding pages: *diaspora, exile, return, place, space, cartography*, and *mapping*. While the meanings of these terms will be fleshed out in greater detail over the course of the ensuing chapters, some preliminary discussion of how I am deploying these concepts is in order.

CARTOGRAPHY AND MAPS

Cartography in this study has an intentionally broad meaning, in accordance with the expansive understanding of mapping that has developed over the past three decades as geographers and historians and theorists of map-making began to deconstruct the image of the map as ideally embodying a perfect, scaled representation of a particular territory. Cartography may present the "illusion" of completely controlling, inhabiting, or representing a particular space, but ultimately, as geographer Denis Cosgrove explains, "mapping is a creative process of inserting our humanity into the world and seizing the world for ourselves."[46] The term "map" may typically signify two-dimensional objects such as a wall map or a driving map, but, as Cosgrove notes, "all sorts of purely mental and imaginative constructs are now treated as maps," from pictures to narratives and more.[47] Maps and mapping in this study will therefore refer not only to visual depictions of particular territories (e.g., hand-drawn maps or Google Earth plottings of destroyed Palestinian villages examined in chapter 1) but also to the geography imaginatively constructed through political speeches and autobiographical reflection (chapter 3). Such an expansive understanding of mapping is justified, I would contend, insofar as it highlights the subjective and interested character of all cartographic production.[48]

As a creative process of grasping the world, cartography's subjectivity cannot be transcended. As Jonathan Z. Smith insists, "the dictum of Alfred Korzybski is inescapable: 'Map is not territory'—but maps are all we possess."[49] Maps gain authority by their "indexical aspect," an embedded claim within maps that they represent territory accurately even as they are inevitably imprecise.[50] Maps are ultimately "self-portraits," reflections of the cartographer's subjectivity.[51] As acts of "interested selectivity," maps present a subjective picture of territory, showing X but not Y, even as the map works to "naturalize" its operations by masking its embodied interests.[52] The map, in other words, presents itself as a fixed and accurate reproduction of a stable terrain. Critical cartographers in turn unmask these naturalizing operations of the map, uncovering not only the map's constructed character but also the constructed (and thus fluid and contested) nature of the places and territory plotted onto the map.[53]

As a creative act of grasping the world, the cartographic enterprise has not surprisingly been intertwined with nationalism, colonialism, and other political and military projects of conquering and controlling territory. The tasks of imagining and demarcating the territory onto which the venture of the nation-state is to unfold make cartography, with its "technologies of spatial abstraction," constitutive of the state.[54] The space of the nation-state, Henri Lefebvre contends, is "contemporaneous with the space of 'plans' and maps."[55] Israeli cartographer Meron Benvenisti underscores that "[c]artographic knowledge is power: that is why this profession has such close links with the military and war."[56] Colonialism—and Orientalism as a form of colonialism—deploys an "imaginative geography" that divides territory into "civilized" and "barbarian." Colonialist cartography thus either actively erases the colonized population from the map or, in its contemporary Israeli manifestation, reflects broader nationalist trends of shoring up sovereign control by walling off the colonized population with massive concrete barriers, electrified fences, military checkpoints, and complex legal regimes.[57] Thus, in the Occupied Territories today one can speak of the "besieging cartography" by which the Israel Defense Forces (IDF) controls the land (and, more significantly, the Palestinian population), with maps guiding and being constructed by the movements of surveillance drones, attack helicopters, tanks, and bulldozers.[58]

If cartography has thus functioned and continues to serve as a handmaiden to colonialism, can counter-cartographies that oppose and subvert colonialism's map-making be imagined? As Denis Cosgrove observes, maps function both as "a memory device and a foundation for projective action."[59] As will be explored in chapters 1 through 4 below, Palestinians have remembered destroyed homes and villages through the construction of atlases, wall maps, and hand-drawn maps reproduced in memory books and websites dedicated to specific villages and through rhetorical map-making in the form of political speeches and memoirs. Through these pictorial and narrative maps, Palestinian refugees chart possible futures of return even as they stand as alternatives to Zionist cartographies. Such plotted forms of resistance exemplify what cartographers have identified as the "counter-mapping" strategies of indigenous groups opposing and subverting colonial, statist maps. A key question with which I will contend is whether these Palestinian refugee counter-mappings of return simply mirror Zionist cartographies of return, envisioning the territory to which people would return as empty, or whether mappings of return might be more like a palimpsests, mappings that reflect and embrace the heterogeneous character of the places in the land.

SPACE AND PLACE

Palestinian refugees, like Taha Muhammad Ali who yearns for "the place itself," actively remember particular *places*, not an abstract space. If maps are typically defined by *space* understood in abstract, geometrical terms (think of the grid boxes onto which many maps are plotted), they also locate specific *places*. Philip Sheldrake offers a concise differentiation between space and place, arguing that "[s]pace is an abstract analytical concept whereas place is always tangible, physical, specific, and relational."[60] Sheldrake elaborates: "Place is space that has the capacity to be remembered and to evoke what is most precious," calling forth human attention and care.[61] Places, like maps, are imaginative constructions, the products of historical attempts to grasp space and invest it with meaning.[62] As an imaginative construction, place, the philosopher Edward Casey contends, is itself "no fixed thing; it has no steadfast essence."[63] Places have no fixed essence because they are products of historical, political contestations over the meaning of particular spatial coordinates. Using and controlling space, turning it into place through naming, daily use, and commemorative actions, are deeply political actions. Thus, for example, the Israeli state has cleared away the rubble of the destroyed Palestinian village of Saffuriya and erected a national park to commemorate the Hasmonean Jewish town of Tzippori; internally displaced persons such as Ali, meanwhile, remember the same place as the village of Saffuriya. Whereas nationalist cartographies would assume that such contests over the historical meanings of place are zero-sum games in which place must be encoded as *either* Palestinian *or* Israeli Jewish, a cartography of palimpsests, I will argue, can accommodate and acknowledge multiple historical meanings carried by a particular place.

DIASPORA AND EXILE

Although in contemporary theological discourse that develops an exilic ecclesiology (e.g., the "resident aliens" theology of Hauerwas and Willimon, or John Howard Yoder's understanding of diaspora as vocation) the terms *diaspora* and *exile* end up being almost interchangeable, in anthropological or sociological literature the two terms are not typically viewed as equivalent. The definition of *diaspora*, in particular, has proven particularly contentious. William Safran advanced an influential, if hotly contested, definition of diasporas as "expatriate minority communities" that: are dispersed from an original "center" to two or more locations; sustain a "memory, vision, or myth about their original homeland"; believe that full acceptance in the host country is impossible; view the ancestral home as a place of return; are committed to the homeland's restoration; and have their identities constituted in large part by their relationships with their homelands.[64] In this limited definition, Jewish communities outside of *eretz yisrael* represent the paradigmatic example of diaspora, although Safran grants that Armenian, Greek, and Palestinian communities also meet the definitional criteria.[65]

Safran's constricted definition has encountered vigorous critique from numerous fronts. Khachig Tölölian argues that clearly and neatly differentiating diaspora from other terms with which it shares a semantic domain—including *immigrant, expatriate, refugee, migrant worker, exile community, ethnic community*—is extremely difficult at best and unproductive at worst.[66] Gabriel Sheffer questions attempts to differentiate the Jewish diaspora as a special or paradigmatic case, arguing that such an approach occludes isomorphism among different diaspora communities.[67] More significant than these micro-critiques, however, is the move by theorists such as Stuart Hall, James Clifford, and Arjun Appadurai to identify diaspora as a discourse and a location in which hybridity is valorized and from which to contest the dominance of the nation-state order.[68] Alex Weingrod and André Levy explain that in the "old discourse" around diaspora (associated with Safran) diaspora communities were homeland-centric, with the homeland portrayed as "a sacred place filled with memories of past glory and bathed in visions of nobility and renaissance." In the "new" diasporic discourse (associated with Hall, Clifford, and others), the focus on homelands recedes into the background, with greater attention paid to "how the phenomenon of 'diaspora' may contradict and ultimately subvert the internal exclusivity of modern nation-states."[69]

This "new" diasporic discourse, however, has been criticized in turn. Pnina Werbner, for example, claims that Hall, Clifford, and Appadurai, in their haste to valorize diaspora as the site and privileged strategy for the subversion of the nationalist order of things, fail to recognize "the continued imbrication of diasporas in nationalist rhetoric," including the continued emphasis within diaspora communities on the homeland.[70] Julie Peteet advances a similar critique when she argues that if Hall's definition of diaspora involves the "scattering and dispersal of peoples who will *never* literally be able to return to the places from which they came," then Palestinians cannot be classified as a diaspora, given Palestinian refugee insistence on the right of return. By removing the homeland-centric element from diaspora's definition, Peteet argues, Hall turns diaspora into a category of minimal explanatory usefulness.[71] Furthermore, as Daniel Boyarin and Jonathan Boyarin contend, the removal or downplaying of a homeland-focus from the definition of diaspora has the problematic effect of denying the applicability of the term to Jewish communities around the world. While the Boyarins agree that overly narrow definitions of diaspora like Safran's that make Jewish diaspora paradigmatic are flawed, they rightly critique any definitional shifts that would, in a move of conceptual supersessionism, define Jews out of diaspora.[72]

I build on the definitions of diaspora and exile put forward by Thomas Tweed in his study of Marian piety among Cuban exiles in Miami and in his theory of religion. Tweed pushes for a more expansive definition of diaspora than that offered by Safran, yet poses an alternative to those definitions exclusively focused on articulating a post-nationalist polity that transcends the particularities of place. The term *diaspora* "points most fundamentally to a group with some shared culture which lives outside the territory that it considers its native place, and whose continuing bonds with that land are crucial for its collective identity." Exile, meanwhile, functions for Tweed as a subset of diaspora: what distinguishes exile from diaspora is whether or not dispersion from the center was voluntary.[73] Underscoring the involuntary character of their dispersion, meanwhile, is the reason why some Palestinians like Edward Said prefer to speak of Palestinian exile (*ghurba* or *manfa*) rather than of Palestinian diaspora.[74] Tweed also allows for ongoing nationalist focus on the homeland within his understanding of diaspora and exile, stressing that for all exiles, no matter which nation they imagine, diasporic nationalism also entails "'geopiety,' or an attachment to the natal landscape."[75] Tweed broadly defines religions as "always-contested and ever-changing maps that orient devotees as they move spatially and temporally" and that "situate the devout in the body, the home, the homeland, and the cosmos."[76] Diasporic religion, in turn, is trans-temporal, in that it "moves practitioners between a constructed past and an imagined future," and translocative, in that it moves participants outward, "forging bonds with others in the homeland and in exile."[77]

Palestinian mappings of exile and return (by Christians or Muslims) thus exemplify what Tweed identifies as diasporic religion, as these cartographies produced by Palestinian refugees connect exiled refugees to one another and to people in the land and help Palestinian refugees imagine a future return to the land. The irony of Palestinian refugee cartography and of Palestinian Christianity as a diasporic religion is that the territory Palestinians map has also been mapped and then conquered by another diasporic religion-turned-triumphant political movement (Judaism-to-Zionism).[78] The special burden of Palestinian Christianity as a diasporic religion, I will argue, is to attempt to map visions of return to the land that embrace the heterogeneous character of the land's places.

CHAPTER OUTLINE

Critically examining how Palestinian Christians have responded to this burden is the task of this investigation, a study that turns to Palestinian Christian cartographies of exile and return in order to argue for the possibility of a form of return to the land not bound to the exclusionary violence of the nation-state. My argument will unfold in two main movements. Over the course of the first two chapters, I flesh out the question driving this study, namely, whether or not Palestinian refugee mappings of return might embody a political theology of return animated by exile and thus represent an understanding of return different from the understanding of return within what Amnon Raz-Krakotzkin has called Zionism's national colonial theology. In the concluding two chapters, I examine specific mapping practices that substantiate my claim that mappings of return not bound to the exclusivist politics of the nation-state are possible.

The first chapter provides a detailed overview and description of different forms of Palestinian refugee cartography while paying careful attention to the wall maps, tour guides, and atlases created by Salman Abu-Sitta and republished in a wide variety of media, including memory books and on websites dedicated to specific destroyed villages. After situating Palestinian refugee cartography within the context of Israeli Jewish fears over the rights of Palestinian refugees to return and compensation, I evaluate these mappings of exile and return in light of the late Edward Said's appropriation of exile as a critical stance and his warnings about Palestinian refugee return mirroring Zionist forms of return. For Said, "exile" designated both a material condition and a critical mode of reflection, while "return" referred not only to a political project of refugee return but also what he called a metaphysics of endlessly deferred return, a permanent condition of being unsettled and "out of place." I connect the polyvalent, and at times ambiguous, character of exile and return in Said's writings to the ongoing debates among Palestinians about the right of return, a debate between self-described realists like Sari Nusseibeh and Rashid Khalidi, on the one hand, who call for Palestinians to accept "virtual" return in exchange for an Israeli affirmation of the right of return in theory, and those, like Salman Abu-Sitta, on the other hand, who insist that the physical return of refugees to their homes and properties from 1948 is "sacred, legal, possible."

Just as Palestinian Christian theologians and church leaders mapped theological responses to Zionism from the place of exile, so, I argue in chapter 2, can Zionism itself be understood as a political theology of exile. As Amnon Raz-Krakotzkin and Gabriel Piterberg have shown, mainstream Zionisms of the left and the right advanced a threefold political theology of Zionism as a return to the Land of Israel (*ha-shiva le-eretz yisrael*), as a return to history (*ha-shiva la-historia*), and as the negation of the exile (*shelilat ha-galut*). Zionism embraced modern Christendom's equation of history with the history of nation-states, and so rejected Jewish life in exile as being outside of history, arguing that return to the Land of Israel understood as sovereign control over that land would reenergize Jewish life by returning the Jewish people to history. In this Zionist political theology, exile has nothing to teach about landed existence.

In order to contest this claim, I turn to the writings of the late John Howard Yoder, whose own Christian political theology of exile drew upon and sought to mirror the Jewish experience of exile. Just as Jewish life in exile stands as a potential critique of Zionism, so does Yoder's missiology of the church as exilic community counter the church's Constantinian accommodations. But, his critics object, Yoder's valorization of exile left him unable to articulate a positive account of landed existence. To answer Yoder's critics, I turn again to Raz-Krakotzkin's account of exilic existence within the land: if the exilic community's life is shaped by, in Yoder's words, "not being in charge," then an exilic theology of life in the land will reject exclusivist claims to sovereignty and will, as Raz-Krakotzkin contends, embrace the binational character of life in the land rather than pursuing strategies of partition.

The third chapter features a form of Palestinian Christian mapping of exile and return that displays the possibilities of a cartography of palimpsests and of reconciled existence between Palestinians and Israeli Jews. In it I examine forms of narrative, visual, and physical return to the ruins of Kafr Bir'im, a destroyed Palestinian Christian village in the northern Galilee, many of whose former inhabitants still live in the Galilee, actively engaged in legal and political struggles to return to the village. I pay particular attention to the place of trees in memories of the village, return visits, and the theological reflections of one prominent displaced Bir'imite, the Greek Catholic Archbishop for the Galilee, Elias Chacour. The pivotal role played by trees in Chacour's autobiographical narrative and his theological analysis exhibits how the arboreal imagination animates Israeli and Palestinian mappings of space and landscapes of return. The planting of trees asserts connection to the land and covers over traces of prior habitation, while oak, fig, olive, and pomegranate trees become sites of memory within the imagined Palestinian refugee landscape. After recounting Bir'im's destruction, I examine Bir'imite practices and discourses around trees, with particular attention to Chacour's autobiographical-theological narrative. What cartographies can the arboreal imagination produce? Is the arboreal imagination necessarily bound up with exclusivist mappings of erasure only, mappings that encode given spaces as *either* Palestinian *or* Israeli Jewish? Or might the arboreal imagination animating the imagined landscapes of Palestinian refugees also produce cartographies of mutuality that accept, even embrace, the complex character of shared space?

The final chapter presents an interpretation of return visits to destroyed Palestinian villages as liturgical actions. I develop this account through a descriptive analysis of the diverse cartographic practices of the Israeli Zochrot Association, an organization dedicated to "remembering the *Nakba* in Hebrew." Zochrot's counter-mapping practices can be interpreted as liturgical in that they point to and embody in the present a vision of a binational future through imaginative narrations and reconstructions of the past. Through engagement with the work of Jean-Yves Lacoste on the topology of liturgy, I argue that such return visits can enact a liturgical subversion of the ethnocratic order through the embodiment of a cartography of palimpsests in which genuine return to the land means a welcoming of difference instead of its erasure. Building on Paul Virilio's analysis of contemporary war, I argue that the transformation of time and place through these exilic vigils of return visits contests the dromocratic domination of space characteristic of the Israeli ethnocratic regime. Specifically, the palimpsest maps created by Zochrot's political actions open up new ways of conceptualizing and living in the places of Israel-Palestine, modes of landed existence shaped by the exilic vigil.

Such is the roadmap for this study. Before embarking on the journey of the ensuing chapters, however, let us return with Taha Muhammad Ali to Saffuriya as he reflects on "the place itself." Ali's poem can be understood as a melancholic resignation to the permanence of Saffuriya's erasure from the map, as he accepts that "the place is not/its dust and stones and open space." It can also be read as a form of counter-mapping, as Ali's verses recreate the erased landscape and as Ali expresses the hope through the peasant woman that the Zionist regime will not be able to "digest" the landscape it has consumed. To these interpretations, however, I would add a third. Ali's poem can, I would suggest, be read as an exilic liturgy, an incantation from exile spoken not with the expectation that the Saffuriya of old will rematerialize but rather with the hope that a new form of life at the place of Saffuriya-turned-Tzippori will become possible. The peasant woman's curse of the kite—"I hope you can't digest it!"—is, I suggested at the beginning, ultimately a hopeful curse: so long as the Israeli apparatus is unsuccessful in completely erasing Palestinian traces from the landscape, the possibility of new forms of mapping, mappings that inscribe both Palestinian and Israeli Jew onto the landscape, persists. This expectant hope is the hope of the exilic vigil, and it is in the spirit of such hope that I have undertaken this study.

Notes

1. Taha Muhammad Ali, "The Place Itself, or I Hope You Can't Digest It," *So What: New and Selected Poems, 1971–2005* (Port Townsend, WA: Copper Canyon, 2006), 156–59.

2. The distinction between "refugee" and "internally displaced person" is a convention of international law, with the distinction pointing to the location to which the person was displaced: if outside of the country, then international law classifies the person as a refugee; if inside the country, then an internally displaced person. Palestinians uprooted from their homes in 1948–49 who ended up in the refugee camps of Lebanon, Syria, Jordan, the then-Jordanian-controlled West Bank, or the Egyptian-controlled Gaza Strip were thus granted refugee status. Uprooted Palestinians who remained in what had become the new state of Israel were viewed as internally displaced persons. The legal distinction should not, however, obscure the similarities in the lived experiences of refugees and internally displaced persons. Both have been alienated from their homes and properties and both are forbidden from returning. Just as Palestinian refugees have over the past two decades sought solutions for their predicament in international law and conventions, so have internally displaced Palestinians turned to international bodies such as the Committee on Economic, Social, and Cultural Rights of the United Nations to press for their return. See Joseph Schlecha, "The Invisible People Come to Light: Israel's 'Internally Displaced' and the 'Unrecognized Villages,'" *Journal of Palestine Studies* 31, no. 1 (Autumn 2001): 20–31.

3. For an examination of the rootedness of Taha Muhammad Ali's poetry in the place of Saffuriya and of Ali's work within the broader context of Palestinian poetry and literature inside Israel, see Adina Hoffman, *My Happiness Bears No Relation to Happiness: A Poet's Life in the Palestinian Century* (New Haven: Yale University Press, 2009).Two terminological notes: Firstly, while the State of Israel would refer Taha Muhammad Ali and other citizens of Palestinian Arab origin as "Israeli Arabs," I follow the preferred self-designation of the majority of Arabs in Israel as Palestinian citizens of Israel. Secondly, throughout this study I will refer to "Israeli Jews" instead of simply "Israelis" or "Jews" in order to underscore that not all citizens of Israel are Jews, an important fact to underscore given that the State of Israel does not recognize an Israeli nationality, but rather a Jewish nationality alongside a multitude of more than 130 other possible "national" classifications, e.g., "Christian," "Druze," "Samaritan," "Bedouin," etc.

4. Constantine Zureik first applied the word *nakba* to Palestinian dispossession in 1948 in his study, *The Meaning of Disaster* (Beirut: Khayat, 1956). The literature on the 1948 war (what most Israeli Jews would call the War of Independence and what Palestinians typically call the *nakba*) is extensive. As will be clear throughout this volume, I assume as a given the overall persuasiveness of the case mounted by the various figures of the so-called "revisionist" school of Israeli historiography such as Benny Morris, Avi Shlaim, and Ilan Pappé. These historians have through archival research undermined traditional Israeli claims about the 1948 war, showing conclusively that: Zionist forces were not a beleaguered band facing the overwhelming might of Arab armies, but were instead better organized and equipped than their foes; Palestinians did not flee upon orders from Arab military leaders, but were instead forcibly expelled from their homes by Zionist forces or fled in fear in the face of advancing Zionist troops as word of multiple massacres spread; and the doctrine of "transfer" was an integral part not only of the right-wing Revisionist Zionism associated with Ze'ev Jabotinsky, but also of left-of-center socialist Zionism. See Benny

Morris, *The Birth of the Palestinian Refugee Problem Revisited* (Cambridge: Cambridge University Press, 2004); Eugene L. Rogan and Avi Shlaim, eds., *The War for Palestine: Rewriting the History of 1948* (Cambridge: Cambridge University Press, 200); Avi Shlaim, *The Iron Wall: Israel and the Arab World* (New York: W. W. Norton, 2001); Avi Shlaim, *Israel and Palestine: Reappraisals, Revisions, and Refutations* (London: Verso, 2010); Ilan Pappé, *A History of Modern Palestine: One Land, Two Peoples* (Cambridge: Cambridge University Press, 2006); and Ilan Pappé, *The Ethnic Cleansing of Palestine* (Oxford: Oneworld, 2006). While Morris, Shlaim, and Pappé generally agree on matters of fact, they diverge in their assessments of the war: while Pappé, for example, is sharply critical of Zionist actions during the war, Morris is broadly sympathetic, even arguing that Zionist expulsions of Palestinian Arabs did not go far enough. In addition to these Israeli Jewish studies, see also Nur Masalha, *The Expulsion of the Palestinians: The Concept of "Transfer" in Zionist Thought, 1882–1948* (Washington, DC: Institute for Palestine Studies, 1993) and Ahmad H. Sa'di and Lila Abu-Lughod, eds., *Nakba: Palestine, 1948, and the Claims of Memory* (New York: Columbia University Press, 2007).

5. Manuel Musallam, speech given at Jenin Camp, Occupied West Bank, Sept. 8, 1993.

6. Glenn Bowman, "The Exilic Imagination: The Construction of the Landscape of Palestine from Its Outside," in *The Landscape of Palestine: Equivocal Poetry*, ed. Ibrahim Abu-Lughod, Roger Heacock, and Khaled Nashef (Bir Zeit: Bir Zeit University Publications, 1999), 53–77.

7. Drew Christiansen, S.J., "Palestinian Christians: Recent Developments," in *The Vatican-Israel Accords: Political, Legal, and Theological Contexts*, ed. Marshall J. Breger (Notre Dame: University of Notre Dame Press, 2004), 309.

8. Following Joseph Maïla's discussion of Arab Christian identity, I would characterize Palestinian Christian identity as transversal: Palestinian Christians are simultaneously Christian and Palestinian. This transversal character distinguishes Palestinian Christian identity (Palestinian and Christian) from Palestinian Muslim (Palestinian therefore Muslim) identity. See Maïla, "The Arab Christians: From the Eastern Question to the Recent Political Situation of the Minorities," in *Christian Communities in the Arab Middle East: The Challenge of the Future*, ed. Andrea Pacini (Oxford and New York: Clarendon, 1998), 25–47.

9. Audeh Rantisi, "The Lydda Death March," in *Burning Issues: Understanding and Misunderstanding the Middle East: A 40-Year Chronicle*, ed. John Mahoney, Jane Adas, and Robert Norberg (New York: Americans for Middle East Understanding, 2007), 318. While the Rantisi family had been Greek Orthodox for centuries, Audeh decided as a young man to pursue ordination within the Anglican Church.

10. Audeh Rantisi, *Blessed Are the Peacemakers: The Story of a Palestinian Christian* (Grand Rapids: Zondervan, 1990), 23–25.

11. Ibid., 27, 41.

12. Ibid., 45.

13. Ibid., 18. Regarding Rantisi's brief encounter with Habash, see "The Lydda Death March," 322.

14. Rantisi, "The Lydda Death March," 324–25.

15. Jean Zaru, *Occupied with Nonviolence: A Palestinian Woman Speaks*, ed. Diane L. Eck and Marla Schrader (Minneapolis: Fortress Press, 2008), 56.

16. Ibid., 12, 4–5.

17. Ibid., 13.

18. Occupied Territories will here refer to the Gaza Strip and the West Bank, including East Jerusalem: the other territories occupied by Israel in 1967 (the Sinai Peninsula, returned to Egyptian sovereignty as part of the Camp David Accords, and the still-occupied Golan Heights, taken from Syria) do not fall within the purview of my study.

19. Zaru, *Occupied with Nonviolence*, 31.

20. Ibid., 45.

21. Ibid., 49.

22. Ibid., 55–56, 23.

23. Salman Abu-Sitta, "Un Pays Aboli de la Carte," in *Le Droit au Retour: Le Problème des Réfugiés Palestiniens*, ed. Farouk Mardam-Bey and Elias Sanbar (Arles: Actes Sud, 2002), 101–18.

24. Edward W. Said, "Palestine: Memory, Invention, and Space," in *The Landscape of Palestine*, ed. Abu-Lughod, Heacock, and Nashef, 9.

25. Julie Peteet, *Landscape of Hope and Despair: Palestinian Refugee Camps* (Philadelphia: University of Pennsylvania Press, 2005), 35. This spatial strategy has continued throughout the peace process of the past two decades, a strategy best summarized by former Israeli Prime Minister Ehud Olmert as "Maximum land, minimum Arabs." For an analysis of this strategy, see David Newman, "Shared Spaces-Separate Spaces: The Israel-Palestine Peace Process," *GeoJournal* 39, no. 4 (Autumn 1996): 363–75.

26. Oren Yiftachel, *Ethnocracy: Land and Identity Politics in Israel/Palestine* (Philadelphia: University of Pennsylvania Press, 2006), 295. Yiftachel defines *ethnocracy* as a regime that "facilitates the *expansion, ethnicization, and control* of a dominant ethnic nation (often termed the charter or titular group) over contested territory and polity. Regimes are defined as legal, political, and moral frameworks determining the distribution of power and resources" (11). The State of Israel, Yiftachel stresses, is but one of many ethnocracies around the world, albeit part of a smaller subset of ethnocracies that present themselves as democratic (12). Yiftachel builds upon and deepens Sammy Smooha's earlier description of Israel as an "ethnic democracy." See Smooha, "Ethnic Democracy: Israel as Archetype," *Israel Studies* 2, no. 2 (Summer 1997): 198–241.

27. See Neve Gordon, "From Colonization to Separation: Exploring the Structure of Israel's Occupation," in *The Power of Inclusive Exclusion: Anatomy of Israeli Rule in the Occupied Palestinian Territories*, ed. Adi Ophir, Michal Givoni, and Sari Hanafi (New York: Zone Books, 2009), 239–67 and Hilla Dayan, "Regimes of Separation: Israel/Palestine and the Shadow of Apartheid," in *The Power of Inclusive Exclusion*, ed. Ophir, Givoni, and Hanafi, 281–321.

28. Shlaim, *The Iron Wall*, chapter 1.

29. For an overview of the legal means deployed by Israel to confiscate Palestinian land and to control Palestinian access to land inside Israel, see Hussein Abu Hussein and Fiona McKay, *Access Denied: Palestinian Land Rights in Israel* (London: Zed, 2003). Souad Dajani brings that history together with the story of Israeli land seizure in the Occupied Territories in her comprehensive study, *Ruling Palestine: A History of the Legally Sanctioned Jewish-Israeli Seizure of Land and Housing in Palestine* (Geneva: Centre on Housing Rights and Evictions and Bethlehem: Badil Resource Center for Palestinian Residency and Refugee Rights, 2005).

30. See Lily Galili, "A Jewish Demographic State," *Journal of Palestine Studies* 32, no. 1 (Autumn 2002): 90–93 and As'ad Ghanem, "Israel and the 'Danger of Demography,'" in *Where Now for Palestine? The Demise of the Two-State Solution*, ed. Jamil Hilal (London: Zed, 2007), 48–74.

31. Eyal Weizman, *Hollow Land: Israel's Architecture of Occupation* (London: Verso, 2007), 58. Israeli cartographers Yehezkel Lein and Eyal Weizman explain that "Israel has created in the Occupied Territories a regime of separation based on discrimination, applying two separate systems of law in the same area and basing the rights of individuals on their nationality. This regime is the only one of its kind in the world, and is reminiscent of distasteful regimes from the past, such as the apartheid regime in South Africa." See Lein and Weizman, *Land Grab: Israel's Settlement Policy in the West Bank* (Jerusalem: B'tselem, 2002), 133. See also Oren Yiftachel and Haim Yacobi, "Barriers, Walls, and Dialectics: The Shaping of 'Creeping Apartheid' in Israel/Palestine," in *Against the Wall: Israel's Barrier to Peace*, ed. Michael Sorkin (New York: New Press, 2005), 138–57. Yiftachel and Yacobi describe a "new political geography" being "etched into the landscape" in which "political space" is "marked by neither two states, nor one, as Palestinians are left in the twilight zone between occupation and ghettoized self-rule" (154).

32. Eyal Weizman, *Hollow Land*, 94.

33. Sari Hanafi, "Spacio-cide and Bio-Politics: The Israeli Colonial Conflict from 1947 to the Wall," in *Against the Wall*, ed. Sorkin, 163.

34. See the essays in *The Power of Inclusive Exclusion*, ed. Ophir, Givoni, and Hanafi.

35. James Ron, *Frontiers and Ghettos: State Violence in Serbia and Israel* (Berkeley: University of California Press, 2003). See also Daniel Bertrand Monk, "Border Spaces/Ghettospheres," in *Against the Wall*, ed. Sorkin, 204–11 and Jad Isaac and Owen Powell, "The Transformation of the Palestinian Environment," in *Where Now for Palestine?*, ed. Hilal, 144–65.

36. Ilan Pappé, "Zionism and the Two-State Solution," in *Where Now for Palestine?*, ed. Hilal, 30–47. See also Ian Lustick, "The Oslo Agreement as Obstacle to Peace," *Journal of Palestine Studies* 27, no. 1 (Autumn 1997): 61–66.

37. Among the many cartographic pronouncements of the demise of the two-state solution, see the analysis of former cartographer for the PLO's Jerusalem-based Orient House, Jan de Jong, in his article "The End of the Two-State Solution—A Geo-Political Analysis," in *Palestinian-Israeli Impasse: Exploring Alternative Solutions to the Palestine-Israel Conflict*, ed. Mahdi Abdul Hadi (Jerusalem: PASSIA, 2005), 315–40. See also Gary Sussman, "The Viability of the Two-State Solution and Israeli Unilateral Intentions," in *Palestinian-Israeli Impasse*, ed. Hadi, 45–66; and Gearóid Tuathail, "Contradictions of the 'Two-State Solution,'" *The Arab World Geographer* 8, no. 3 (2005): 168–71.

38. Julie Peteet, *Landscape of Hope and Despair*, 38.

39. Gabriel Piterberg, "Can the Subaltern Remember? A Pessimistic View of the Victims of Zionism," in *Memory and Violence in the Middle East and North Africa*, ed. Ussama Makdisi and Paul A. Silverstein (Bloomington and Indianapolis: Indiana University Press, 2006), 177.

40. Edward W. Said, "Palestine: Memory, Invention, and Space," 12.

41. *The Epistle to Diognetus: Greek Text with Introduction, Translation, and Notes*, ed. H. G. Meecham (Manchester: Manchester University Press, 1935), 5.

42. Stanley Hauerwas and William H. Willimon, *Resident Aliens: Life in the Christian Colony* (Nashville: Abingdon, 1989).

43. W. D. Davies, *The Gospel and the Land: Early Christianity and Jewish Territorial Doctrine* (Sheffield, UK: JSOT Press, 1994), 375, 367. Geographer Yi-Fu Tuan observes that religion can "either bind a people to place or free them from it." Tuan, *Space and Place: The Perspective of Experience* (Minneapolis: University of Minnesota Press, 1977), 152. Davies clearly presents Christianity as freeing people from ties that bind them to particular territories.

44. Eyal Weizman, *Hollow Land*, 15–16.

45. Daniel Bertrand Monk, *An Aesthetic Occupation: The Immediacy of Architecture and the Palestine Conflict* (Durham, NC: Duke University Press, 2002), 131–32.

46. Denis Cosgrove, *Geography and Vision: Seeing, Imagining, and Representing the World* (London and New York: I. B. Tauris, 2008), 168.

47. Ibid., 2.

48. For a collection of "maps" that radically broadens the notion of mapping to include a panoply of artistic ruminations on place and space, see Annelys de Vet, *Subjective Atlas of Palestine* (Rotterdam: 010 Publishers, 2007).

49. Jonathan Z. Smith, *Map Is Not Territory: Studies in the History of Religion* (Chicago and London: University of Chicago Press, 1993), 309.

50. "Mapping Ghosts: Visible Collective Talks to Trevor Paglen," in *An Atlas of Radical Cartography*, ed. Lize Mogel and Alexis Bhagat (Los Angeles: Journal of Aesthetics and Protest, 2007), 44.

51. Jai Sen, "Other Worlds, Other Maps: Mapping the Unintended City," in *An Atlas of Radical Cartography*, ed. Mogel and Bhagat, 13.

52. Denis Wood, *The Power of Maps* (New York and London: Guilford, 1992), 1–3.

53. Sam Gill, "Territory," in *Critical Terms for Religious Studies*, ed. Mark C. Taylor (Chicago: University of Chicago Press, 1998), 310.

54. Matthew Sparke, *In the Space of Theory: Postfoundational Geographies of the Nation-State* (Minneapolis: University of Minnesota Press, 2005), 9.

55. Henri Lefebvre, *The Production of Space* (London: Blackwell, 1991), 194.

56. Meron Benvenisti, *Sacred Landscape: The Buried History of the Holy Land since 1948* (Berkeley: University of California Press, 2000), 13.

57. Edward W. Said, *Orientalism* (New York: Vintage, 1979), 54. Wendy Brown has recently argued that Israeli wall- and fence-building in the Occupied Territories, as technologies of "separation and domination in a complex context of settler colonialism," should be viewed in comparative perspective as an example of how nation-states today seek to deflect "from crises of national cultural identity, from colonial domination in a postcolonial age, and from the discomfort of privilege obtained through super-exploitation in an increasingly interconnected and interdependent global political economy." See Brown, *Walled States, Waning Sovereignty* (New York: Zone Books, 2010), 30, 133.

58. Stephen Graham, "Constructing Urbicide by Bulldozer in the Occupied Territories," in *Cities, War, and Terrorism: Towards an Urban Geopolitics*, ed. Stephen Graham (London: Blackwell, 2004), 193.

59. Cosgrove, *Geography and Vision*, 168.

60. Philip Sheldrake, *Spaces for the Sacred: Place, Memory, and Identity* (Baltimore: Johns Hopkins University Press, 2001), 7.

61. Ibid., 1, 154.

62. "Place is space which has historical meanings, where some things have happened which are now remembered and which provide continuity and identity across generations." Walter Brueggemann, *The Land: Place as Gift, Promise, and Challenge in Biblical Theology*, 2nd ed. (Minneapolis: Fortress Press, 2002), 5. Brueggemann's formulation leaves something to be desired: a better statement would have been "Place is space that human beings have invested with historical meaning."

63. Edward Casey, *The Fate of Place: A Philosophical History* (Berkeley: University of California Press, 1998), 286.

64. William Safran, "Diasporas in Modern Societies: Myths of Homeland and Return," *Diaspora* 1, no. 1 (1991): 83–84.

65. William Safran, "The Jewish Diaspora in a Comparative and Theoretical Perspective," *Israel Studies* 10, no. 1 (Spring 2005): 36–60.

66. Khachig Tölölian, "The Nation-State and Its Others: In Lieu of a Preface," *Diaspora* 1, no. 1 (1991): 3–7.

67. Gabriel Sheffer, "Is the Jewish Diaspora Unique? Reflections on the Diaspora's Current Situation," *Israel Studies* 10, no. 1 (Spring 2005): 1–35.

68. See, for example, Stuart Hall, "Cultural Identity and Diaspora," in *Identity: Community, Culture, Difference*, ed. Jonathan Rutherford (London: Lawrence & Wishart, 1990), 222–37; James Clifford, "Diasporas," *Cultural Anthropology* 9, no. 3 (August 1994): 302–38; and Arjun Appadurai, *Modernity at Large: Cultural Dimensions of Globalization* (Minneapolis: University of Minnesota Press, 1996).

69. Alex Weingrod and André Levy, "On Homelands and Diasporas: An Introduction," in *Homelands and Diasporas: Holy Lands and Other Places*, ed. André Levy and Alex Weingrod (Stanford: Stanford University Press, 2005), 5, 8.

70. Pnina Werbner, "The Place Which Is Diaspora: Citizenship, Religion, and Gender in the Making of Chaordic Transnationalism," in *Homelands and Diasporas*, ed. Levy and Weingrod, 30.

71. Julie Peteet, "Problematizing a Palestinian Diaspora," *International Journal of Middle East Studies* 39, no. 4 (October 2007), 628.

72. See Daniel and Jonathan Boyarin, "Diaspora: Generational Ground of Jewish Identity," *Critical Inquiry* 19, no. 4 (1993): 693–725 and *Powers of Diaspora: Two Essays on the Relevance of Jewish Culture* (Minneapolis: University of Minnesota Press, 2002).

73. Thomas A. Tweed, *Our Lady of the Exile: Diasporic Religion at a Cuban Catholic Shrine in Miami* (New York and Oxford: Oxford University Press, 1997), 84, 83.

74. Edward Said, *After the Last Sky: Palestinian Lives* (New York: Columbia University Press, 1999), 115.

75. Tweed, *Our Lady of the Exile*, 87.

76. Thomas A. Tweed, *Crossing and Dwelling: A Theory of Religion* (Cambridge, MA: Harvard University Press, 2006), 74.

77. Tweed, *Our Lady of the Exile*, 139, 97.

78. Glenn Bowman, "'A Country of Words': Conceiving the Palestinian Nation from the Position of Exile," in *The Making of Political Identities*, ed. Ernesto Laclau (London: Verso, 1994), 138.

1

"Homecoming Is Out of the Question"

Palestinian Refugee Cartography and Edward Said's View from Exile

"Forgetfulness leads to exile, while remembrance is the secret of redemption." The Palestinian refugee activist Salman Abu-Sitta deploys this quotation, which he attributes to the Baal Shem Tov, as one of the epigraphs to his "register of depopulated locales in Palestine," one of Abu-Sitta's initial attempts to document the dispossession and forced exile of Palestinians by Zionist militias in 1948, named by Palestinians as the *nakba*.[1] Memory for Abu-Sitta represents a moral demand placed upon refugees: failure to cultivate memory, the epigraph suggests, will prolong refugees' exile, whereas proper attention to memory will hasten redemption understood as the physical return of refugees to their homes.[2]

Abu-Sitta displays little interest in the mystical Hasidic framework within which the Baal Shem Tov's conceptions of exile and redemption operated, one in which exile referred most fundamentally to the estrangement of the people Israel (and by extension, humanity) from God, with redemption correspondingly understood as the mystical cleaving of the soul to God. The epigraphic appeal to the Baal Shem Tov does not point to a mystical dimension to Abu-Sitta's effort to document the ravages of the *nakba*, but rather reflects how Abu-Sitta self-consciously locates the Palestinian refugee case within the symbolic discourse of Jewish exile and return. This discursive move is reinforced by another epigraph in Abu-Sitta's registry of over five hundred destroyed Palestinian towns and villages, a citation from Lam. 5:1–2: "Remember, O God, what has befallen us; behold, and see our disgrace! Our inheritance has been turned over to strangers, our homes to aliens."[3] Abu-Sitta maps Palestinian exile onto Jewish exile and Palestinian refugee memory onto Jewish remembrance of *eretz yisrael*. In the face of Zionist discourses that claim

Palestine as the land on which the exiled Jewish people will find redemption through return (renewed national existence and the reentry into history for secular Zionists, the hastening of the Messiah's return for religious Zionists), Abu-Sitta claims the metaphors of exile, return, and redemption for Palestinians. Abu-Sitta's archival and cartographic efforts thus represent "part of an ongoing project to document the collective memory of the 'unchosen' but determined people."[4]

Unlike maps produced by state actors which often seek to erase the political ideologies encoded within various cartographic features (choices about what names to use, what to mark, what borders to draw, what legendary material to use, etc.), Abu-Sitta's maps and atlases are unabashedly political, forming part of a broader campaign for Palestinian refugee rights of return, compensation, and restitution. Abu-Sitta's cartographic productions, meanwhile, stand alongside a wide variety of other Palestinian refugee mappings of exile and projected return presented in encyclopedias, memory books, and websites. The heart of this chapter consists of a descriptive analysis of these various forms of cartographic production, what some cartographic theorists call "counter-mappings," and a critical evaluation of what functions these counter-mappings of exile and return serve. Do they stand as memorials of a past and places never to be recovered? Do they foster the creation of new diasporic forms of community? Do they help to galvanize political action on behalf of Palestinian refugee rights, including return?

Most pertinent to the question of this study, do the "counter-mappings" produced by Palestinian refugees mirror what Israeli cartographer and critic Meron Benvenisti has called the "flawless Hebrew map," that is, Zionist mappings that clear the Palestinian landscape so that the Jewish national project might unfold on a smooth cartographic plane?[5] Most Israeli Jews, including Benvenisti, perceive Palestinian refugee cartography as mirroring Zionist mapping in precisely this way, and thus experience Palestinian refugee calls for return as a profound existential threat. Palestinians, meanwhile, are divided regarding the feasibility of refugee return and on the role it should play in a comprehensive peace agreement with Israel. Thus, after critically analyzing the functions played by different Palestinian mappings of exile and return, I contextualize Palestinian refugee cartography within Israeli Jewish fears about return and within intra-Palestinian debates about the practicality and the realism of return, debates in which Abu-Sitta and his maps have played key roles.

In the final section of this chapter, I turn to the reflections of the Palestinian-American critic Edward Said on exile as both a physical condition and a critical stance to provide a lens through which to interpret Palestinian refugee cartographies. While Said joined Abu-Sitta in decrying and mobilizing against the hardships and dispossessions of exile, Said also, unlike Abu-Sitta, identifies a positive function for exile, insisting that the view from exile offers a decentered place from which to critique injustice and the abuse of power. Said's ruminations on exile and return, I contend, help to illuminate what different meanings "return" might have, including what return shaped by an exilic perspective might look like. If, as we will see, Said insists that "homecoming is out of the question" for Palestinian refugees, what other possible meanings, if any, might return have?

THE PROLIFERATION OF PALESTINIAN MEMORY PRODUCTION

The past fifteen years have witnessed an explosion of memory production by Palestinian refugees in the form of "memory books" highlighting specific villages destroyed during the *nakba* of 1948; oral histories; memoirs; fictional narrations; and Internet websites focused on particular towns or villages or dedicated to an encyclopedic summation of the *nakba*'s destruction.[6] Some of this memory production has been actively supported, promoted, and organized by nongovernmental organizations and transnational political networks, such as the Badil Resource Center for Palestinian Residency and Refugee Rights and the Al-Awda Right to Return Coalition, committed to mobilizing activism in defense of Palestinian refugee rights of return, compensation, and restitution.[7] Other forms of Palestinian refugee memory production have been more individualized and localized, such as the writing of memoirs or the launching of websites dedicated to particular Palestinian villages.

Both types of Palestinian refugee memory production emerged or intensified in the mid-1990s. To be sure, memory books and other forms of cultural production dedicated to remembering the *nakba* existed in the 1980s and even earlier.[8] Yet, as Israeli anthropologist Efrat Ben-Ze'ev observes, "Palestinian commemoration has been prospering in the last decade," particularly in the genres of written testimonies, Internet sites, and film.[9] Ben-Ze'ev rightly resists positing any simple correlation between the proliferation of Palestinian refugee memory production and the emergence of new technologies such as the Internet, arguing that "even in their absence, archives and village ethnographies and memorial books could have been produced all along, yet they have blossomed only over the last decade." Ben-Ze'ev is less convincing, however, when she seeks to explain why Palestinian refugee memory production has exploded, attributing the phenomenon to a generational shift, with the second and third generations of Palestinian refugees driven to "recapture the past so that when voices fade away, there will be a permanently available record. To this end, new methods are developed and substitutes for a homeland are enveloped in books and viewed on television and computer screens."[10]

While the aging and passing away of the generation that directly experienced the dispossession of 1948 does undoubtedly serve as a catalyst for the proliferation of Palestinian refugee memory production, Ben-Ze'ev fails to take into consideration the Palestinian political context within which this proliferation has occurred. Specifically, Ben-Ze'ev does not adequately recognize the impact of the Oslo Accords and the establishment of the Palestinian Authority (PA) in parts of the Occupied Territories on Palestinian refugee and internally displaced communities. In contrast, Randa Farah has correctly explained that Palestinian refugees in the wake of the Oslo Accords came to recognize that the political framework created by the agreements displaced the Palestinian refugee right of return in favor of the "right to self-determination" understood as "the establishment of a sovereign state": in this framework, "the right of return, compensation and restitution would be restricted to citizenship rights and perhaps relocation within the Palestinian statelet on the West Bank and Gaza only."[11] Palestinian Christian novelist and poet (and Israeli citizen) Anton Shammas bleakly evaluated the Oslo accords as having turned Palestine of 1948 into "a territory without a map," a "mapless country that exists only in the oral traditions and the written texts of poetry and fiction. A key to a house in Yafa, then, is bound to become a collector's item that opens no door, a threatless tool of the imagination."[12]

In the face of this grim assessment, however, Palestinian refugee memory production, including map-making, has proliferated, continuing up until the present, as Palestinian refugees—and internally displaced Palestinians within Israel—began to mobilize in defense of their rights of return, compensation, and restitution, convinced that the PLO, once viewed as the defender of those rights, was no longer a trusted advocate.[13] Palestinian refugees sense, Laleh Khalili maintains, that only "dogged insistence" on their rights will "prevent their options from becoming entirely circumscribed by much more powerful actors."[14] Confronted by a Zionist cartographic and planning regime that works to efface traces of the Palestinian landscape, Palestinian refugees undertake their own cartographic endeavors, aware that they face the stark choice of "map or be mapped!"[15]

The word *nostalgia*, Svetlana Boym has explained, was coined in 1688 as a pseudo-Greek term by Swiss doctor Johannes Hofer to denote "the sad mood originating from the desire to return to one's native land."[16] While, as Rochelle Davis grants, "it is easy to attribute Palestinians' feelings to a nostalgic longing for the long-absent past and their lost lands," one must also account for the role played by Palestinian refugees' current living conditions as stateless refugees, denied basic rights in numerous contexts. Many Palestinian refugees understandably assert the right of return and map visions for such return in the face of political and legal regimes that deprive them of the basic protections afforded to citizens.[17] Accordingly, Davis rightly concludes, "geographic nostalgia for the village places and the peasant lifestyle is rooted both in local memories and experiences and in Palestinians' current status as landless and dispossessed refugees."[18]

Palestinian refugee memory production over the past fifteen years or so, including memory production created on and disseminated via digital media such as the Internet, should thus be viewed in large measure as an attempt to mobilize Palestinian refugees (and sometimes sympathetic allies) in defense of rights of compensation, restitution, and especially return, rights that are viewed as under severe threat. Forgetfulness of one's origins, failure to transmit memories from one generation to another and record these memories for posterity: the fear that these will prolong exile helps to drive Palestinian refugee memory production. In the face of the Zionist rejection of Palestinian refugee return, international indifference, and an ineffectual and compromising Palestinian leadership for whom the refugee question is a source of irritation, Palestinian refugees pin their hopes on memory, in the expectation that memory, as Abu-Sitta's appropriation of the Baal Shem Tov would have it, might prove to be the "secret to redemption."

MAPPING MEMORY: ENCYCLOPEDIAS, VILLAGE BOOKS, WEBSITES, AND ATLASES

Palestinian refugee memory production has proliferated in a wide variety of media. In this section, I will examine some of the media by which Palestinian refugees have sought to map and transmit memories of home, to locate themselves in exile, and to chart possible futures of return. My purpose is not to provide an exhaustive overview of the types of Palestinian refugee memory production and the media by which such memory production takes shape and is disseminated. I will not, for example, pay close attention to films, memoirs, or fictional accounts produced by Palestinian refugees, and will give only glancing consideration to memory books in chapters 3 and 4. Instead, my focus here will be on the ends served by various forms of Palestinian refugee memory mapping.[19]

MEMORY AS ENCYCLOPEDIC DOCUMENTATION

One function played by Palestinian refugee memory is documentary, a drive to record in encyclopedic breadth all that was lost during the *nakba*: not only the villages, towns, and landscapes (with their distinctive environmental markers such as hills, springs, flora, and fauna), but also the customs and folklore tied to village life. Comprehensive publications in the 1970s and 1980s such as the multi-author *Palestinian Encyclopedia*, published in Damascus, or Mustafa Dabbagh's magisterial eleven-volume *Our Land, Palestine*, sought to document and thus to memorialize the land and a lost way of life.[20] These volumes, however, also advanced a territorial claim that went beyond the memorial or the documentary: Dabbagh's encyclopedia, after all, bore the title *Our Land* [*Biladuna*].

This claim of possession falls away, however, with the one-volume—but still encyclopedic in scope—publication by the Institute for Palestine Studies of *All That Remains*, a descriptive listing of each of the Palestinian towns and villages destroyed between 1948 and 1949.[21] The editors of *All That Remains* drew on cartographic surveys and registers compiled by the British Mandate government, such as the *Palestine Index Gazetteer, Survey of Palestine, 1941–1945*, and the British Land Survey Map of 1944, alongside oral histories and archival research carried out by Palestinian nongovernmental organizations like the Birzeit Research and Documentation Center and the Galilee Center for Social Research, in order to compile what they claimed to be a comprehensive and authoritative listing of 413 Palestinian towns and villages destroyed during the 1948 war.[22] Each village or town then received its own listing (alphabetically within each region), including basic demographic facts (population, religious breakdown, etc.) and a brief historical overview, along with information about how the village was destroyed, where the villagers ended up, and what remains from the village endure on the landscape.

All That Remains presents itself not as a blueprint for prospective action but instead as a weighty (literally) tribute, "a gesture of homage" to the "collective memories" and "sense of ancestral affiliation" of the hundreds of thousands of Palestinians from the 413 destroyed towns and villages, an "acknowledgment" of their suffering and a "tribute to their credentials as three-dimensional beings."[23] Such acknowledgment and tribute, the editors stress, do *not* represent "a call for the reversal of the tide of history, nor for the delegitimization of Zionism."[24] Rather, the encyclopedia stands as "a call" for "a break into the chain of causation which has, since the beginning of the Zionist colonization of Palestine, created the dimensions of the tragedy of the Palestinian people as we know it today." This "chain of causation" can be broken, the editors suggest, if triumphant Zionism as an "exultant builder" would acknowledge, "if only on prudential grounds," the "debris left in its wake."[25] The editors of *All That Remains*, led by historian Walid Khalidi, thus anticipated the arguments advanced later in the 1990s by other Palestinian academics and politicians like Rashid Khalidi and Sari Nusseibeh, that insisting on Palestinian refugee return is impractical and that the best that can be hoped for is thus an Israeli recognition of at least partial responsibility for Palestinian refugee dispossession. These arguments will be examined in greater detail below.

CONVENING A DIASPORIC PUBLIC SPHERE: PALESTINIAN REFUGEE MEMORY ON THE WEB

If *All That Remains* was the product of mostly elite actors based in academic institutions, then memory books and websites dedicated to specific Palestinian villages are mostly compiled by "non-elite actors—neither the politically powerful nor the globalized professionals," persons who within their own particular contexts might form "an educated local elite" but who "remain enmeshed in and an inextricable part of their small communities."[26]

Describing itself as the virtual domicile for an uprooted people ("The Home of Ethnically Cleansed and Occupied Palestinians"), the Palestine Remembered website (with full content in both Arabic and English, along with more limited content in Hebrew) plays multiple roles. Not only does the site present itself as a comprehensive database for information about Palestinian towns and villages destroyed in 1948, but it also creates transnational forms of community among dispersed refugees and resources and spurs political action in defense of Palestinian refugee rights.

The site's self-proclaimed political agenda as outlined in Palestine Remembered's mission statement is to debunk the "Zionist myth" that Palestine was an empty land, to raise awareness among Palestinian refugees of their rights under international law, to frame the Palestinian-Israeli conflict in terms of Palestinian dispossession and expulsion, and to humanize Palestinian refugees for others, especially for Israeli Jews.[27] The site offers basic primers on the Palestinian-Israeli conflict and the Right of Return ("The Conflict 101" and "ROR 101"), designed to equip Palestinian refugee activism with an ideological framework and a historical narrative.[28] To foster this political activism, Palestine Remembered considers part of its mission to be creating "an easy medium where refugees can communicate, organize, and share their experiences amongst themselves." Refugees can sign up as site members and then register on the "411-Directory Service" of a particular village, noting name (or more often screen name), clan (*hamula*) affiliation, and current country of residence. Message boards, meanwhile, offer refugees the opportunity to sign the village's virtual guestbook and record marriage, obituary, and graduation announcements. Through these services, "ex-villagers and their descendants can establish social ties across borders that cannot be crossed," maintaining and recreating the village and tribal bonds ruptured by dispossession and exile and nurturing new transnational publics.[29]

In its goal of providing "a comprehensive source of information about the villages and cities that were ethnically cleansed, looted, and destroyed by the Israeli army," Palestine Remembered also functions less as an objective, encyclopedic reference and more as an interactive medium by which refugees share memories with one another, a medium that tries to "amplify" the "voices in cyberspace" and to "preserve the memories and experiences" of Palestinian refugees.[30] While in its compilation of ordered facts in encyclopedic form about specific villages Palestine Remembered resembles (and borrows from) the structure and content of published reference sources such as *All That Remains*, Palestine Remembered also calls on Palestinian refugees to become active participants in the shaping of the historical record through various interactive media.[31] While other websites seek to provide either concentrated information about one particular village or, as in the case of AlNakba.org, founded by the Arab Studies Society and the Khalil Sakakini Cultural Center in Ramallah, a comprehensive overview of Palestinian dispossession from 1948, Palestine Remembered stands out from the rest thanks to the degree of interactivity built into the site.[32] Refugees contribute to the site's content by uploading photos and audio and video files containing oral history narratives about Palestinian life before, during, and after the *nakba*. Most intriguingly for the purposes of this investigation, refugees can also register on the site to plot the erased Palestinian landscape back onto the map using Google Earth technology, a form of interactive cartographic construction.[33]

Through these interactive functions, Palestine Remembered becomes a virtual form of what Pierre Nora has called a *lieu de mémoire*, a site of memory, the fundamental purpose of which is "to stop time, to block the work of forgetting, to establish a state of things, to immortalize death, to materialize the immaterial."[34] With most of Palestine Remembered's refugee contributors based in the diaspora and thus unable to visit destroyed village sites in present-day Israel, the website substitutes for the ruins, cactus plants, and fruit trees of the actual location, serving as a virtual *lieu de mémoire*. Separated from their villages of origin by physical and legal barriers, Palestinian refugees share Nora's recognition that memory does not erupt spontaneously, that memory must be cultivated and produced through the creation of archives and the celebration of anniversaries. In short, they concur with Nora that "without commemorative vigilance, history would sweep" away the remembered locations.[35]

The memory productions presented on Palestine Remembered are not univocal in character. Rather, they reflect what Laleh Khalili has termed "the polysemic nature of commemorative practices."[36] On the one hand, the website as a *lieu de mémoire* inscribes Palestinian refugee memories into a broader Palestinian nationalist narrative of dispossession and return (while reasserting the centrality of the refugee cause to Palestinian nationalism). On the other hand, the focus on particular villages and local identities reflects to some degree the post-nationalism of the post-Oslo era, the reassertion of more localized identities, and the fragmentation of the broader Palestinian nationalist identity—especially in the wake of the Palestinian statist project being thwarted by the territorial fragmentation of the Occupied Territories by dividing walls and fences, Israeli-only bypass roads, and expanded settlements. This dual meaning of commemorative practices on Palestine Remembered emerges from what Khalili identifies as "the tension between top-down nationalist narratives (which nevertheless resonate with the refugees themselves) and more locally grounded subaltern narratives."[37]

As a memory site composed of multiple media (e.g., photographs, audio files, video testimonies, and online cartography), Palestine Remembered stands as an example of what Arjun Appadurai terms a *mediascape*, an "image-centered, narrative-based" account of strips of reality, "out of which scripts can be formed of imagined lives."[38] Appadurai identifies the communities created by such mediascapes as "diasporic public spheres."[39] Following Appadurai, one can thus interpret the transnational communities created by Palestine Remembered gathering dispersed refugees living in diverse locations around shared memory practices centered on specific villages as "diasporic public spheres." Websites like Palestine Remembered, Rochelle Davis explains, allow "Palestinians to bridge the diasporic geography of their lives in order to connect the past to the present, photographs to stories, and family histories to Palestinian histories," in turn creating a diasporic public sphere.[40]

Appadurai arguably overreaches, however, in his assessment of such diasporic public spheres as "the crucibles of a postnational order."[41] Appadurai's claim that "the nation-state, as a complex modern political form, is on its last legs" prevents him from recognizing the resilience of the nation-state as a political form.[42] True, the proliferation of Palestinian memory production on websites such as Palestine Remembered reflects profound disillusionment among Palestinian refugees that the PLO-led nationalism that culminated in the Oslo "statelet" could protect Palestinian refugee interests. To that extent, mediascapes like Palestine Remembered do indeed contain "the seeds of more dispersed and diverse forms of transnational allegiance and affiliation."[43]

Yet that is surely not the complete story. A more nuanced interpretation of the Palestine Remembered mediascape would recognize that it not only represents a diasporic public sphere, but it also seeks to reinscribe Palestinian refugee rights of return, compensation, and restitution into the narrative of Palestinian nationalism. The diasporic public spheres convened on Palestine Remembered may indeed reflect "nonnational identities and aspirations," but not to the exclusion of Palestinian national identities. Localized village and regional identities are asserted alongside self-identification with the larger Palestinian nation.[44]

"SACRED, LEGAL, POSSIBLE": SALMAN ABU-SITTA'S CARTOGRAPHY OF RETURN

Among the individuals and organizations dedicated to documenting the dispossession and forced exile of Palestinians in 1948, arguably none has been as active and productive as the civil engineer and longtime member of the Palestine National Council Salman Abu-Sitta, a refugee from Bir as-Sabi' (now the Israeli city of Beersheva). The founder of the Palestine Land Society in London, Abu-Sitta, like many other Palestinian refugee activists, became active in the defense of Palestinian refugee rights in the mid-1990s, at a time when Palestinian refugees perceived their rights as under threat.

Through extensive study of maps produced by the Ottoman, British Mandate, and Israeli authorities, Abu-Sitta has, beginning in the mid-1990s, compiled registries of destroyed Palestinian villages and then has produced maps and atlases resituating these erased locales on the cartographic plane. Abu-Sitta's project of documenting the "collective memory" of Palestinian refugees takes multiple forms. In addition to registries compiling lists of destroyed villages by districts and subdistricts, along with available information about those villages, Abu-Sitta has produced multiple cartographic representations of the Palestinian past, the *nakba*, and prospects for return. In his magisterial *Atlas of Palestine, 1948* and the more recent *Atlas of Palestine, 1917–1966*, Abu-Sitta seeks to offer a comprehensive overview of Palestine's landscape prior to the catastrophe, combining survey maps produced by the British Mandate authorities with aerial photographs also taken by the Mandate government.[45] The "Palestine 1948" wall map, published in 2008 to mark sixty years of Palestinian exile, and the maps in *From Refugees to Citizens at Home*, meanwhile, fulfill two functions: the archival one of restoring the erased Palestinian landscape to the map, and the polemical one of presenting a pictorial argument (in cartographic form) for why Palestinian refugee return is "no Utopian project" but is instead an eminently practical matter.

The maps Abu-Sitta constructs purport to demonstrate that the vast majority of Palestinian refugees originate from towns or villages whose ruins are now located either on agricultural or state land such as the parks and nature reserves created after the Israeli state expropriated the properties of refugees and internally displaced persons under the terms of the Israeli Absentee Property Law of 1950. In an ironic reversal of how the Oslo Accords divide up the Occupied West Bank into Areas A, B, and C (identifying whether the PA or the Israeli military government has responsibility for security and civilian affairs), Abu-Sitta, in all of his cartographic publications, divides up the Israeli map into Areas A, B, and C in order to identify areas of relatively high- or low-population density. From these maps, Abu-Sitta claims to show that 80 percent of Palestinian refugees come from low-population density areas, with former village lands now having become a combination of state lands (forests, national parks, etc.) or agricultural land for *kibbutzim* and *moshavim*. Palestinian refugee return, Abu-Sitta therefore contends, would not result in Israeli Jewish displacement, and would thus be relatively feasible and practical: large arrows pointing from refugee camps back into locations in Israel dramatically picture the proposed return.

The Return Journey, for its part, has less of an archival or overtly polemical agenda, focused more on the practical tasks of a guidebook. Over the grid boxes of a Hebrew-language road atlas, Abu-Sitta restores destroyed Palestinian locales to the map, naming these sites in Arabic, Hebrew, and English. Abu-Sitta envisions *The Return Journey* serving as a practical guidebook to "assist those Palestinians able to do so to visit the site of the towns or villages of their original homes," to "enable visitors to learn more about the history of the country," and to "encourage Jewish Israelis to explore the Palestinian experience of 1948."[46] Denis Wood has argued that "[t]he very point of the map [is] to present us not with the world we can *see*, but to point *toward* a world we might *know*."[47] As Rochelle Davis explains, "by listing names of places," Palestinian map-makers and map-users "show their knowledge of that place" and thus "imprint their presence on the land through this authority and knowledge."[48] Making and using maps of a particular village or of the land of Palestine as a whole implies an intimate knowledge of—and thus connection to—the land.

Abu-Sitta's maps have been in turn used by numerous other Palestinian refugee organizations, from committees dedicated to the memory of particular villages like 'Iqrit of Saffuriya, to websites such as the encyclopedic Palestine

Remembered, to activist networks like the Al-Awda coalition focused on mobilizing in defense of Palestinian refugee rights. Taken together as a whole, Abu-Sitta's cartographic productions not only function to reassert Palestinian presence in the face of a regime that has effaced and continues to obscure that presence, but also to point toward an imagined future of refugee return, presenting such return as practical and possible rather than as utopian illusion. His maps, Abu-Sitta underscores, constitute "a proposed plan for the return of Palestinian refugees to their homes. It is not Utopia."[49]

The right of return presented and defended cartographically by Abu-Sitta is, in his phrase, "sacred, legal, possible."[50] This sacralized account of Palestinian refugee return is not based on a theological account of the land itself as holy. Unlike Islamist organizations such as Hamas or the Islamic Movement in Israel, Abu-Sitta does not subscribe to a theological description of all of Palestine as *waqf*, property set aside for religious purposes. Nor is Abu-Sitta's description of the right of return as sacred primarily dependent on the presence of self-identified holy places on the landscape, such as mosques, churches, and *maqams* linked to traditional saints. True, Abu-Sitta does refer to Palestine as the "Holy Land," a designation supported by the fact that "its soil is studded with holy sites of all kinds, mosques, churches, synagogues, sheikhs, maqams, shrines and other sites for which only ruins remain."[51] In *The Return Journey* guide, Abu-Sitta identifies nearly 5,000 such religious sites, building on a previous 1976 field survey carried out by Shukri Arraf and on documentation of nearly one thousand Muslim and Christian religious shrines compiled by the Al-Aqsa Association, an organization associated with the Islamic Movement in Israel.[52]

Abu-Sitta's documentary and cartographic productions differ, however, from this seemingly similar effort by the Islamist Al-Aqsa Association to document all of Palestine's holy places in that Abu-Sitta's focus is not on the shrines as *waqf* or as proof of Islam's claim on the land but as expressions of the Palestinian national spirit. Abu-Sitta is struck by the endurance of religious shrines even as the dominant religion in the land shifted: "Over centuries, Palestinians revered these sites regardless of their religion or even when they converted from one religion to another. This is a proof that Palestinians remained the same people, especially in the hilly areas, whatever their tongue or their faith was."[53] True, like the Islamist Al-Aqsa Association, Abu-Sitta disapprovingly notes the repurposing of sacred buildings: "Some mosques," he writes, "are turned into other functions: a bar, a restaurant, a museum or a stable."[54] Such Israeli appropriation of Palestinian mosques, however, is simply representative for Abu-Sitta of the broader Zionist expropriation of Palestinian space. Abu-Sitta is just as affronted by the erasure of hundreds of towns and villages from the map as he is by the repurposing of these mosques. This is because for Abu-Sitta the discourse of sacredness operates within a nationalist framework, with the term "sacred" describing primarily the unbreakable connection of the Palestinian people (both Christian and Muslim) to the land. Given this sacred bond of land and people, the right of Palestinian refugees to return to their homes is accordingly "sacred to all Palestinians. It has remained their fundamental objective since 1948. Their determination on the return issue has endured despite warfare, suffering, and enormous social and political hardships. In this, the refugee from Iqrit, who is an Israeli citizen, the refugee from Lydda, who is a Jordanian citizen, the refugee from Haifa, who is stateless in Syria or Lebanon, and the refugee from Jaffa, who is a U.S. citizen, have the same determination."[55] The right of return is sacred for Abu-Sitta because it is "an indestructible core of the Palestinian psyche."[56] Remembering, tending, and nurturing the sacred bond between people and land is thus critical, according to Abu-Sitta, to maintain refugee commitment to return. Remembering, in short, is "the key to redemption."

THE MAP AS MEMORY DEVICE AND BASIS FOR PROJECTIVE ACTION

How should the maps and cartographic constructions produced by Abu-Sitta and reproduced on websites like Palestine Remembered be interpreted? What political messages do they convey? What political futures do they embody and foster? One way to think about Palestinian refugee cartography is as an example of what Edward Said has called "counter-maps" and of what numerous cartographers have termed "counter-mapping," the effort of an indigenous people to challenge colonialist mappings of space.[57] Without the resources of the state, indigenous groups must mobilize resources to plot their own accounts of space. So, for example, whereas colonialist cartography in twentieth-century Palestine proceeded with the support and under the auspices of first the British Mandate authorities (committed under the Balfour Declaration to ensuring the establishment of a Jewish national home in Palestine) and then the State of Israel, Palestinian counter-cartography had to make do without state support.[58]

Cartographic theorist Denis Cosgrove explains that a map is "at once a memory device and a foundation for projective action."[59] Products of human endeavor, maps reflect "a creative process of inserting our humanity into the world and seizing the world for ourselves." All maps permit the "illusion" that space can be "represented completely."[60] The possibilities afforded by contemporary mapping technologies like Google Earth only intensify this "illusion of total synopsis and truthful vision."[61] It is not surprising that Palestinian refugees and their descendants, uprooted from their homes and prevented from return, turn to the seeming stability the map offers and grasp at the promise of controlling space that cartographic construction holds forth.

A striking feature of the maps produced by Abu-Sitta is how they call attention to their constructed character and to the propositions they embody. Critical cartographers have demonstrated that maps are always social constructions, that they are not direct mirrors of the landscape, and that they always encode, by the manner in which they present map data and by what they choose to present and render absent, the interests of the map-makers.[62] Typically, however, maps *naturalize* themselves, presenting themselves as objective representations of territory and masking the interests they embody.[63] As Denis Wood and John Fels explain, "Maps objectify by winnowing out our personal agency, replacing it with that of a reference object so constructed by so many people over so long a time that it might as well have been constructed by no one at all."[64] The maps in *Atlas of Palestine, 1948* or in *The Return Journey*, by contrast, are cartographic palimpsests, highlighting overlapping layers of national presence. As intentionally produced palimpsests, these maps call attention to the agency behind their construction.

All maps consist of propositions: not just the basic proposition of "this is there," but also higher-order propositions, such as "this is there and *therefore it is also*."[65] Abu-Sitta's maps, maps in memory books, and maps on websites like Palestine Remembered call attention to these propositions, claiming *this village was there, and therefore the Zionist erasure of the village from the landscape and the map must be countered*. However, because many of these maps (e.g., Abu-Sitta's maps in *The Return Journey*) are palimpsests, they potentially communicate more than these basic propositions. Abu-Sitta's palimpsest maps, with destroyed Palestinian villages reinscribed over the Hebrew map, can be interpreted, to be sure, as "counter-maps" in the simple, straightforward manner articulated by Wood in his *Rethinking the Power of Maps*, maps that assert Palestinian presence and control over and against Israeli Jewish presence. I would contend, however, that Abu-Sitta's cartographic productions, by reproducing and not erasing the Hebrew map, point to the possibility of a deeper form of counter-mapping, a counter-mapping animated by the implied propositions that Palestinian return need not mean the erasure of the Hebrew map.

As Issam Aburaiya and Efrat Ben-Ze'ev suggest, alternative cartographies, ones that make room for and embrace heterogeneous spaces, are both possible and an urgent necessity.[66] Any particular space, Henri Lefebvre has suggested, opens itself up to an infinite number of cartographic interpretations. "How many maps, in the descriptive or geographical sense, might be needed to deal exhaustively with a given space, to code and decode all its meaning and contents?" Lefebvre asks. "It is doubtful," he continues, "whether a finite number can ever be given in answer to this sort of question."[67]

A critical issue at stake here is whether or not the cartographic imagination is wedded to state power. J. B. Harley is undoubtedly correct that "[m]aps are preeminently a language of power, not of protest," and that cartography typically operates as a "teleological discourse, reifying power, reinforcing the status quo, and freezing social interaction within charted lines."[68] The maps created by the new Israeli state, what Benvenisti calls the "flawless Hebrew map," are representative of such statist cartography. Nationalist cartographies, Matthew Sparke explains, tend to impose the template of the imagined nation-state "proleptically on a heterogeneous past."[69] The existence of nation-states is intimately intertwined with cartographic production. As Denis Wood and John Fels observe, "outside the world of maps, states carry on a precarious existence; little of nature, they are much of maps, for to map a state is to assert its territorial expression, to leave it off to deny its existence."[70] Its past erased from the map, the Palestinian nation has an inherently tenuous existence. Cartographic productions like those of Abu-Sitta can be viewed as attempts, in the absence of an effective state apparatus, to unify and stabilize an increasingly fragmented Palestinian nation, even as they additionally mobilize refugee activism for return.

But does Palestinian cartographic resistance end up mirroring the mapping regime it opposes? Joe Bryan expresses concern that indigenous counter-mapping efforts might unwittingly adopt colonial understandings of space.[71] Denis Wood, meanwhile, is deeply skeptical that Abu-Sitta's counter-mapping represents anything other than a mimetic replication of Zionism's commitment to the nation-state: just as Zionists drew up counter-maps to the cartographic productions of the British Mandate, so, argues Wood, does Abu-Sitta advance "counter-counter-maps," with both projects wedded to statist politics.[72] While Bryan and Wood rightly point to a real danger of counter-mapping efforts, I contend over the ensuing chapters that counter-mappings are possible that disrupt the exclusivist logic of the nation-state and that some refugee counter-maps, including Abu-Sitta's, can be interpreted in precisely this fashion. Rachel Havrelock argues that the act of mapping within the context of the Palestinian-Israeli conflict tends to foster the illusion of separate and homogenous national territories. While I agree with Havrelock in this assessment, I also join her in her stated hope that other cartographic forms are possible.[73]

Palestinian Refugee Cartography and Debates
on the Right of Return

Many Israel Jewish commentators perceive Palestinian refugee counter-mappings as an existential threat. Abu-Sitta includes as another epigraph to his register of destroyed Palestinian villages a telling quotation from the Israeli Jewish peace activist, Uri Avneri: "I have seen maps from 1948, where hundreds of villages and towns which have disappeared are noted on maps distributed by Palestinians in the diaspora. These maps are more dangerous than any bomb."[74] As Avneri's quote makes clear, some Israelis interpret these forms of cartographic construction as part of a win-or-lose cartographic battle. Arnon Golan, for example, assesses cartographic portrayals of the *nakba* and projected return thus: "The Palestinian imaginary map conceals a future threat, whose realization may be attempted, resulting in the eradication of the Jewish map."[75] Meron Benvenisti, meanwhile, sees "the ferocity of the Israeli-Palestinian conflict and its vengeful nature" encoded in both Zionist map-making, which pictured Palestine as an empty land onto which the Zionist national project might unfold, and in Palestinian refugee map-making, which he views as a mirror of Zionist cartography, equally determined to erase that which does not fit with the nationalist project. Such maps, Benvenisti claims, sound a cartographic battle-cry: "I'll destroy your map just as you destroyed mine."[76]

The fears expressed by Avneri, Golan, and Benvenisti about Palestinian refugee cartography emerge from their assumption that Palestinian mappings of return must necessarily mirror Zionist mappings of the same. Thus, if Zionist cartography portrayed the land as an empty, homogeneous space onto which the Zionist national project might unfold, and if this cartographic erasure of Palestinians went hand-in-hand with the actual dispossession of Palestinians, then Palestinian return is naturally assumed to entail the dispossession and cartographic erasure of Israeli Jews. Issam Aburaiya and Efrat Ben-Ze'ev grant that the "Palestine-Israel conflict is often portrayed as a zero-sum game, allowing only two options for the definition and identity of the land—Arab or Jewish, Palestinian or Israeli. . . . Within this abstract context, multiple rendering of space is rarely tolerated."[77] Whether or not such "multiple rendering of space" is compatible with discourses of return animates this chapter and this inquiry as a whole.

The anxious Israeli Jewish assessment of Palestinian refugee cartography translates politically into a solid Israeli rejectionist stance regarding Palestinian refugees. While, as will be examined in chapter 4, some Israeli Jews have dedicated themselves to "remembering the *nakba* in Hebrew" and to provoking discussion within Israeli Jewish society about Palestinian refugee return, the

State of Israel adamantly refuses to consider any form of refugee return because it would threaten the "Jewish character" of Israel, with "Jewish character" understood in terms of a state with a Jewish demographic majority.[78] If Palestinian refugee cartography is experienced as a threat, it is because, as Ian Lustick and Ann Lesch explain, "It is not an exaggeration to describe Jewish Israelis as terrified at the prospect of a return of Palestinian refugees to Israel," a terror driven by "images of an uncontrolled and open-ended process leading to the demographic, cultural, and political submergence of Israel as a Jewish state and, ultimately, the disappearance of the Land of Israel as a place where a Jewish society and polity could thrive."[79] In the face of Israeli intransigence regarding refugee return, Palestinian politicians and academics have debated whether or not Palestinian refugee rights should be insisted upon or potentially traded for other political goods in the course of final status negotiations. In this section, I give a brief overview of this debate in order to situate Palestinian refugee cartography within Palestinian politics. Not only is Palestinian cartographer Abu-Sitta an active participant in this debate, but he is also a source of cartographic information and an inspiration for a wide variety of Palestinian civil society organizations seeking to intervene in the Palestinian conversation around the right of return.

Scores of books and articles have been written about the Palestinian refugee case touching on its historical origins; the status of Palestinian refugees within international law and the context of best practices regarding refugee return in other peace agreements; and the desire (or lack thereof) of refugees to return. In this section I will not examine such fiercely contested questions as: Are refugee rights of return, compensation, and restitution enshrined in international law?[80] If so, do they apply to Palestinian refugees? If they do, are they potentially outweighed by an Israeli Jewish right to self-determination (a question to which I will return in chapter 2)? Are there precedents in international peace treaties involving refugees that would weigh for or against Palestinian refugee return?[81] Should Palestinian refugee rights be viewed as being offset by the rights to restitution and compensation of *mizrahi* Jews in Israel who immigrated to Israel from countries such as Egypt, Yemen, and Iraq, with some of that emigration from those Arab countries driven by the anti-Jewish policies and practices they had adopted?[82] How many Palestinian refugees would exercise the right to return if allowed to return by Israel?[83] As intriguing as those questions are, answering them does not address the question animating my broader investigation, namely, if there can be a form of return to the land that does not mirror Zionist return and is not bound to the form of the nation-state. After all, Palestinian refugee rights might be guaranteed by international law and precedent, but that does not indicate whether or not Palestinian refugee return mirrors Zionist return.

Palestinian refugees correctly sense a shift within the PLO on the question of refugee rights from the Oslo accords onwards. As argued above, recognition of this shift has helped provoke the dramatic increase of Palestinian refugee memory production. Even as the PLO continues to talk about the importance of securing "justice" for Palestinian refugees, Palestinian political scientist Manuel Hassassian notes that "the Palestinian refugees know only too well that words like justice and rights were made for political abuse."[84] The PLO's Negotiation Department articulates a rights-based approach to the Palestinian refugee case rooted in international law, yet talk of refugee return has dropped out of the discourse of the leadership of the PLO and the PA in the Occupied Territories. When upper-level PLO or PA officials do mention the right of return, they deliberately leave its meaning vague, mindful of the fact that being too explicit in one direction or the other would either antagonize Palestinian refugees or the Israeli government.[85] Palestinian refugees, however, have interpreted the clear message behind the ambiguity, namely, that the PLO and its instruments like the PA have substituted the goal of liberating all of Palestine through the return of refugees with the goal of creating a state in the Occupied Territories of East Jerusalem, the West Bank, and the Gaza Strip.[86] For Islamist political movements such as Hamas and Islamic Jihad, meanwhile, Palestinian refugee rights also fade into the background, superseded by the goals of reclaiming all of Palestine as *waqf* or of renewing Islamic practice within Palestinian society.

Even as the PLO/PA leadership has cultivated a studied ambiguity about Palestinian refugee rights in the context of a final status agreement with Israel, senior officials have offered tacit support for so-called "Track Two" (civil society) attempts to draft a Palestinian-Israeli peace agreement such as the Geneva Initiative and the Nusseibeh-Ayalon agreement, both of which do not include full recognition and implementation of Palestinian refugee rights.[87] Sari Nusseibeh, an Oxford-trained philosopher, current president of Al-Aqsa University, and former PLO representative in Jerusalem, long argued that if Palestinians have decided to push for a two-state resolution to the conflict, then, given the Zionist insistence on maintaining Israel's Jewish character understood in demographic terms, Palestinians would have to relinquish the right of return, making do at best with an acknowledgment in principle of the right and the virtual exercise of that right through truncated return to a new Palestinian state in the Occupied Territories.[88] For Nusseibeh, Palestinian refugee cartographies are the products of "fantasy," a failure to come to terms with the fact that the

Palestinian landscape is no more: Palestinians must thus relinquish the illusory right to return to a place that no longer exists in favor of the right of living in freedom and independence.[89] "We have two rights," Nusseibeh stated. "We have the right of return, in my opinion. But we also have the right to live in freedom and independence. And very often in life one has to forgo the implementation of one right in order to implement other rights."[90] Palestinian-American historian Rashid Khalidi basically concurs with Nusseibeh, claiming that Palestinian refugees, in face of Israel's refusal to accept any form of refugee return, must aim for "justice within the realm of the possible."[91] That means above all an Israeli Jewish acceptance of moral responsibility for the Palestinian refugee crisis: although compensation for Palestinian refugees should potentially play a part of a final status accord, Khalidi underscores that "acknowledgment that a wrong has been done by those who did it, or their successors, is perhaps more important to a lasting political solution."[92]

Palestinian civil society organizations like the Badil Resource Center for Refugee and Residency Rights and transnational networks like the Al-Awda Right to Return Coalition have attempted to coalesce and galvanize Palestinian refugee opposition to proposals like those advanced by Nusseibeh and Khalidi. Contesting claims by proponents of proposals like the Geneva Initiative that compromise on Palestinian refugee rights represents the "realist" position, right of return advocates point to Abu-Sitta's maps to argue that refugee return is feasible (and thus realistic) and to refugee determination to continue demanding their rights (demonstrating that a *Realpolitik* framework must not only account for the positions advanced by the Israeli state but also for the demands of Palestinian refugees).[93]

However, these critics grant that Nusseibeh and Khalidi have done Palestinian political discourse a favor by raising the question of what type of two-state solution Palestinians can accept. Nadim Rouhana, Israeli-Palestinian sociologist, for example, argues that the controversy created by Nusseibeh's proposals have the benefit of pushing Palestinians to define the national movement's goals: to secure the right of return within the context of "one binational state over the whole territory of historical Palestine" or "to achieve a Palestinian state without the right of return in practice, but with the principle upheld according to a formula negotiated with Israel."[94]

An activist organization such as Badil, meanwhile, like Abu-Sitta and many other individuals and organizations in the Al-Awda Right of Return Coalition, argues against a two-state solution that would enshrine Israel's right to protect a Jewish demographic majority. Badil writes: "Nusseibeh's conception of a two-state solution—i.e. a Palestinian state and a Jewish state—violates the basic international norm governing the relations between states, and the relations between a state and its inhabitants—i.e., equality of non-discrimination." The Israeli insistence on preserving the State of Israel as a "Jewish state," Badil contends, "discriminates against individual Palestinian refugees who are prevented from exercising their right of return and restitution of property; internally displaced Palestinians who are citizens of Israel but also barred from exercising their right of return and restitution of property; Palestinian citizens of Israel in general who are excluded by virtue of Israel's definition of itself as a 'Jewish state'; and, all other 'non-Jewish' citizens and residents."[95] A two-state solution without the right of return is no durable solution, these critics claim, based as it would be on the foundation of a discriminatory, ethnocratic polity.[96]

"THE ENTIRE WORLD IS AS A FOREIGN PLACE": EDWARD SAID ON EXILE AND RETURN

The late Palestinian-American critic Edward Said did not directly address (appreciatively or negatively) the arguments advanced by Khalidi and Nusseibeh in favor of Palestinians accepting Israeli recognition of the right of return in principle while implementing return virtually to a reconfigured Palestinian state to be created in the Occupied Territories rather than to the refugees' original village locations. The Said of the late 1970s and most of the 1980s championed a two-state solution to the conflict, and accordingly stressed that "for most of us there will always remain the sense of deep, haunting loss, that Jaffa, Haifa, and the Galilee will not once again be as they were in 1948, that thousands of us have lost what we have lost forever."[97] By the advent of the Oslo accords, however, Said had become deeply disillusioned with the two-state approach and had begun arguing that Palestinians needed to look beyond the nation-state as the *telos* for their political energies.[98] This Said expressed admiration for Salman Abu-Sitta's cartographic enterprise and for the efforts of Badil and Al-Awda to create transnational networks of advocacy on behalf of Palestinian refugee rights, including the right of return.[99] Yet, at the same time, Said raised critical questions about the meaning of return, worried that Palestinian discourse around refugee return might too easily end up replicating the Zionist form of return that had created the Palestinian refugee case in the first place. Said repeatedly stressed the ravages on national, communal, and individual life exacted by exile, and so did not dismiss talk of return.[100] Nevertheless, Said cautioned that Palestinians should be careful not to forget the positive lessons of exile, the critical perspective that the exilic location can impart. Exile, after all, has profoundly shaped Palestinian identity:

"we do in fact form a community, if at heart a community built on suffering and exile."[101] Exile is "the fundamental condition of Palestinian life, the source of what is both over- and underdeveloped about it, the energy for what is best, say, in the components of its remarkable literature . . . and in its extraordinary network of communications, associations, and extended families."[102]

An exemplar of what Abdul JanMohamed calls the "specular border intellectual," Said refused the comforts of being easily "at home" in any one culture or polity, convinced that it is the responsibility of the intellectual—understood as any individual ready to speak truth to and within her own context—to maintain a sense of being "out of place," inhabiting a liminal space from which to critique one's own nation, culture, and people.[103] Said, in brief, embraced exile as the proper *place* of the critic.[104] Exile, for Said, is not simply a physical reality (although Said emphasized that the materiality of exile must never be forgotten, lest it be aestheticized beyond recognition), but also names a metaphorical condition.[105] Building on Paul Virilio, Said called this condition *counter-habitation*, one of living a migrant existence within public spaces.[106] If Zionism, for Said, represented an "ideology of difference" underwriting a politics of separation, then exilic politics as counter-habitation accepts existence amidst difference.[107]

Only exilic counter-habitation, Said suggested, will be adequate to resist colonialist forms of geography that leave no room for heterogeneous places.[108] The question that must be posed to Abu-Sitta's cartographic project is whether or not the form of return advocated by Abu-Sitta falls captive to what Said called the "symmetry of redemption" characteristic of mainstream Zionist conceptualizations of return, a form of return whose "horrid clanging shutters" close off the Other (the Palestinian Other, for Zionism, or the Jewish Other, for Abu-Sitta) from view.[109] What type of sacralization of space is at play in these maps given Abu-Sitta's emphasis not only on the mundane practicalities of refugee return, but as well on the "sacred" character of Palestinian refugee rights? Abu-Sitta's cartographic production arguably has the effect of sacralizing all Palestinian space destroyed and erased in 1948, not only the ruins of previously "sacred" spaces such as mosques, churches, and cemeteries. Rather than seeking to emulate the Zionist form of return, Said insisted on the way in which Palestinians disrupt the all-too-easy symmetry of exile and return in Zionist thought, a symmetry that ignores and erases the Palestinian presence. "We are 'other,' an opposite, a flaw in the geometry of resettlement and exodus," a disruption to the smoothness and homogeneity of the Zionist map, Said contended.[110]

Distinguishing between secular and religious criticism, Said establishes a contrast between what he calls, on the one hand, the "open secular element," the secular criticism of the exilic intellectual marked by a "constantly postponed metaphysics of return" that privileges "restless nomadic activity over the settlements of held territory," and, on the other hand, the closed symmetry of religion. Palestinian exile and dispossession, Said observed, occurs "alongside and intervening in a closed orbit of Jewish exile and a recuperated, much-celebrated patriotism of which Israel is the emblem. Better our wanderings, I sometimes think, than the horrid clanging shutters of their return. The open secular element, and not the symmetry of redemption."[111] The cartographic reinscription of the Palestinian landscape represents a practical assertion of rights and identity, not an effort to recreate an idealized, pristine past and pour the presence of the past back into the present. "Every effort we make to retain our Palestinian identity is also an effort to get back on the map," Said argued. "This is a secular effort—as are most of the struggles of our recent political history—and I would insist that religious considerations are secondary, are consequences, not causes. But the map, like the land itself, or like the walls of our houses, is already so saturated and cluttered that we have had to get used to working within an already dense and worked-over space."[112]

Said's repeated—one might say incessant—identification of exilic criticism with the secular, contrasting it to the supposed dogmatism of the religious, runs throughout his critical work. Ironically, however, the key text that inspires Said's exilic outlook comes from the medieval Augustinian theologian Hugo of St. Victor as mediated by the twentieth-century German Jewish literary critic Erich Auerbach. In almost all of his major works Said turns to a passage from Hugo's *Didascalion* quoted at the end of Auerbach's magisterial overview of Western literature, *Mimesis*, a passage Said calls "Hugo's exilic credo," an "ascetic code of willed homelessness":[113]

> It is therefore, a source of great virtue for the practiced mind to learn, bit by bit, first to change about in visible and transitory things, so that afterwards it may be able to leave them behind altogether. The person who finds his homeland sweet is still a tender beginner; he to whom every soil is as his native one is already strong; but he is perfect to whom the entire world is as a foreign place. The tender soul has fixed his love on one spot in the world; the strong person has extended his love to all places; the perfect man has extinguished his.[114]

What Said appropriated from Hugo via Auerbach as a humanist credo simultaneously echoes the exilic church described in 1 Peter and the *Epistle to Diognetus*. Hugo's Augustinianism, meanwhile, leads one to see reverberations of Augustine's *City of God* in this exilic code. That Said was deaf to the theological background of Hugo's text reflects the overall woodenness of Said's binary opposition of the "secular" to the "religious."[115] Closer attention to Christian (and Jewish) theological understandings of exile would have (or at least should have) led Said to recognize that the "religious" is not incompatible with the "exilic" (and, ideally, to call into question a simple binarism of the secular against the religious).[116] Said arguably recognized at some level that this binary opposition of secular-religious breaks down, given his tongue-in-cheek self-identification as "the last Jewish intellectual." If Zionism presents a closed circle of exile and return, the Jewish diaspora, as exemplified by Auerbach and Theodor Adorno, offers a different, more critical model of exile, a model embraced by Said.[117]

The Saidian question to be asked about Palestinian refugee return is thus: Must Palestinian refugee return simply mirror the mainstream Zionist form of return (depicted by Said as a "religious" form of return), which in its tracings of new Zionist cartographies was inextricably intertwined with the erasure of Palestinian space? Do Abu-Sitta's mappings of Palestinian refugee return constitute such a mirroring of Zionist return? Said underscored that Palestinian exile teaches that "[h]omecoming is out of the question. You learn to transform the mechanics of loss into a constantly postponed metaphysics of return."[118] Specifically, homecoming as defined either by recapturing an imagined past or by incorporation into the nation-state is out of the question for Said. Do Abu-Sitta's cartographic productions, however, operate with such a nationalist or romanticized notion of homecoming?

I would contend that Abu-Sitta's maps *can* (but need not) be interpreted as escaping the statist character of most national maps. Matthew Sparke argues that in the case of most national maps (in his case he focuses on Canadian national maps) "the abstract effect of the state and territorial homogeneity on which it is secured are . . . flatly presented as admitting no alternatives."[119] For nation-state cartography, one-to-one correlations exist between nation and circumscribed territory. However, alternatives to nationalist cartography exist, Sparke maintains. Sparke thinks specifically of maps superimposing First Nation mappings onto the contemporary Canadian colonial landscape, maps that thus display "the palimpsest produced by the whole series of precolonial, colonial, and postcolonial inscriptions."[120] Rather than producing a "cartographic national anthem," the map-as-palimpsest exhibits what Sparke, drawing on

Edward Said, calls "contrapuntal cartographies."[121] Such contrapuntal cartography maps Said's vision of a reconciled political future for Palestinians and Israeli Jews that transcends the colonial form of the nation-state.[122] Sparke's Saidian conception of "contrapuntal cartography," a cartography of palimpsests, helps visually to explain Rochelle Davis's claim that Palestinian refugee mappings of place "oppose but do not necessarily negate Zionist ideas about this same land, Israel, which Zionists see as a homeland and staging ground for the history of the Jewish people. What Palestinians struggle against is the right of Jews to form a state that excludes Palestinians from their lands, livelihoods, and rights."[123]

Abu-Sitta's maps of the *nakba* and Palestinian refugee return permit being decoded, I contend, as examples of such contrapuntal cartography. The maps in the *Return Journey* and *From Refugees to Citizens at Home* atlases display a form of return that does not wall off or erase the Palestinian or the Jewish other from view. This form of return does not conceptualize territory in terms of the smooth space of nationalist cartographies but instead as a palimpsest in which particular sites reveal and embrace a multiplicity of histories and identities. Abu-Sitta's palimpsest maps reproduce cartographic traces of the more than 500 towns and villages destroyed in 1948, traces that persist as irritants, "tucked away, under and within the folds of history, a lesion within memory," traces capable of becoming sites of memory that disrupt the abstract, homogeneous, flat space of nationalist imaginations and around which new political visions of heterogeneous spaces might coalesce.[124] The form of Palestinian refugee return embodied in these palimpsest maps is not a simple mirror of Zionist return, and so does not encode the erasure of Israeli Jewish spaces in a manner parallel to how Zionist return erased Palestinian spaces. *The Return Journey* does not ignore the Hebrew map, but instead inscribes destroyed Palestinian towns and villages back onto that Hebrew map, even naming those locales in Hebrew as well as Arabic.

Avneri, Benvenisti, and Golan are undoubtedly correct that Abu-Sitta's cartographic constructions subvert Zionist cartographies that project an empty space within which a Jewish demographic majority might be secured. Subversion of Zionist cartography, however, need not mean the erasure of Israeli Jewish spaces. Rather, Palestinian refugee cartography as exemplified in Abu-Sitta's maps points to a future in which Palestinian and Israeli Jewish places exist side-by-side, and sometimes as a palimpsest, not in a relationship of unrelieved hostility. In Palestine-Israel today exclusivist nationalisms are ascendant and the ideologies and practices of dispossession seem more firmly entrenched than ever. Cartographic battles over sacred landscapes are the order of the day. Yet within such cartographic conflict, maps for a binational future of heterogeneous space emerge: such maps suggest that the "secret of redemption" lies not in the smooth, homogeneous spaces of the nation-state but rather in an embrace of the heterogeneous character of the landscape and its peoples.

Notes

1. Salman Abu-Sitta, *The Palestinian Nakba, 1948: The Register of Depopulated Localities in Palestine* (London: The Palestinian Return Centre, 1998), frontispiece.

2. Liisa Malkki notes that in refugee imaginations "homeland" is often as much a "moral destination" as a "territorial or topographic entity." Malkki, "National Geographic: The Rooting of Peoples and the Territorialization of National Identity among Scholars and Refugees," *Cultural Anthropology* 7, no. 1 (February 1992), 35–36.

3. Abu-Sitta, *The Palestinian Nakba*, frontispiece. Abu-Sitta does not indicate which Bible translation he is citing.

4. Ibid., 5.

5. Meron Benvenisti, *Sacred Landscape: The Buried History of the Holy Land since 1948* (Berkeley: University of California Press, 2000), 40–44.

6. For the most comprehensive discussions of memory books, see Rochelle A. Davis, *Palestinian Village Histories* (Stanford: Stanford University Press, 2011) and Susan Slyomovics, *The Object of Memory: Arab and Jew Narrate the Palestinian Village* (Philadelphia: University of Pennsylvania Press, 1998), 1–28.

7. In addition to sponsoring annual artistic competitions around Palestinian refugee themes and publishing memory books about particular villages (e.g., Kafr Bir'im), Badil has led the way in trying to document the grounding in international law of Palestinian refugee rights of return, compensation, and restitution. See http://www.badil.org. For the Al-Awda coalition, see http://www.al-awda.org. Memory work is often supported and promoted by state and para-state organizations. While the PLO and the Palestinian Authority have both produced materials to memorialize the *nakba* and destroyed Palestinian villages, Palestinian refugee memory production has mostly been carried out by nongovernmental, civil society, and familial groups. Without a sovereign state, Palestinians lack a governing authority that could conduct the cartographic memory work that most states produce.

8. See, for example, the thirteen memory books compiled by the Bir Zeit University Research and Documentation Center in the 1980s.

9. Efrat Ben-Ze'ev, "Transmission and Transformation: The Palestinian Second Generation and the Commemoration of the Homeland," in *Homelands and Diasporas: Holy Lands and Other Places*, ed. André Levy and Alex Weingrod (Stanford: Stanford University Press, 2005), 136. See also Diana Allan, "Mythologising *Al-Nakba*: Narratives, Collective Identity and Cultural Practice among Palestinian Refugees in Lebanon," *Oral History* 33, no. 1 (Spring 2005): 47–55.

10. Ben Ze'ev, "Transmission and Transformation," 137.

11. Randa Farah, "Palestinian Refugees: Dethroning the Nation at the Crowning of the 'Statelet?'" *interventions* 8, no. 2 (July 2006): 230, 237.

12. Anton Shammas, "The Art of Forgetting," *New York Times Magazine* (December 26, 1993), 33.

13. As Rochelle A. Davis observes, "Palestinians in the diaspora feel further than ever from a political settlement that would include them in any meaningful way." See Davis, *Palestinian Village Histories*, 13.

14. Laleh Khalili, "Commemorating Contested Lands," in *Exile and Return: Predicaments of Palestinians and Jews*, ed. Ann M. Lesch and Ian S. Lustick (Philadelphia: University of Pennsylvania Press, 2005), 19.

15. For "map or be mapped!" see Joe Bryan, "Where Would We Be without Them? Knowledge, Space, and Power in Indigenous Politics," *Futures* 41 (2009): 24.

16. Svetlana Boym, *The Future of Nostalgia* (New York: Basic Books, 2001), 3.

17. Davis, *Palestinian Village Histories*, 23.

18. Ibid., 178.

19. Palestinian map-making extends beyond the refugee-focused and -produced maps that I examine here. Palestinian nongovernmental organizations in general (alongside Israeli human rights organizations) have been prolific producers of maps documenting the Israeli confiscation of Palestinian land and settler-colonial expansion in the Occupied Territories.

20. See *The Palestinian Encyclopedia* [Arabic], 4 volumes (Damascus: Hay'at al-Mawsu'ah al-Filastiniyyah, 1984) and Mustafa Dabbagh, *Our Land, Palestine* [Arabic], 11 volumes (Hebron: Matbu'at Rabitat al-Jami'iyyin bi-Muhafizat al-Khalil, 1972–86).

21. Walid Khalidi, ed., *All That Remains: The Palestinian Villages Occupied and Depopulated by Israel in 1948* (Washington, DC: Institute for Palestine Studies, 1992).

22. Ibid., xvii–xix. The number of destroyed Palestinian population centers identified by *All That Remains* (413) is markedly less than the number highlighted by Abu-Sitta (over 530). The difference between these figures can be explained by at least three factors: a) Abu-Sitta uncovered some village locales missed by the earlier effort; b) Abu-Sitta counted as multiple locales some population centers counted only as one by the *All That Remains* editors; and c) the *All That Remains* editors did not count the encampments of semi-nomadic Bedouin agriculturalists in an-Naqab/the Negev desert. *All That Remains*, xviii.

23. Ibid. *All That Remains*, xxxiv.

24. Ibid.

25. Ibid.

26. Rochelle A. Davis, *Palestinian Village Histories*, 5.

27. See http://www.palestineremembered.com/MissionStatement.htm.

28. See "The Conflict 101, or The Palestinian-Israeli Conflict for Beginners," at http://www.palestineremembered.com/Acre/Palestine-Remembered/Story725.html and "ROR 101" at http://www.palestineremembered.com/Acre/Right-Of-Return/index.html, consisting of the text from Salman Abu-Sitta's *Palestinian Right to Return: Sacred, Legal, Possible* (London: Palestinian Return Center, 1999).

29. Ben-Ze'ev, "Transmission and Transformation," 136.

30. See http://www.palestineremembered.com/MissionStatement.htm.

31. Salman Abu-Sitta, *Atlas of Palestine, 1948* (London: Palestine Land Society, 2005) and Salman Abu-Sitta, *The Atlas of Palestine, 1917–1966* (London: Palestine Land Society, 2010).

32. See http://www.alnakba.org. The site offers markedly less material than Palestine Remembered, and provides almost no opportunities for interactivity. Examples of village-specific sites created by an individual or community group include pages highlighting the villages of Iqrit (http://www.iqrit.org), Lifta (http://www.liftasociety.org), and Kafr Bir'im (http://www.birem.org). Some village-specific sites provide limited opportunities for interaction, e.g., guest books and boards for announcements.

33. Chapters 3 and 4 will highlight particular ways that Palestinians and Israeli Jews use websites to document and map destroyed Palestinian villages and create networks to mobilize for activism on behalf of the Palestinian right of return. Such activism is an example of what Mark Palmer has coined "indigital" activism, i.e., the deployment of digital technologies as part of indigenous struggles for rights and recognition. See Palmer, "Engaging with *Indigital* Geographic Information Networks," *Futures* 41 (2009): 33–40.

34. Pierre Nora, "Between Memory and History: Les Lieux de Mémoire," *Representations* 26 (Spring 1989): 19. For Nora's understanding of memory and history developed through a

narration of the French past, see the four volumes of *Rethinking France: Les Lieux de Mémoire* (Chicago: University of Chicago Press, 2000–2010).

35. Nora, "Between Memory and History," 12.

36. Laleh Khalili, *Heroes and Martyrs of Palestine: The Politics of National Commemoration* (Cambridge: Cambridge University Press, 2007), 10.

37. Laleh Khalili, "Place of Memory and Mourning: Palestinian Commemoration in the Refugee Camps of Lebanon," *Comparative Studies of South Asia, Africa and the Middle East* 25, no. 1 (2005): 31.

38. Arjun Appadurai, *Modernity at Large: Cultural Dimensions of Globalization* (Minneapolis: University of Minnesota Press, 1996), 35.

39. Ibid., 22. See also Rochelle Davis's discussion of the diasporic connections created through the circulation of memory books and through new technologies such as the Internet. Davis, *Palestinian Village Histories*, 223–25.

40. Davis, *Palestinian Village Histories*, 162.

41. Appadurai, *Modernity at Large*, 22.

42. Ibid., 19.

43. Ibid., 20.

44. Ibid., 167.

45. Salman Abu-Sitta, *Atlas of Palestine, 1948* and Abu-Sitta, *Atlas of Palestine, 1917–1966*.

46. Abu-Sitta, *The Return Journey: Guide to Destroyed and Remaining Villages and Holy Places in Palestine* (London: Palestine Land Society, 2007), 243. Mark Monmonier has examined various ways in which maps establish a series of interdictions on movement: Abu-Sitta's *Return Journey*, in contrast, invites Palestinian refugees to embark on imagined and actual journeys to places from which they have been barred. Monmonier, *No Dig, No Fly, No Go: How Maps Restrict and Control* (Chicago: University of Chicago Press, 2010).

47. Denis Wood, *The Power of Maps* (New York and London: Guilford, 1992), 12.

48. Davis, *Palestinian Village Histories*, 155.

49. Abu-Sitta, *From Refugees to Citizens at Home* (London: Palestinian Return Centre, 2000), 5.

50. Abu-Sitta, *Palestinian Right to Return*, 66.

51. Abu-Sitta, *The Return Journey*, 232.

52. For a primary account of the Islamic Movement in Israel, see Ra'id Salah, "The Islamic Movement in Israel: An Interview with Shaykh Ra'id Salah," *Journal of Palestine Studies* 36, no. 2 (Winter 2007): 66–76.

53. Abu-Sitta, *The Return Journey*, 232.

54. Ibid. See also Michael Dumper, *Islam and Israel: Muslim Religious Endowments and the Jewish State* (Washington, DC: Institute for Palestine Studies, 1994).

55. Abu-Sitta, *From Refugees to Citizens at Home*, 15.

56. Abu-Sitta, *Palestinian Right to Return*, 66.

57. See Edward Said, *Peace and Its Discontents: Gaza-Jericho, 1993–1995* (London and New York: Vintage, 1996), 26–28. For a discussion of counter-mapping within the field of critical cartography, see Joel Wainwright and Joe Bryan, "Cartography, Territory, Property: Postcolonial Reflections on Indigenous Counter-Mapping," *Cultural Geographies* 16 (2009): 153–78.

58. For an examination of British Mandate mapping practices, see Dov Gavish, *A Survey of Palestine under the British Mandate, 1920–1948* (London and New York: RoutledgeCurzon, 2005).

59. Denis Cosgrove, *Geography and Vision: Seeing, Imagining, and Representing the World* (London and New York: I. B. Tauris, 2008), 168.

60. Ibid.

61. Ibid., 156.

62. Wood, *The Power of Maps*, 1.

63. Ibid., 3.

64. Denis Wood and John Fels, *The Natures of Maps: Cartographic Constructions of the Natural World* (Chicago and London: University of Chicago Press, 2008), 8.

65. Ibid., 7.

66. Issam Aburaiya and Efrat Ben-Ze'ev insist that "as time goes by, other maps—multiple maps for each space—continuously emerge. The imaginary maps that would not necessarily run along ethnic lines might hold the secret for a more tranquil future in Israel/Palestine." Aburaiya and Ben-Ze'ev, "'Middle-Ground' Politics and the Re-Palestinianization of Places in Israel," *International Journal of Middle East Studies* 36 (2004): 651.

67. Henri Lefebvre, *The Production of Space*, trans. Donald Nicholson-Smith (Oxford: Blackwell, 1991), 85.

68. J. B. Harley, *The New Nature of Maps: Essays in the History of Cartography* (Baltimore: Johns Hopkins University Press, 2002), 79.

69. Matthew Sparke, *In the Space of Theory: Postfoundational Geographies of the Nation-State* (Minneapolis: University of Minnesota Press, 2005), 5.

70. Denis Wood and John Fels, "Designs of Signs: Myth and Meaning in Maps," *Cartographica* 23, no. 1 (1986): 64.

71. See Joe Bryan, "Where Would We Be without Them?"

72. Denis Wood, *Rethinking the Power of Maps* (New York: Guilford, 2010), 232–54.

73. "The map and its legends create a unified Israel and a unified Palestine distinct from one another. They produce the national groups by resisting the fact that Israel and Palestine overlap and by ignoring their respective internal divisions." Rachel Havrelock, *River Jordan: The Mythology of a Dividing Line* (Chicago: University of Chicago Press, 2011), 2–3. Yet Havrelock proceeds to argue that binational mappings of territory that acknowledge and accept co-presence with others as a positive good are possible (16).

74. Abu-Sitta, *The Palestinian Nakba*, frontispiece.

75. Arnon Golan, "The Spatial Outcome of the 1948 War and Prospects for Return," in *Israel and the Palestinian Refugees*, ed. Eyal Benvenisti, Chaim Gans, and Sari Hanafi (Berlin: Springer, 2007), 56–57.

76. Meron Benvenisti, *Sacred Landscape*, 54.

77. Ben-Ze'ev and Aburaiya, 651.

78. "My top priority," writes Shlomo Gazit, "is the continued existence of Israel as a *Jewish* state—a *Jewish* state and not an *Israeli* state." As the rest of his article makes clear, the Jewishness of the Israeli state depends upon securing and maintaining a Jewish demographic majority. Gazit, "Solving the Refugee Problem—An Israeli Point of View," in *The Palestinian Refugees: Old Problems—New Solutions*, ed. Joseph Ginat and Edward J. Perkins (Norman: University of Oklahoma Press, 2001), 235.

79. Ian S. Lustick and Ann M. Lesch, "The Failure of Oslo and the Abiding Question of the Refugees," in *Exile and Return*, ed. Lustick and Lesch, 3–16.

80. For a representative case arguing that Palestinian refugee rights are *not* guaranteed by international law, see Yaffa Zilbershafts, "International Law and the Palestinian Right of Return to the States of Israel," in *Israel and the Palestinian Refugees*, ed. Benvenisti, Gans, and Hanafi, 191–218. For a sampling of arguments that international law does in fact secure Palestinian refugee rights, see Terry Rempel, ed., *Rights in Principle—Rights in Practice: Revisiting the Role of International Law in Crafting Durable Solutions for Palestinian Refugees* (Bethlehem: Badil Resource Center for Palestinian Residency and Refugee Rights, 2009); Lex Takkenberg, *The Status of Palestinian Refugees in International Law* (Oxford: Oxford University Press, 1998); Susan Akram, Michael Dumper, Michael Lynk, and Iain Scobbie, eds., *International Law and the Israeli-Palestinian Conflict: A Rights-Based Approach to Middle East Peace* (London: Routledge, 2010); and Scott Leckie, *Housing, Land, and Property Restitution Rights of Refugees and Displaced Persons* (Cambridge and New York: Cambridge University Press, 2007).

81. For case studies that place the Palestinian refugee situation, often treated as *sui generis*, within comparative perspective, see Michael Dumper, ed. *Palestinian Refugee Repatriation: Global Perspectives* (London and New York: Routledge, 2006).

82. For overviews of this question see Michael R. Fischbach, "Palestinian and Mizrahi Jewish Property Claims in Discourse and Diplomacy," in *Exile and Return*, ed. Lesch and Lustick, 207–24; Jan Abu Shakrah, "Deconstructing the Link: Palestinian Refugees and Jewish Immigrants from Arab Countries," in *Palestinian Refugees: The Right of Return*, ed. Naseer Aruri (London: Pluto, 2001), 208–16; and Yehouda Shenhav, "Arab Jews, Population Exchange, and the Palestinian Right of Return," in *Exile and Return*, ed. Lesch and Lustick, 225–45. Shenhav persuasively argues: "The reasons and motivations by which the Arab Jews immigrated to Israel are diverse. Some were coerced by the conditions in Arab countries and as a result of Zionism and Arab nationalism. Some came voluntarily and intentionally. Others were brought against their own will by the Zionist movement and Jewish organizations. Whatever the motivation, it should not be equated with the Palestinian inhabitants of Palestine prior to 1948. The linkage between those populations and their properties is a manipulative practice of the state and should be abandoned from the political discourse" (241).

83. Under political conditions in which Israeli acknowledgment of the right of return is not on the horizon, obtaining an accurate sense of what percentage of Palestinian refugees would choose to return proves difficult, as respondents to public opinion polls or subjects of oral interviews will routinely emphasize their determination to return as a way of underscoring their insistence on return as a right. See Sari Hanafi, "The Sociology of Return: Palestinian Social Capital, Transnational Kinships and the Refugee Repatriation Process," in *Israel and the Palestinian Refugees*, ed. Benvenisti, Gans, and Hanafi, 3–40.

84. Manuel Hassassian, "The Political Refugee Problem in the Light of the Peace Process," in *The Palestinian Refugees: Old Problems—New Solutions*, ed. Ginat and Perkins, 75.

85. Official PLO proclamations insist on the right of return. So, for example, the PLO Negotiations Affairs Department claims that Palestinians have the right to recognition of Israeli responsibility; recognition and implementation of the principle of the right of return; restitution of Palestinian refugee properties; and full compensation when restitution is not possible. Yet, as Menachem Klein notes, "the right of return is absent from some of the most important statements made by senior PLO officials." Klein, "The Negotiations for the Settlement of the 1948 Refugees," in *Israel and the Palestinian Refugees*, ed. Benvenisti, Gans, and Hanafi, 465. In the face of this ambiguity, Palestinian NGOs have stepped in to bring greater clarity to the demand for the recognition of the right of return. See Elazar Barkan, "Considerations toward Accepting Historical Responsibility," in *Exile and Return*, ed. Lesch and Lustick, 91 and Menachem Klein, "From a Doctrine-Oriented to a Solution-Oriented Policy: The PLO's 'Right of Return,' 1964–2000," in *The Palestinian Refugees: Old Problems—New Solutions*, ed. Ginat and Perkins, 46–56.

86. George E. Bisharat, "Exile to Compatriot: Transformations in the Social Identity of Palestinian Refugees in the West Bank," in *Culture, Power, Place: Explorations in Critical Anthropology*, ed. Akhil Gupta and James Ferguson (Durham, NC and London: Duke University Press, 1997), 224. See also Jaber Suleiman, "The Palestinian Liberation Organization: From the Right of Return to Bantustan," in *Palestinian Refugees: The Right of Return*, ed. Aruri, 87–103. The release by the Al Jazeera satellite television network of the so-called "Palestine Papers" documenting ongoing negotiations by PLO/PA and Israeli government officials confirmed Palestinian refugee suspicions that senior PLO and Fatah leaders were prepared to relinquish refugees' right of return in exchange for statehood and territorial concessions. See Clayton Swisher, *The Palestine Papers: The End of the Road?* (Chatham, UK: Hesperus, 2011), esp. 38–53.

87. The Nusseibeh-Ayalon plan, named after its drafters, Sari Nusseibeh and Ami Ayalon, envisions an international fund to compensate Palestinian refugees, while stating clearly that any Palestinian refugee return would be to the new State of Palestine, not to homes and villages inside Israel. For the text of the Nusseibeh-Ayalon plan, see http://www.peacelobby.org/nusseibeh-ayalon_initiative.htm. Meanwhile, the Geneva Initiative (sometimes referred to as the Beilin-Abu

Mazen plan, after its main drafters, Meretz politician Yossi Beilin and Mahmoud Abbas, or Abu Mazen, now the head of the PLO and the PA) included the same basic stipulations as the Nusseibeh-Ayalon plan, while allowing for limited Palestinian refugee return to Israel contingent on Israel's agreement. See http://www.geneva-accord.org/. Donna Arzt advanced a similar proposal in her study, *Refugees into Citizens: Palestinians and the End of the Arab-Israeli Conflict* (New York: Council on Foreign Relations, 1997).

88. Nusseibeh first advanced this position in the study he co-authored with the Israeli Jewish political scientist, Mark Heller, *No Trumpets, No Drums: A Two-State Settlement of the Israeli-Palestinian Conflict* (New York: Hill & Wang, 1993). He later proposed that Palestinian refugee return be traded for the State of Israel recognizing Palestinian sovereignty in East Jerusalem. See Sari Nusseibeh, *Final Status: Jerusalem and Return* (Houston: James A. Baker III Institute for Public Policy of Rice University, 2007).

89. Nusseibeh, *Final Status*, 37–38.

90. Sari Nusseibeh, *Once upon a Country: A Palestinian Life* (New York: Farrar, Straus & Giroux, 2007), 446.

91. Rashid Khalidi, "The Palestinian Refugee Problem: A Possible Solution," *Palestine-Israel Journal of Politics, Economics, and Culture* 3, no. 4 (Autumn 1995): 72. Neither for Khalidi nor for Nusseibeh (nor for PLO nor PA officials who accept their approach to the refugee situation) does relinquishing the right of Palestinian refugees to return go hand-in-hand with acknowledging the supposed right of the State of Israel to be a "Jewish" state. Although the PLO recognized the State of Israel's right to exist in the Oslo Accords (without Israel acknowledging the right of a Palestinian state to exist), Israeli officials have increasingly cited Palestinian unwillingness to recognize Israel's right to exist as a Jewish state as representing an insurmountable obstacle to a final, comprehensive peace agreement. Such a demand is objectionable for at least two reasons. First, for Palestinians to state that Israel has a right to exist as a Jewish state (in the demographic sense upheld by Netanyahu and other Israeli officials) implies that Palestinian dispossession in 1948–49 was a necessary, moral good, as it made way for the realization of that right. To accept for pragmatic reasons the impossibility of refugee return for uprooted refugees is quite different from retroactively providing moral sanction to the uprooting of those refugees. Second, for the PLO to recognize Israel as a Jewish (again, in the demographic sense) state would unfairly prejudice the status of Palestinian Arabs inside Israel, who have increasingly been organizing to press for greater communal and individual equality within Israel. For a summary of Palestinian objections to the demand that Palestinians recognize Israel as a Jewish state, see Ahmad Samih Khalidi, "Why Can't the Palestinians Recognize the Jewish State?" *Journal of Palestine Studies* 40, no. 1 (Summer 2011): 78–81. In chapter 2, I will return to the question of what it means to think of Israel as a Jewish state, suggesting that in some binational scenarios the state's Jewishness could be affirmed in a nondemographic manner.

92. Rashid Khalidi, "Truth, Justice, and Reconciliation: Elements of a Solution to the Palestinian Refugee Issue," in *The Palestinian Exodus, 1948–1998*, ed. Ghada Karmi and Eugene Cotran (Reading, UK: Ithaca Press, 1999), 222–23.

93. Rosemary Sayigh, "Back to the Center: Post-Oslo Revival of the Refugee Issue," in *The Struggle for Sovereignty: Palestine and Israel, 1993–2005*, ed. Joel Beinin and Rebecca L. Stein (Stanford: Stanford University Press, 2006), 130–39.

94. Nadim N. Rouhana, "Truth and Reconciliation: The Right of Return in the Context of Past Injustice," in *Exile and Return*, ed. Lesch and Lustick, 274–75.

95. Badil Resource Center for Palestinian Residency and Refugee Rights, "Initial Remarks Concerning Comments by Sari Nusseibeh on Palestinian Refugee Rights" (October 24, 2001). Available at http://badil.org/en/documents/category/52-other-papers?start=20.

96. Nusseibeh, for his part, has since rethought his advocacy for a two-state solution, as Israeli colonization of the Occupied Territories has progressively undermined the territorial basis for such an approach. Back in 2008, Nusseibeh told a reporter for the Israeli newspaper *Haaretz*: "Unless a major breakthrough happens by the end of this year, in my opinion we should start

trying to strive for equality" within one state, working to "bring Fatah around to a new idea, the old-new idea, of one state." Quoted in Akiva Eldar, "'We Are Running Out of Time': Interview with Sari Nusseibeh," *Haaretz* (August 14, 2008). Nusseibeh followed that line of thinking in his study, *What Is a Palestinian State Worth?* (Cambridge, MA: Harvard University Press, 2011), in which he contends that Palestinians would be better off abandoning the struggle for statehood, given how Israeli colonization of the Occupied Territories has rendered a two-state solution all-but-impossible. In a similar manner, Beshara Doumani contends that the Palestinian national movement's fixation on statehood led in practice to the denial of key Palestinian rights, in particular Palestinian refugee rights. See Doumani, "Palestine versus the Palestinians? The Iron Laws and the Ironies of a People Denied," *Journal of Palestine Studies* 36, no. 4 (Summer 2007): 49–64.

97. Yet even as he upheld a compromise for a "ministate" within Mandate Palestine, Said also emphasized that the broader vision of a humanity not defined by race or nationality would continue to have influence in the region, potentially transforming it beyond the nation-state system. Edward Said, *The Question of Palestine* (New York: Vintage, 1979), 175.

98. For Said's political commentary during and after the Oslo period, see *The Politics of Dispossession: The Struggle for Palestinian Self-Determination, 1969-1994* (London and New York: Vintage, 1995); *Peace and Its Discontents: Gaza-Jericho, 1993–1995* (London and New York: Vintage, 1996); *The End of the Peace Process: Oslo and After* (London and New York: Vintage, 2000); and *From Oslo to Iraq and the Road Map* (New York: Pantheon, 2004).

99. Edward Said, "Introduction: The Right of Return at Last," in *Palestinian Refugees: The Right of Return*, ed. Aruri, 6. Said particularly appreciated Abu-Sitta's immersion in the details of cartography, given the fact that one of Said's critiques of the Oslo accords was that Palestinian negotiators made numerous bad decisions based on their ignorance of the geography of the Occupied Territories, an ignorance compounded by the Israeli negotiators' comprehensive geographical knowledge: "[the Palestinians] had no detailed maps of their own at Oslo; nor, unbelievably, were there any individuals on the negotiating team familiar enough with the geography of the Occupied Territories to contest decisions or to provide alternative plans." Edward Said, "Palestinians under Siege," *London Review of Books* (24 December 2000), 22.

100. Exile, Said underscored, is "a condition legislated to deny dignity," "a discontinuous state of being" which cuts people "off from their roots, their land, their past." Edward W. Said, *Reflections on Exile and Other Essays* (Cambridge, MA: Harvard University Press, 2000), 175, 177.

101. Said, *After the Last Sky: Palestinian Lives* (New York: Columbia University Press, 1999), 5.

102. Said, *The Question of Palestine*, 69.

103. Abdul R. JanMohamed, "Worldliness-without-World, Homelessness-as-Home: Toward a Definition of the Specular Border Intellectual," in *Edward Said: A Critical Reader*, ed. Michael Sprinker (Oxford: Blackwell, 1992), 96–120 and Yifen Beus, "After the Last Sky: A Liminal Space," in *Paradoxical Citizenship: Edward Said*, ed. Silvia Nagy-Zekmi (Lanham, MD: Lexington, 2006), 211–20. Said used the phrase "out of place" to describe his existential condition and as the title of his autobiography. See Edward Said, *Out of Place: A Memoir* (New York: Alfred A. Knopf, 1999).

104. As John Ochoa explains, the critic "must be always in exile, always both outside and within," in a "heterotopic place." See Ochoa, "Said's Foucault, or the Places of the Critic," in *Paradoxical Citizenship: Edward Said*, ed. Nagy-Zekmi, 55. See also Ilan Pappé, "The Exilic Homeland of Edward W. Said," *interventions* 81 (March 2006): 9–23.

105. Edward Said, *Representations of the Intellectual: The 1993 Reith Lectures* (New York and London: Vintage, 1994), 39.

106. Edward Said, *Culture and Imperialism* (New York: Vintage, 1994), 402. See also Paul Virilio, *L'Insécurité du territoire* (Paris: Stock, 1976), 88ff.

107. Edward Said, "An Ideology of Difference," *Critical Inquiry* 12, no. 1 (Autumn 1985): 38–58. Ilan Pappé felicitously describes Said's exilic approach as one of *stable exilic intellectualism*: Said's valorization of exile does not come at the expense of connection to place, but instead enables a different, exilic way of relating to and of inhabiting place. See Pappé, "Exilic Homeland," 10.

108. Edward Said, *The Question of Palestine*, 77.

109. Edward Said, *After the Last Sky*, 150.

110. Ibid., 17.

111. Ibid., 150. Said's famous "Canaanite" reading of Michael Walzer's treatment of the exodus narrative reflects Said's assessment that Walzer's political philosophy, when put to the task of analyzing the Palestinian-Israeli conflict, operates within precisely this "closed orbit" of the "symmetry of redemption" through return from exile. See Said, "Michael Walzer's *Exodus and Revolution*: A Canaanite Reading," in *Blaming the Victims: Spurious Scholarship and the Palestinian Question*, ed. Edward Said and Christopher Hitchens (London: Verso, 1988), 161–78 and Michael Walzer and Edward Said, "An Exchange," *Grand Street* 5, no. 4 (1986): 246–59.

112. Said, *After the Last Sky*, 62.

113. Said, *The World, the Text, and the Critic* (Cambridge, MA: Harvard University Press, 1983), 7. Other places where Said appeals to Hugo of St. Victor include: *Reflections on Exile*, 185; *Orientalism* (New York: Vintage, 1979), 259; and *Culture and Imperialism*, 406–7.

114. Hugo of St. Victor, *Didascalion*, trans. Jerome Taylor (New York: Columbia University Press, 1961), 101.

115. For a critical examination of Said's opposition of "secular" to "religious" criticism, see William D. Hart, *Edward Said and the Religious Effects of Culture* (Cambridge: Cambridge University Press, 2000).

116. John Barbour emphasizes the similarities between Said's exilic criticism and "religious" approaches to exile, identifying Said as a hybrid between Thomas Tweed's supralocative and translocative forms of religious mapping of place. Barbour, "Edward Said and the Space of Exile," *Literature and Theology* 21, no. 3 (September 2007): 299. Said himself appeared to recognize at points that the secular-religious opposition breaks down, as when he praised the Sabeel Ecumenical Liberation Theology Center, headed by the Anglican priest Naim Ateek, for its "secular" form of Christian witness. See Said, "Keynote Address," in *Holy Land—Hollow Jubilee: God, Justice, and the Palestinians*, ed. Naim Ateek and Michael Prior (London: Melisende, 1999), 17–32. For an argument that Said's secular-versus-religious criticism opposition was never intended to be interpreted in a rigid fashion, see Mathieu Courville, "The Secular Masks of Religion: A (Re)constructive Critique of W. D. Hart's *Edward Said and the Religious Effects of Culture*," *Studies in Religion/Sciences Religieuses*, 34, no. 2 (2005): 233–49.

117. "I am the last Jewish intellectual," Said stated in an interview with Aviv Lavie. "You do not know anyone else like that. All the other Jewish intellectuals are masters from the suburbs. From Amos Oz to those who live here in America, so that I am the last one, the authentic follower of Adorno. I will articulate it like this: I am a Jewish Palestinian." Said, *Power, Politics, and Culture: Interviews with Edward W. Said*, ed. Gauri Viswanathan (New York: Pantheon, 2001), 458. Sarah Hammerschlag's critique of Said for supposedly "acting as an occupier" by usurping, in supersessionist fashion, Jewish identity from self-identified Jews, is strikingly tone-deaf to the playful, deliberately ironic character of Said's interview with Lavie. Said, *contra* Hammerschlag, was not trying to make a point about whether or not a Zionist Israeli author like Amos Oz is "Jewish," nor was Said ignorant of the many Jews, both inside and outside of Israel, who live out the type of exilic politics of place Said championed. Rather, Said was simply underscoring the irony that he, as a member of a people uprooted by Zionists, was now articulating an exilic politics often identified as "Jewish." This ironic development in turn serves to undermine the strict partition between "Jewish" and "Palestinian" identities that Zionist and Palestinian nationalist imaginations create and police. See Hammerschlag, *The Figural Jew: Politics and Identity in Postwar French Thought* (Chicago and London: University of Chicago Press, 2010), 23–24.

118. Said, *After the Last Sky*, 50.

119. Sparke, 21.

120. Ibid., 19.

121. Ibid., 4. Said borrowed the contrapuntal metaphor from music, and develops it for cultural and political analysis most notably in *Culture and Imperialism* and *Representations of the Intellectual*. The exilic awareness of multiple worlds is, Said explained, a contrapuntal awareness. Said, *Representations of the Intellectual*, 186. Palestinians and Israeli face the urgent task, Said argued, of narrating contrapuntal histories. Said, "Afterword: The Consequences of 1948," in *The War for Palestine: Rewriting the History of 1948*, ed. Eugene L. Rogan and Avi Shlaim (Cambridge: Cambridge University Press, 2001), 218. In addition to being a literary critic, Said was an accomplished amateur musician and occasional music critic. For an example of Said's discussion of the contrapuntal in music and its connection to politics, see *Parallels and Paradoxes: Explorations in Music and Society*, with Daniel Barenboim (New York: Vintage, 2004).

122. The "contrapuntal cartography" articulated by Sparke and arguably present in Said's work indicates that while Bryan has valid concerns about indigenous mapping projects, i.e., that they unwittingly replicate colonial categories and binarisms, not all Palestinian refugee cartography remains captive to colonialist forms of mapping. See Joe Bryan, "Where Would We Be without Them?" and D. Turnbull, "Mapping Encounters and (En)Countering Maps: A Critical Examination of Cartographic Resistance," *Knowledge and Society* 11 (1998): 15–44.

123. Davis, *Palestinian Village Histories*, 18.

124. Lena Jayyusi, "Iterability, Cumulativity, and Presence: The Relational Figures of Palestinian Memory," in *Nakba: Palestine, 1948, and the Claims of Memory*, ed. Ahmad H. Sa'di and Lila Abu-Lughod (New York: Columbia University Press, 2007), 108.

2

Reclaiming the Place of Exile for Political Theology

In the refugee mappings examined in the preceding chapter, exile is primarily presented as a *location* to escape through return. Yet, I contend, these cartographies of return from exile, when they create palimpsests and reveal the land to consist of heterogeneous places and overlapping identities, do more than simply overcome or erase exile. Instead, these mappings suggest the possibility of an exilic form of return, a vision of inhabiting particular places in Israel-Palestine shaped by the lessons of exile. The "return journeys" charted by Abu-Sitta and other Palestinian refugees at their best create such palimpsests, and therefore project not only a departure *from* exile but also display having been shaped *by* exile.

In this chapter I defend the claim that mappings of return might be shaped by an exilic ethos through an analysis of two competing political theologies of exile: first, what Israeli political theorist Amnon Raz-Krakotzkin has called the national colonial theology of Zionism, with its doctrinal insistence on the "negation of exile" (*shelilat ha-galut*); and second, the late John Howard Yoder's exilic ecclesiology and missiology, with its embrace of *galut* as vocation.[1] Through a close discussion of how the negation of exile fits within a Zionist political theology in which the Jewish people are redeemed from exile through physical return to the land of Israel and through (re)entry into "real" history understood as the history of nation-states, I follow Raz-Krakotzkin, Gabriel Piterberg, and others in insisting that the negation of exile fuels cartographies of return that erase Palestinians from the map.

To counter this Zionist political theology of exile, I turn to an analysis of how Yoder named exile as the shape of the church's mission, a posture of "not being in charge" and of seeking the *shalom* of the cities and lands in which the church finds itself. While Yoder's theological appraisal of exile unfolds within a sometimes problematic account of Christianity's relationship to

Judaism, these flaws are not fatal. As I will show, one can separate Yoder's exilic ecclesiology from the supersessionist dimensions of his theology of Judaism. Furthermore, contrary to Yoder's critics who charge that Yoder's theology of exile cannot provide a positive account of landedness, I will show how Yoder's work subverts easy binary oppositions of exile to return. Instead, a careful reading of Yoder's treatment of exile uncovers a vision of return shaped by exile, a theology of life in the land molded by the exilic commitment to building the *polis* for others with whom one enters into shared political existence.

In the concluding section of this chapter, I consider how Yoder's political theology of exilic landedness intersects in productive and provocative ways with critiques of the nationalist assumptions underpinning traditional Zionism and proposals for binational accommodation that transcend versions of the two-state solution to the Israeli–Palestinian conflict still wedded to such nationalist presuppositions. Raz-Krakotzkin and other Israeli Jewish political theorists and activists describe the binational polities they defend as "exilic" or "diasporic" in character. To live in an exilic manner need not mean a cosmopolitan repudiation of all particular places, but can rather name a specific way of inhabiting those places that affirms their always already heterogeneous nature. Proponents of an exilic binationalism thus contest traditional forms of Zionism not by opposing exile to return or exile to landedness, but instead by opposing Zionism's theological negation of exile and by defending an alternative political theology of exile in which exile conditions understandings of land and return.

THE NEGATION OF EXILE IN ZIONIST POLITICAL THEOLOGY

In order to claim exile as a positive category for developing a constructive theology of land and return, particularly within the context of the Palestinian-Israeli conflict, one must first address how Zionism has conceptualized exile as a negative condition to be overcome through return to the land. "Zionism challenged all the aspects of traditional Judaism," contends Yosef Salmon, and nowhere is that challenge more evident than in Zionism's "attitude to the religious concepts of diaspora and redemption."[2] Exile, in traditional Jewish terms, named an ontological condition of the Jewish people (and by extension the world as a whole) awaiting in expectant, eschatological longing the redemption that the arrival of the messiah would bring. For Zionism, exile acquired a new meaning as a weak and degenerate spiritual and mental state. The Zionist "negation of exile" (*shelilat ha-galut*) in turn referred not simply to the (re)establishment of national Jewish life in the land of Israel, but also to the overcoming of this purportedly negative exilic mentality.[3]

To observe that Zionism challenged traditional Jewish life and thought, including interpretations of exile, is *not* to view Zionism as a complete break with the Jewish past. Rather, it is simply to underscore how Zionism involves a radical reinterpretation and reframing of key Jewish concepts such as exile and return.[4] Amos Funkenstein observes how Zionism and then the State of Israel replace "the sacred liturgical memory with secular liturgical memory—days of remembrance, flags, and monuments," and at the heart of this transformation is a re-narration of the history of Jewish exile.[5] Zionism appropriates traditional notions of exile, return, and redemption and radically reframes them within what Raz-Krakotzkin has called a "national colonial theology" supported by three doctrinal pillars: the negation of exile (*shelilat ha-galut*), the "return to the land" (*ha-shiva le-eretz yisrael*), and the "return to history" (*ha-shiva la-historia*).[6] "With the concepts of the negation of exile and the return to history," Raz-Krakotzkin asserts, "the Jewish Zionist implantation in Palestine comes to be considered as the restoration of Jewish sovereignty, the return of the Jewish people to a land presented as its own (and supposedly empty), and as the success of Jewish history, the fulfillment of millenarian aspirations. The return to history is presented as the return to national and political sovereignty which the Jews had known in biblical antiquity and in the Second Temple period."[7]

Jewish life in exile, from the perspective of mainstream Zionism, is negated as abnormal or even diseased, a problematic condition to be remedied through *aliyah*, or ascent, to the land of Israel and through the "return" of the Jewish people to the history of nation-states. The Zionist act of settling the land thus takes the place of traditional Jewish pilgrimage, with immigration to the land accorded national-spiritual character; conversely, Israelis who emigrate from Israel receive the pejorative label *yordim* (the ones who descend). Exile is presented by Zionism as "a defective existence, incomplete or abnormal, a situation in which 'the spirit of the nation' could not fully express itself": the Jewish nation could only find its fulfillment in its own land and with its own state.[8] For Ella Shohat, Zionism's theological reframing of traditional Jewish concepts is captured by the Hebrew phrase "*mi-gola le-geoola*" ("from diaspora to redemption"), a phrase that offers "a teleological reading of Jewish history in which Zionism formed a redemptive vehicle for the renewal of Jewish life on the demarcated terrain, no longer simply spiritual and textual but, instead, national and political."[9] *Aliyah* thus negates exile through the redemptive project of *kibbutz galuiot*, or the "ingathering of the exiles."[10]

Zionism as a national colonial theology articulates and reinforces a series of binary oppositions between exile, on the one hand, and homeland and return, on the other. Laurence Silberstein documents how this central binary of homeland/exile is developed within Zionist writings, with homeland as a "productive," "unifying" force "nurturing to Jewish national culture" standing opposed to exile as "destructive," "fragmenting," and "life-threatening."[11] For Zionism as national colonial theology, then, exile and homeland, or exile and return, are pitted against one another in stark opposition, with the assumption that projects of return can only mean the negation of exile and that an embrace of exile must entail a refusal of return.

Zionism as a political theology constructs a historical schema in which exile represents an abnormal rupture in the life of the Jewish people. As Yael Zerubavel explains, this Zionist periodization of history is "based on the primacy of the people-land bond," with the past "divided into two main periods, Antiquity and Exile," a past that leads up to the modern national revival of Zionism.[12] This historical schema encodes Antiquity as positive and Exile as a "hole" between Antiquity and national rebirth in the form of Zionism, with "an acute lack of positive characteristics attributed" to Jewish life during the period of exile.[13] "Zionist collective memory not only defied Exile and its spirit," Zerubavel observes, "it also blamed it for a deliberate suppression of the national memory of the ancient struggles for liberation."[14] This depreciation of exile, Piterberg claims, derives from what for Zionism is an "uncontestable presupposition," namely, that "from time immemorial, the Jews constituted a territorial nation," and from the corollary that "non-territorial existence must be abnormal, incomplete, and inauthentic."[15]

The historical myth within which the negation of exile was situated, like other forms of Romantic nationalism, posited "a homogeneous national past." Rather than narrate the experience of Jewish communities in terms of their embeddedness within and interaction with diverse cultures, institutions, and practices, Zionist historians insisted on the homogeneous experience of the Jewish people (moving from antiquity to exile to national revival), with many of those historians insisting on a "scientific," biological basis to the Jewish nation.[16]

The negation of exile, as noted above, was not simply a polemic against a particular geographical location. Instead, it was above all a critique of the "exile mentality" that had debilitated the once-proud Jewish nation. This critique assumes gendered, anti-Jewish, and Orientalist dimensions. The young, masculine pioneer (or *sabra*, in Hebrew, after the prickly-pear cactus fruit) contrasts with the weak, effeminate Jew of the diaspora. "Posited in gendered language as the masculine redeemer of the passive Diaspora Jew, the mythologized sabra simultaneously signified the destruction of the diasporic Jewish identity," Shohat asserts.[17] The weak, passive, feminized Jew, within the context of the Zionist account of Jewish history, was the product of the "demeaning and regressive lifestyle" forced upon and cultivated by Jewish communities in the diaspora. Only with return to the land would Jews regain the masculine vigor they had enjoyed in biblical times.[18]

The harsh, polemical portrait of diaspora Jewish communities painted by Zionists tellingly mirrored European anti-Jewish stereotypes. Accordingly, as Yitzhak Laor observes, "Most Zionists, especially on the Left, and even religious Zionists, accepted that nineteenth-century hatred toward the Jews was the fault of its victims."[19] Just as different exclusivist forms of European Romantic nationalism contended that Jews were foreign matter who did not quite fit or belong, either biologically or culturally, within Europe's nation-states, so did Zionism claim that Jews had an abnormal existence within Europe, a condition that could only be cured through the normalization of Jewish life in the form of an independent Jewish nation-state. Within this framework, vigorous Jewish cultures of the diaspora such as Yiddish were denigrated and devalued as Zionism expounded "a denial of previous exilic histories and traditions."[20]

Not only was Jewish life within Europe *galuti* (in the sense of abnormal, weak, diseased)—Jewish existence in the Arab world came under even greater criticism among Zionist thinkers. As a movement begun by European Ashkenazi Jews, Zionism propagated an Orientalist discourse in which "Judeo-Arab culture was disdained as a sign of '*galut*.'"[21] Arab Jews—be they from Egypt, Iraq, or Morocco—would have to "abandon their diasporic culture." For *mizrahi* Jews from the countries of the Middle East, this "meant abandoning Arabness and acquiescing in assimilationist modernization for 'their own good.'"[22] On the one hand, this emphasis on the need of *mizrahi* Jews to abandon their Arabness simply reflects the broader Zionist insistence on the importance of Diaspora Jews overcoming the exilic, *galuti* mentality through the Zionist act of settlement. On the other hand, however, it is also symptomatic of the pervasive Orientalist assumptions that permeated Zionist discourse, assumptions that subordinated Arab to European culture.[23] For Zionism, the status of Jews as Europe's internally colonized Other could ironically only be overcome by Jews becoming European colonizers. Yitzhak Laor states that "Zionism thought it would politically resolve the exile within Europe—Jews as 'Orientals inside the Occident'—not just by an Exodus, by going elsewhere, but by going to the heart of the colonial hinterland of Europe, the East, not to become part of that East but in order to become representatives of the West 'over there,' far away from the exile we were subjected to 'here,' inside Europe."[24] Marginalized within Europe as non-European, Jews could become European by undertaking a European-style colonial project in Palestine. And just as Ashkenazi Jews had played the role of the Oriental Other within Europe, so in the context of Zionist settlement and the new State of Israel would Palestinian Arabs and *mizrahim* assume the place of the internally colonized Other.

Taken together, the "negation of exile," "return to the land," and "return to history" tropes place Zionism squarely in the context of European Romantic nationalism and colonialism. The "history" designated by the Zionist "return to history," Raz-Krakotzkin explains, is the history "of the nineteenth century, which makes the nation the exclusive, sovereign subject. The return to history signifies the return to national sovereignty and is accompanied by the rejection of the passivity attributed to the Jew of the diaspora who lives in the messianic expectation of divine intervention."[25] The discourse around the negation of exile, meanwhile, "reveals the properly theological dimension of the national conscience," with the "secularism" of "secular Zionism" uncovered as "the nationalization of the theological myth reformulated through concepts borrowed from European romanticism."[26] Piterberg elaborates that within the framework of nineteenth-century European nationalism, the "nation is the autonomous historical subject par excellence, and the state is the *telos* of its march towards self-fulfilment." Zionism is accordingly based on the presupposition that "only nations that occupy the soil of their homeland, and establish political sovereignty over it, are capable of shaping their own destiny and so entering history."[27] For Judaism to become a "normal civilized nation," it must escape the "distortion" and "pariahdom" marking the abnormal "state of being a non-nation-state."[28]

The "return to history" trope within Zionist national colonial theology not only reflects nineteenth-century assumptions of Romantic nationalism, it also tellingly echoes Christian theologies of repudiation which cast exile as divine punishment upon the Jewish people for their rejection of Jesus as the Messiah. "Christianity considers the exile of the Jews as their 'departure from history,'" Raz-Krakotzkin observes, "that is to say, their departure from the context of grace. Exile is the consequence of their sins, above all their refusal of the Good News. Their exile is the proof of their condition as sinners, and only theirs—and as a consequence, it is proof of the truth of Christianity."[29] Rabbinic Judaism, in contrast, presented an account of exile that contested the Christian depiction of Jewish exile as corroborating Christianity's truth, insisting that Jewish exile was "emblematic of the world: an unredeemed world, which is itself in *galut*."[30] Zionist historians and advocates abandoned this account of *galut*, however, in turn accepting the Christian presentation of exile as a particular exclusion of the Jews from the history of salvation—except now the exclusion was from the history of nation-states. To "return to history" meant for Judaism to transform into a "normal" national body in control of its own destiny in a sovereign state on its own territory. Ironically, becoming normal in this sense also meant acquiescing to the Christian denial of the Jewish people's election by God for a particular vocation in the world. "Virtually all Zionists—at least the overwhelmingly secular majority of the first three *aliyot*—shared an insistence that the Jews must be a 'normal' people," states Paul Mendes-Flohr. "In the name of the desired normalization, they consciously sought to jettison the idea of election."[31]

Zionism entailed not only "the assimilation of Christian attitudes toward history, but a total denial of the history and historicization of the Jews."[32] The rich, diverse experiences of Jewish communities in Europe, North Africa, the Middle East, and beyond are flattened out and homogenized into the category of *galut*, the complex ways in which those communities interacted with their surrounding cultures rendered irrelevant within the Zionist historical schematization except for their status as examples of abnormality and disease to be cured through the simultaneous return to history and the land. A critique of Zionism's political theology will require the reinsertion of exile as that which Zionism has negated back into history, to narrate history from an "exilic" perspective. Such a critique will be developed over the rest of this chapter.[33]

A significant dimension of this critique will be reckoning with how the Zionist negation of exile was intertwined with another negation, namely, the negation of the Palestinian presence in the land within which the supposed problem of Jewish exile was to be resolved. As already discussed, the Zionist appraisal of exile deviates sharply from rabbinic Judaism's conceptualization of exile as a metaphysical condition marking all of earthly existence. The negation of exile goes hand-in-hand with a triumphalist account of history. "In traditional Judaism," Raz-Krakotzkin explains, "exile is not solely the condition of the Jews, but characterizes the situation of the world in general."[34] By highlighting absence and the incompleteness of human existence, "the concept of exile opposes itself to any attempt to underwrite 'the history of the conquerors.'"[35] Negating exile, in contrast, goes hand in hand with justifying the history of the victors, a history that erases the past of the conquered. The negation of exile shapes a "Zionist conscience" that rests on "effacing and repression," on the erasure not only of Jewish life in diaspora but also of Palestine's history prior to the Zionist return.[36] Mainstream Zionist imagination conceptually erases Palestinians from view, heralding the settlement of a land without a people for a people without a land, and such conceptual erasure proves a perilously short distance from actual practices and policies of the forcible dispossession of Palestinians.[37] Just as the exiled Jewish people lived outside of history, according to the Zionist historical schema, so, too, was the land of Israel presented as "empty," "condemned to exile as long as there was no Jewish sovereignty over it: it lacked any meaningful or authentic history, awaiting its own redemption with the return of the Jews."[38] However, because the land of course was not literally empty, Zionist return to history and the land would be inevitably and inextricably bound to practices and policies of uprooting and dispossession, with returning Jewish exiles creating new exiles in turn. The negation of exile thus did not eliminate exile, but instead simply displaced it onto Palestinians. The supposedly "insoluble" Jewish question, observed Hannah Arendt, "was indeed solved—namely, by means of a colonized and then conquered territory." This "solution," she continued, "merely produced a new category of refugees, the Arabs, thereby increasing the number of the stateless and rightless." [39]

COUNTERING *SHELILAT HA-GALUT*: JOHN HOWARD YODER'S MISSIOLOGY OF EXILE

The Zionist negation of exile thus plays a critical role within a national colonial theology and a corresponding colonial practice that creates new exiles in turn. The Zionist vision of return is predicated upon a binary opposition between exile and return and assumes that return can only be redemptive if it involves the nation establishing demographic hegemony within a circumscribed territory. In order to contest Zionism as an ideology and practice, I argue, one must begin by challenging *shelilat ha-galut* and then by exploring what a theological appropriation of exile might contribute to a theology of land and return not bound to nationalist politics. I will launch this challenge to Zionism's negation of exile through a critical description and analysis of the exilic theology and missiology developed over nearly a quarter century by the Mennonite ethicist John Howard Yoder. As early as 1973, responding to early forms of liberation theology that turned to the Exodus as the primary biblical model of liberative action, Yoder proposed that theologians explore the political possibilities embedded within the biblical depiction of exile.[40] Over the next two decades Yoder returned to the theme of diaspora and exile (he tended to use the two terms interchangeably) in multiple contexts—and especially in his occasional essays on the separation of Christianity from Judaism—constructing a vision of God's people embracing diaspora as a missiological vocation, a charge of seeking one's own *shalom* by seeking the *shalom* of the cities in which God's people find themselves exiled. One year before his death in 1997, Yoder collected several of the essays in which he investigated the historical and theological roots of the Jewish-Christian schism, essays in which the theme of exile plays a central role, and self-published those essays as a Shalom Desktop Packet. Then, after Yoder's death, the Jewish theologian Peter Ochs and the Christian theologian Michael Cartwright, with the encouragement of Yoder's self-appointed publicist Stanley Hauerwas, edited these essays for publication.[41] My concern in this section will not be to examine all of the dimensions of Yoder's account of the Jewish-Christian schism, but will instead be with highlighting Yoder's theological embrace of exile, or *galut*, as vocation, with the aim of discerning whether or not a positive valuation of exile might surprisingly nurture theologies of landedness and return that are less exclusivist than those shaped by exile's negation.

Through the essays in *The Jewish-Christian Schism Revisited*, Yoder sought to articulate "one basic alternative perspective" about the separation of Christianity from Judaism.[42] Specifically, Yoder maintained that the schism "did not have to be," observing that for at least a couple of centuries "to be a Jew and to be a follower of Jesus were not alternatives."[43] The shift from an intra-Jewish debate about whether or not Jesus is the promised Messiah to a division between "Christianity" and "Judaism" can be attributed in large measure, Yoder argued, to the phenomenon of "Constantinianism," by which Yoder meant less the political machinations of Emperor Constantine and more a shift in self-understanding: a shift from God's people understanding themselves to be in exile in the world, dispersed by God in mission, to self-identification with the Roman Empire. This shift, Yoder claimed, meant the loss of the church's "Jewish rootage," the loss of the theological vision that sustains God's people in exile, including the loss of a "readiness to live in the diaspora style of the Suffering Servant."[44] The rift, then, between Christians and Jews was not historically necessary, and today, Yoder believed, the divide could start to be overcome through a recognition of a common calling to seek the *shalom* of the cities of their exile, a calling that Yoder believed had been better preserved within the rabbinic Judaism of the diaspora than in a Christianity that had become all-too-much at home in the world, spiritually captive to the dominant social order.[45]

Exile, for Yoder, represents an ethic, theology, and spirituality of "not being in charge," of embracing "Galut as vocation."[46] This missiological interpretation of exile emerges from Yoder's narration of the people Israel's history as a story of a people called by God to be radically dependent upon God alone. The people Israel's fundamental identity "was not defined first by a theoretical monotheism, by cult or *kaschrut*, nor by the Decalogue," Yoder stated. "It was rather defined by the claim of the tribes to 'have no king but

JHWH [*sic*]/Adonai," a claim that developed from the Abrahamic and Mosaic trust in God and that stood in uneasy tension with, and at times pointed toward the rejection of, Israelite monarchy.[47] The people Israel, in Yoder's account, are called to embody this paradigmatic existence of radical reliance upon God alone in order to bear witness to God's wisdom and righteousness. The arc of the biblical narrative, from Abraham to Jesus, bears witness to this vocation. "What begins in Abraham, and crests in Jesus," Yoder insisted, "is not merely a different set of ideas about the world or about morality: it is a new definition of God. A God enters into relations with people who does not fit into the designs of human communities and their rules."[48]

The connective thread tying Abraham's radical reliance on God to the insistence in the holy war traditions that God, not the people, will fight, to Jeremiah's admonition to the uprooted people Israel to seek the peace of the city of their exile (Jer. 29:7), is the calling to trust in God alone for one's protection and salvation and to embody a communal politics of "not being in charge" commensurate with that trust. Yoder explained that this trust in God "opens the door to his saving intervention. It is the opposite of making one's own political/ military arrangements. Jeremiah's abandoning statehood for the future is thus not so much forsaking an earlier hope as it is returning to the original trust in JHWH [*sic*]."[49] Israelite kingship (or, to be anachronistic, "statehood") was, in this telling of the biblical narrative, something of an anomaly, subject to critique from within the scriptural witness that points back to Israel's reliance on God.[50] The exile in Babylon thus represented not a disruption in God's plans for his people, but rather an opportunity to return to radical dependence on God. "The move to Babylon was not a two-generation parenthesis, after which the Davidic or Solomonic project was supposed to take up again where it had left off. It was rather the beginning, under a firm fresh prophetic mandate, of a new phase of the Mosaic project."[51] The people Israel's exile is a sending out into mission, a point Yoder drove home in his paraphrase of the injunction in Jer. 29:7 as "Seek the salvation of the culture to which God has sent you."[52]

Biblical exile, in Yoder's telling, thus cannot be simply reduced to divine punishment, but in fact opens a new chapter in the people Israel's learning to depend on God alone, bearing witness through that reliance to God's wisdom and righteousness. Jesus as the promised Messiah fulfills what it means for the people Israel to live in covenantal faithfulness to God amidst the exile of the world. In Jesus Christ, Yoder emphasized, one finds "the fulfillment and not the abolition of the meaning of Torah as covenant of grace."[53] Concerned with rebutting the charge of Marcionism often leveled against Christian pacifists, Yoder stressed that Jesus' call to enemy-love unfolds and fulfills an "original intent . . . within the Torah itself, which points to the renunciation of violence and the love of enemy."[54] Jesus should not therefore be interpreted as abolishing Judaism but as continuing and fulfilling it.[55] Similarly, Paul should not be interpreted (as is common in more popularized accounts) as founding a new religion, but rather as defining "one more stream within Jewry," a stream that "had been prepared for by the phenomenon of 'Jeremiah,' i.e. by the acceptance of *galut* as mission centuries before." Paul's insistence on the inclusion of Gentiles into the covenant had been prepared, Yoder argued, by what he termed the "missionary" outreach of Jewish communities in exile, an outreach that attracted "God-fearing" Gentiles to synagogue life.[56] While followers of Jesus disagreed with other Jews about whether or not Jesus was the Messiah and the extent and nature of Gentile inclusion into synagogue life, these were and could have remained intra-Jewish debates.

This positive judgment concerning exile in turn informs Yoder's understanding of postbiblical history. While Christianity abandoned the path of radical dependence on God alone, entering into fateful compromises with empire (summed up for Yoder by the term "Constantinianism"), rabbinic Judaism kept alive the "not in charge" way of life proclaimed by Jeremiah and fulfilled in Jesus. Thus, Yoder claimed that "for over a millennium the Jews of the diaspora were the closest thing to the ethic of Jesus existing on any significant scale anywhere in Christendom."[57] Diaspora Judaism, Yoder asserted, was "the oldest and the toughest 'peace church,'" and embodied "mission without provincialism, cosmopolitan vision without empire."[58] Jewish communities in exile thus incarnated what Yoder famously called the "politics of Jesus," the doxological, political practices of the community gathered in eschatological anticipation.[59] Jewish life in exile was sustained by a faith in a transcendent God on whom God's people are radically dependent: "since God is sovereign over history, there is no need to seize (or subvert) political sovereignty in order for God's will to be done."[60] And this faith shaped a particular form of communal life, namely, decentralized worship gathered around the reading of the Torah.[61] Just as the church is called to incarnate a political witness that consists of sacramental social processes such as baptism, communion, mutual admonition, and listening to and speaking in the Spirit (all of which are practices that spawn "secular" analogues), so diaspora Jewish communities, Yoder maintained, actually embodied this witness in their communal lives, a witness that accords "with the grain of the universe."[62]

Diasporic existence inculcates a particular epistemological stance, argued Yoder. To accept *galut* as vocation is to accept that one's own cultural location is radically contingent and historical and to be disabused of any pretensions that one's language or rationality is somehow more universal or less particular than that of others. God's people living in exile renounce in principle the claim that "the place where they stand is in some sense more reasonable, more universal, than other places."[63] To live diasporically means not only to accept the necessity of translation and being multilingual if one is going to communicate and to live up to the missiological charge of seeking the city's salvation. It means recognizing that the good news the synagogue or the church has to share "cannot be imposed by authority, or coercively. It is rendered null when assent is imposed."[64] God's exiled people cannot count on political power or a supposedly universal rationality to persuade others to heed its message, but must instead cultivate disciplines of patience and openness as they join others in working together for the peace of the city.[65]

If rabbinic Judaism stood for Yoder as exemplary of what Christian political witness should have been, Zionism, in turn, represented for him a Jewish counterpart of Christian Constantinianism, a falling away from the vocation of embodying a counter-politics of radical dependence on God alone amidst empires that glory in military might.[66] "The whole point of Hebrew identity since Abraham is a call to be doing something else amidst the world's power arenas," Yoder insisted. "It is only by being something different that Jewry in fact has survived; it is only in order to be something morally different that Jewry is called to survive."[67] Zionism, with its drive for the Jewish people to be a nation like other nations, threatens to compromise this calling. Ironically, Zionism thus stands as the "culmination" of Judaism's "Christianization," a process that included Jewish communities relinquishing their "missionary" outreach in the face of Christian restrictions and that at root stemmed from a renunciation of election and an abdication of the calling to embody a diasporic politics. Yet, in the midst of Zionism triumphant, a Jewish minority, represented by thinkers and groups as diverse as Martin Buber, Steven Schwarzschild, and the anti-Zionist, ultra-Orthodox *neturei karta*, in different ways have rejected "the model of nationalism, triumphalism, and the very notion that Jews should want to be like their neighbours even in external social organization."[68]

EXILE, RETURN, AND PLACE

In assessing and engaging Yoder's account of the Jewish-Christian schism and his articulation of *galut* as vocation for God's people who learn to live in radical dependence upon God alone, Christian as well as Jewish theologians have raised at least four broad, interrelated critiques of Yoder's position. First, that Yoder presented an insufficiently nuanced narration of Jewish history, overplaying the missionary character and the pacifism of Jewish communities in the diaspora while simultaneously downplaying visions of return to the land within diaspora Judaism. Second, that Yoder's vision of Christians and Jews discovering a shared vocation of living the embodied witness of communities in exile threatens to obscure or even deny any positive theological value to Jewish difference. Third, that Yoder's reading of Scripture as a story of God's people learning radical dependence upon God alone, issuing in an embrace of *galut* as vocation, fails to attend to the diversity of theologies of land in the Bible, including traditions that focus on inhabiting, possessing, and returning to the land. And finally, that Yoder's exilic theology does not have the resources with which to develop a positive theological account of landed existence.

My primary concern in this section will be to address the third and fourth critiques, as they directly speak to the broader concern of this study, namely, whether or not exile can shape projects of return so that return need not be bound to the violent, exclusivist politics of the nation-state. However, briefly addressing the other two critiques is important in order to determine the positive kernel of Yoder's approach that can be salvaged and thus to assess whether or not the problematic moves Yoder made can be disentangled from his championing of *galut* as vocation. In brief, I join Michael Cartwright, Peter Ochs, and Daniel Boyarin, among others, in their sympathetic critiques of Yoder's theology of the Jewish-Christian schism as inadvertently betraying supersessionist tendencies. Daniel Barber summarizes these concerns well when he notes that "Yoder's use of diaspora ends up engendering an essentialist account of Judaism" insofar as his rhetoric at times veers in the direction of excluding as non-Jewish any nonpacifist, nonmissionary, return-focused aspects of Jewish life in the diaspora.[69] Peter Ochs echoes Barber's complaint, concerned that Yoder's account of diaspora Judaism is supersessionist to the extent that it is reductionistic. "Yoder's non-nonsupersessionist tendency lies not in what he admires about rabbinic Judaism," Ochs maintains, "but in what he strictly excludes from it," such as any "defensive," nonmissionary dimensions to the *mishna*. Yoder either errs by exaggerating and mischaracterizing the missionary and pacifist character of diaspora Judaism or by excluding nonmissionary, nonpacifist elements of diaspora Judaism from the supposed essence of true Judaism.[70] Yoder thus erred, according to Cartwright, by eclipsing "the difference between Christians and Jews in the name of a common destiny," the destiny of seeking the peace of the city of one's exile.[71] Meanwhile, Daniel Boyarin, more sympathetic to Yoder's critique of Zionism than either Cartwright or Ochs, concurs that Yoder's characterization of

Judaism as the oldest and most durable "peace church" functions as a "gesture of 'appropriation' that reads so many Jews somehow right out of Judaism." Yoder's call to Christians and Jews "to begin to imagine ourselves as one thing, as one community, to disinvest ourselves in difference," to imagine the Jewish-Christian schism as not necessary, ironically mimics the supersessionist gesture, except that instead of Judaism being negated and replaced by Christianity, Jewish difference is simply denied as the supposed essence of Judaism is collapsed into the supposed essence of Christianity.[72] Boyarin agrees with Yoder in contesting simplistic historical narrations of a clean break between "Judaism" and "Christianity" in the first or second century, joining other scholars in showing how complex interactions irreducible to the terms "rupture" or "schism" between Jews who accepted Jesus as the messiah and those who did not persisted up into the fifth century CE.[73] Yet Boyarin rejects what he views as Yoder's unwarranted extrapolation from this historical record to the normative claim that the difference between Jew and Christian can be overcome through mutual embrace of an exilic identity.

Even as I join Cartwright, Ochs, and Boyarin in lamenting how Yoder's theological interpretation of the Jewish-Christian schism ends up repeating supersessionist moves in a new form by denying Jewish difference, I also agree with Boyarin that Yoder's exilic theology can be disentangled from this lingering supersessionism. Specifically, rather than seeing "*galut* as vocation" as a shared, common essence that marks and defines "true" Judaism and "true" Christianity, one can instead highlight how *galut* functions positively both "as a predicate common to both Christianity (as Yoder advances it) and Judaism" (as advanced by Boyarin, Raz-Krakotzkin, Piterberg, Shohat, and others). This convergence between predicates does not collapse Judaism and Christianity into one another, thus negating Jewish-Christian difference, but instead simply highlights the possibility of intersection and cooperation.[74] Collaboration and mutual support between Jews and Christians can become possible around the task of recovering exilic traditions within Christianity and Judaism, even as Jews and Christians recognize and affirm the differences that separate them and the possibility of mutual learning from and challenge to those differences.

While Yoder's exilic theology can thus be arguably salvaged from his supersessionist tendencies, one must still answer critiques that Yoder was tone-deaf to the polyvocal character of the scriptural witness about landedness and that he failed to offer an account of return to and life in the land. Gerald Schlabach presents one version of this critique when he argues that Yoder's Jeremian theology must be balanced by the Deuteronomic injunction to settle and live justly in the land (e.g., Deuteronomy 6–9). Yoder's exilic theology,

Schlabach contends, does not provide resources for thinking about landed existence in a literal, not simply a figurative, sense.[75] Cartwright, meanwhile, accuses Yoder of captivity to a "monological hermeneutic that sought to *limit* the range of possible meanings of the text of Scripture." Had Yoder paid more careful attention to rabbinic modes of interpretation, Cartwright suggests, Yoder might have learned "to read Scripture polyphonically."[76] With Cartwright and Schlabach, one can affirm that Scripture undoubtedly does present a polyphony of voices on the question of the people Israel's landed existence. I will contend, however, that only when one assumes that exile and return or exile and landedness stand in diametrical opposition to one another does an affirmation of scriptural polyphony on the question of land appear to pose a challenge to Yoder's exilic theology.

Yoder's critics assume that his theology of *galut* as vocation cannot offer a compelling theology of land and return because they conceive of exile and return in binary terms. Yet biblical scholarship does not uncover such a stark opposition between the two terms. Norman Habel and Walter Brueggemann have authored definitive studies outlining the multiple theologies of land at play within the Hebrew Bible, theologies that stand in significant tension with one another but that also comment and build upon each other in often surprising ways.[77] Yet even within this multiplicity of land theologies, Brueggemann argues, one cannot avoid how exile becomes a "defining interpretive metaphor" within the Tanakh and then later within the Jewish history.[78] To grapple seriously with the Bible's multiple land traditions, Brueggemann maintains, leads one to accept that exile and return do not stand in an either/or relationship to one another. Brueggemann explains that one can understand the people Israel's land histories in different ways:

> The first is a history of risking homelessness that yields the gift of home. The second is the deep yearning for home, but in ways that result in homelessness. And in the third history, from exile to Jesus, we learn that Jesus' embrace of homelessness (crucifixion) is finally the awesome, amazing gift of home (resurrection). The learning is radically dialectical. It will not do, as one might be inclined to do with a theology of glory, to say that God's history is simply a story of coming to the land promised. Nor will it do, as one might be tempted in a theology of the cross, to say God's history is a story of homelessness. Either statement misses the main affirmation of the unexpected way in which land and landlessness are linked to each other.[79]

Put another way: an embrace of *galut* as vocation need not mean a valorization of landlessness or a cosmopolitan rootlessness. A cursory reading of Jeremiah's appeal to the exiles might lead one to think that Jeremiah is affirming homelessness, but that would be to ignore the fact that Jeremiah calls upon the exiles to build homes and plant trees, to become rooted and landed, in Babylon. Exile for the displaced Israelites in Babylon is thus not *homelessness* or *landlessness*, but rather entails the discovery of a new form of home and a novel manner of landedness. Daniel Smith-Christopher asserts that the experience of exile teaches God's people that its embodied political witness need not be bound to sovereign power. Exile reveals that all places and all lands have become possible sites from which God's people can "engage in resistance, even outside of nationalist aspirations or imperial connivance."[80] Even when the people Israel return to the land from Babylon, as Yoder stressed, they do so "without political independence or a king": inhabiting the land has taken on a new, exilic quality.[81] The Hebrew Bible, as Timothy Gorringe observes, "is framed by landlessness and dispossession. We are not reading a text written by conquerors, but by losers," and an acknowledgment of how the canonical text's multiple land theologies are framed by exile and dispossession should help dampen any attempts to appropriate Scripture on behalf of triumphalist projects.[82]

A recognition of the importance of exile as a frame to the Hebrew Bible and as a theme that continues on into the church's dispersion into mission in the New Testament does not underwrite a completely placeless theology. To be sure, the story of *galut* as vocation, which culminates with the Jeremian call and the risen Jesus' dispersion of his disciples to the whole world, is a story about how, in the words of W. D. Davies, "not only the bonds of death" but also "the bonds of the land" have been loosened for Christians.[83] It is, granted, a story of how a "certain static land theology has been broken open in such a way as to designate all places on the map as potentially holy."[84] Yet the loosening of the bonds of the land and the breaking open of static land theologies do not mean landlessness. Rather, they point to new modes of living in the land, forms of landedness not reducible to the struggle to obtain exclusive sovereignty and to homogenizing cartographies that attempt to establish one-to-one correlations between nation and territory.

Yoder's interpretation of Scripture as affirming *galut* as vocation should not be read as Yoder excising or ignoring scriptural traditions about inhabiting, possessing, or returning to land. Instead, for Yoder, exile inflects how God's people inhabit, possess, or return to land. Reflecting on what it means to inhabit or possess land exilically will help to answer the fourth and final challenge to Yoder's exilic theology, namely, that he did not develop a positive description of landed existence, neither for Jews in *eretz yisrael* nor for Palestinians. Cartwright states one version of this challenge when he claims that Yoder's valorization of exile threatens to break the triad of people–Torah–land that defines Jewish existence by removing land from the conceptual grouping.[85] Ochs, meanwhile, accuses Yoder of being captive to a "logic of twos," to binary thinking that considers the only two options for relation to land to be exile or oppressive landedness. "Yoder's exclusive choice *for* an exclusively exilic Judaism shares the same logic as the Maccabees' and Zealots' choice *for* an exclusively nonexilic Judaism of land and national power," Ochs maintains.[86] For Yoder, Ochs insists, "there is no middle between Israel's exilic separation from the land and the Maccabees' nationalist strategy for remaining in it."[87]

These critiques leveled by Cartwright and Ochs, I argue below, miss the mark, reflecting not Yoder's binary thinking about exile and land but rather a lingering binarism operative in their own thought, a binarism that leads them to assume when Yoder championed *galut* as vocation that he envisioned a landless, rootless existence for the people Israel and the church.[88] Yet one should not be too critical of Ochs and Cartwright, for Yoder himself wondered if his theology of *galut* as vocation could be received as good news by displaced peoples. Is there, Yoder wondered, "something about this Jewish vision of the dignity and ministry of the scattered peoples of God which might be echoed or replicated by other migrant peoples? Might there even be something helpful in this memory which would speak by a more distant analogy to the condition of peoples overwhelmed by imperial immigration, like the original Americans or Australians, or the Ainu or the Maori?"[89] Or, one might add, the Palestinians? What, in brief, does the Jeremian vision of seeking the peace of the cities of one's exile have to say to Palestinian refugees who yearn to return to their homes and who map out plans for return? Could Yoder's answer be no more than: relinquish all dreams of return and accept one's exile as permanent? Or might Yoder's exilic theology in fact have resources to suggest how return should take place and how returning Palestinians might justly inhabit the land where their destroyed villages once stood?

Yoder presented his most detailed answers to these questions in his essay, "Earthly Jerusalem and Heavenly Jerusalem," a paper originally delivered at a B'nai B'rith conference and later included in his collection of essays on the Jewish-Christian schism. Yoder began by reflecting on the significance of Jerusalem as the Davidic capital and eventual site of the Tabernacle and Temple. Jerusalem, Yoder observed, "had belonged to none of the tribes. The Lord's choice of Jerusalem left behind their tribal judges' seats and their local holy places. Even on earth, extraterritoriality was part of [God's] self-definition."[90] God's transcendence relativizes and stands against any absolute, exclusivist claims to territory. "The transcendence of the Most High," Yoder stated, "is acted out in the fact that the place of his manifestation is not our own turf."[91] To speak of a "celestial Jerusalem" that stands above yet is mapped over the "earthly Jerusalem" is to underscore God's transcendence, with "the otherness of God" signified by the "otherness of Jerusalem." God dwells among God's people, yet God's people cannot grasp or possess God. God's otherness thus "points us away from possessiveness and toward the redefinition of providence so as to favour the outsider." [92]

The recognition that the land belongs to God, that we are all exiles who ultimately have our dwelling in God (Ps. 90:1), brings with it a rejection of political forms that exclude and oppress. "Authentic reverence before divine sovereignty must accordingly mean a critical judgment upon nationhood/ statehood in its modern as well as its medieval forms," Yoder insisted—and, as seen above, that included a critical judgment on Zionism as a form of modern nationalism.[93] Any claim to territory and a place in the land, Yoder maintained, must be evaluated according to "whom it excludes or expels; whether our enemies are God's enemies or his children." God's people do not fulfill their witness as a paradigm nation by replicating nationalist politics of exclusion and dispossession, but are instead called to embody a politics of exile in the land. "Those who enter Jerusalem's gates sing that it is 'built to be a city where people come together in unity' (Ps. 122.3)," Yoder observed. Accordingly, he concluded, "Those people are qualified to work at the building of the city who build it for others."[94]

Building the city for others: that was the call of Jeremiah to the exiles in Babylon, to seek the *shalom* of the city to which they had been displaced. A theology of land and return should thus not be built upon the negation of exile, but should instead incorporate its lessons, with God's people possessing particular places not only for their own sake but for the sake of the widow, the orphan, the stranger, the refugee.[95] As Nathan Kerr explains, to live exilically "in relation to a 'place' that is not one's own, for the sake of that place's transformation and conversion to the coming kingdom of God, is not necessarily to privilege exile and dispossession as over-against land and return." Instead, an exilic theology of land will conceive of land not in terms of exclusive possession, but rather in terms of "dispossession," with the land becoming "a 'shared space' of encounter with and conversion to the other."[96] Joining Yoder in negating the negation of exile thus means accepting one's exilic status, even when one is at home, and recognizing that one truly inhabits and takes possession of particular places not by seeking to escape one's exilic status but rather through efforts to create polities that welcome and incorporate the exiles (the refugees, the internally displaced) created by the exclusionary politics of the nation-state.

Exile in the Land: Political Theologies of Binationalism

What type of political arrangements in Palestine-Israel are commensurate with a political theology of exile in which the task of inhabiting particular places is shaped by the Jeremian call to seek the *shalom* of the city to which one has been dispersed? Building on Yoder's account of diaspora and exile, Dan Barber claims that to imagine diaspora is "to signify space apart from the borders of identity by which space, with the aid of history-telling (of origins, ends, and necessities) has been carved up."[97] The negation of exile forms part of a larger historical schema in which the Jewish nation-state, marked off by militarized borders created through strategies of partition, becomes the *telos* of Jewish history. To contest these spacio-political realities, I argue, requires a recovery of the positive role for exile in a political theology of land and return. In the case of Palestine-Israel, that will mean advocating for binational political formations that embrace the presence of Palestinian and Jewish Others as positive goods to be celebrated rather than as foreign matter to be cordoned off and excluded through policies and procedures of separation. Yoder's exilic theology of place, I suggest, thus converges in productive and provocative ways with how Israeli political theorists and activists have recovered exilic traditions in order to project shared Palestinian-Israeli futures not bound to the exclusionary violence of the nation-state.

If one accepts the understandings of exile and return at play within the Zionist national colonial theology, then it becomes difficult-to-impossible not to interpret Palestinian refugee calls to return as mirroring the Zionist negation of exile and its focus on returning to history by returning to a nation-state existence within the land. Julie Peteet pessimistically suggests that "in this conflict, there can only be one return, one exile, and one victim."[98] Just as Zionism negates the exile for the sake of historical redemption in the form of return to the land and the establishment of the nation-state, so does Palestinian nationalism at times mirror the historical schema underlying Zionism. Elias Sanbar, for example, replicates the Zionist "return to history" doctrine when he claims that "by departing from space, the Palestinians, about whom the world agreed to say 'they do not exist,' also departed from time."[99] Living in exile Palestinians were outside of history, and this abnormal existence could only be overcome through "the ideology of the Return," an "ideology which constituted the basis of the national renaissance arising out of the exile" and which had three elements: "land, which is transported, time, which is restored, and a name, which is preserved."[100] When exile and return are considered to be diametrically opposed to one another, then the Palestinian-Israeli conflict becomes a contest about *which* exile and *which* return are the true exile and the true return.

To think of exile and return, or exile and landedness, as mutually intertwined and imbricated realities rather than as fundamentally opposed states of being points in the direction of a binational resolution to the Palestinian-Israeli conflict, a resolution that does not take the nation-state model for granted. However, before explaining how a political theology of exile supports binationalism, it will help first to situate this discussion within contemporary political realities that have made binationalism an increasingly attractive political model and within the context of critiques and defenses of binationalism. Zionism had aimed to normalize Jewish existence by negating the exile, to enfranchise Jewish communities disenfranchised by life in European ghettoes and marginalized by European nationalisms, but in a bitter irony Zionism has "created the biggest ghetto in Jewish history, a super-armed ghetto, capable of continually expanding its confines, but a ghetto nonetheless."[101] This militarized fortress/ghetto Israel currently rules over a binational reality—a binational reality in which nearly four million stateless Palestinians in the Gaza Strip, East Jerusalem, and the West Bank live without citizenship rights and in which over a million Palestinians inside Israel face numerous forms of discrimination thanks to the state's ethnocratic policies. Israeli policies and practices (and peace processes) attempt to wall off the Palestinian presence (be it inside Israel, the Occupied Territories, or the region's refugee camps) with procedural, legal, and physical barriers, attempting to keep the demographic threat to the Jewishness (understood solely in demographic terms) of the State of Israel at bay.[102] Advocates of binational political arrangements reject these strategies of separation, of seeking (futilely) to wall off the binational reality through militarized borders and discriminatory legal regimes, arguing that the existing binational reality must be accepted as a promise rather than confronted as a threat.[103]

The most common critique of binational proposals—leveled by Palestinian and Israeli Jewish political analysts alike—argues that binationalism encourages naïve, utopian thinking. Proponents of binationalism, critics contend, gloss over the stark power imbalance between the State of Israel and the Palestinians, a power imbalance that enables Israel to resist any pressure it might face to allow refugee return and transition from its current ethnocratic character into either a state of all its citizens or into part of a binational federation. Taking these political realities seriously, this argument goes, means adopting a pragmatic and accommodating politics of the possible.[104] Critiques of binationalism typically intersect with critiques of Palestinian refugee return, as opponents of such return rightly note that any sizable return of Palestinian refugees would alter the demographic composition of the State of Israel, thus threatening the state's Jewish character (when the Jewishness of Israel is understood solely in demographic terms). Insisting on the right of return stands in tension with advocacy for a two-state solution to the Palestinian–Israeli conflict, at least with two-state solutions premised on the nationalist assumption that the state should reflect and primarily serve the needs and interests of the dominant, majority nation: significant return of Palestinian refugees to Israel in the context of a two-state solution would lead not to a Palestinian state and an Israeli Jewish state, but to two states with Palestinian majority populations.[105] The Palestinian refugee right of return conflicts with the supposed right of Israel to maintain itself as a Jewish state, understood as a state with a Jewish majority.[106]

Proponents of binationalism respond to these critiques by contesting the purported right or justice of the Israeli state creating and maintaining Jewish demographic hegemony at the expense of Palestinian refugees and their right of return. While international law does protect some rights of communal and cultural self-definition, argues Israeli lawyer Michael Kagan, it does not grant ethnocratic states such as Israel the right to maintain structures and policies that reinforce the ethnocratic system, especially when such structures and policies come at the expense of rights clearly recognized within international law, such as the right of refugees to viable solutions, including the choice among return to their homes, repatriation in the host country, and resettlement in a third country.[107] To the claim that the Zionist vision of establishing Jewish demographic hegemony was a just vision, especially in light of the Jewish experience in Europe, critics like Raz-Krakotzkin respond by underscoring the stark reality behind this claim, namely, that "in order to establish a Jewish state and to ensure Jewish hegemony and Jewish majority, expulsion and exclusion were inevitable."[108] Zionism understood in demographic terms is a Zionism wedded to the negation of exile, and for such a Zionism, visions of peace will always entail separation from Palestinians. The politics of separation, meanwhile, always spells dispossession and marginalization for Palestinians.[109]

Finally, to the assertion that it is utopian and unrealistic, binationalism's defenders counter that similar objections could be leveled against the two-state solution. As Israeli colonization of the West Bank and East Jerusalem has intensified since 1967 under governments of the center-left as well as the center-right, the territorial basis of a two-state solution that would entail Palestinians relinquishing the right of return in exchange for a Palestinian state in 22 percent of Mandate Palestine (the Gaza Strip, the West Bank, and East Jerusalem) has been progressively undermined. Self-proclaimed realism, in turn, presses Palestinians to accept a state in smaller and smaller parts of this 22 percent of Mandate Palestine, as it would be allegedly unrealistic to expect the dismantling of Israeli colonies in the Occupied Territories. As with most forms of *Realpolitik*, realism is here defined solely in terms of the interests of the powerful. The desires and demands of Palestinian refugees, or of Palestinians whose lands have been confiscated to build new settlements or whose water resources have been confiscated for use by Israel, do not factor into the calculus of what constitutes realism. Binationalism's defenders insist instead on beginning with the contemporary reality that a binational sharing of the land of Israel-Palestine already exists: it is simply a binationalism of domination and dispossession through the imposition of internal and external partitions. The realistic path forward, binationalists argue, is not one of doubling down on strategies of partition and separation, but is rather one of transforming the present binational reality of domination and separation into a binationalism of mutuality and interdependence.[110] While the failed peace processes of the past two decades, driven by the short-term interests of the moment, have been beholden to strategies of partition, a more realistic approach will take a longer view, recognizing that a true realism will accept that "in the long run the solution will be a bi-national state, in which both nations will be able to run their national lives together."[111]

This binationalism for which I argue in this study must be differentiated from the one-state solution (also often called the unitary or the one democratic state solution) in which national and communal differences are erased or at least subordinated to the central importance of the individual citizen. For at least its first decade the PLO advocated a one-state solution to the conflict.[112] As Israeli colonization has progressively undermined the territorial basis of any two-state solution to the conflict, the unitary state solution has experienced a resurgence, with some Palestinian and Israeli Jewish commentators alike advocating for a future of one, democratic state of Palestine-Israel representing all of its citizens equally.[113] Seemingly progressive, the unitary democratic model is problematic in that it mirrors the Enlightenment assumption that communal and religious attachments must be transcended—or at least definitively subordinated—as the individual citizen becomes the locus of political subjectivity. This modernist move in turn echoes Christian supersessionism in that it assumes that any divine vocation entrusted to the Jewish people has been overcome, replaced by the nation and its citizens as the bearers of historical, political destinies. Rather than a one-state solution that eclipses Palestinian-Israeli Jewish difference, a binationalist politics is required that affirms such difference while not translating that difference into the basis of a politics of partition. This type of binationalism emphasizes the mutual interdependence that future political arrangements in Israel-Palestine will require, an interdependence that will take the form of a federation or confederation of smaller, sometimes overlapping, communal units, political forms that disrupt the homogenizing logic of nation-state models.[114] Consociational binationalism acknowledges the heterogeneous character of the land and its people, affirming the way in which time and spatial maps of identity overlap one another, creating and uncovering what Mizrahi scholar Ella Shoat calls "a dynamic palimpsest of identity formations."[115]

This type of consociational binationalism is reflected in Yehouda Shenhav's proposal for what he calls a *demokratiya hesderit*, a division of the region into smaller territories in which various religious and national communities would live in a loose confederation of independent cantons.[116] Numerous other federal or confederal forms of binationalism have been championed.[117] Common to all of them, however, is an insistence on the common character of the land and on mutuality and sharing (rather than on separation and dispossession) between Palestinians and Israeli Jews. These visions of binational mutuality serve as a reminder that not all Palestinians and Israeli Jews have viewed partition as inevitable: the call to a binational future has been sounding since Zionism's earliest days. One thinks, for example, of Hannah Arendt's aspiration for "a Palestinian entity in which there would be no majority or minority status distinctions," but instead mutuality between Palestinian Arabs and Jews.[118] Or one could point to Judah Magnes, Martin Buber, and the *Brit Shalom* circle.[119]

Several contemporary Israeli Jewish advocates of binationalism have made the striking connection between championing binationalism, on the one hand, and countering *shelilat ha-galut*, or negating the negation of exile, on the other. In doing so, they provide a positive reply to Edward Said's question of whether or not the language and conceptualizations of diaspora might "become the not-so-precarious foundation in the land of Jews and Palestinians of a bi-national state in which Israel and Palestine are parts, rather than antagonists of each other's history and underlying reality."[120] Raz-Krakotzkin, for example, asserts that true peace between Israeli Jews and Palestinians will require "a different definition of Jewish existence and sovereignty" than the demographic nation-statism of mainstream Zionism.[121] To achieve "a comprehensive redefinition of the Jewish collectivity in Palestine," Raz-Krakotzkin maintains, Israeli Jews must look beyond how *shelilat ha-galut* denigrated Jewish life in the Arab world, and in the process adopt the "in-betweenness of the Mizrahi condition," a condition in which Arab and Jew are not viewed as opposed or incompatible but as intertwined.[122] Leaving behind the negation of exile in turn opens up understandings of redemption other than the ascendance of the nation–state. "Bi-nationalism, unlike the present paradigm," Raz-Krakotzkin states, "would provide a context that incorporates the population of the refugee camps in the image of redemption. Such a bi-nationalism would be undertaken with a sense of responsibility, based on the historical understanding that the birth of Israel and the Palestinian tragedy are not two separate events, but one and the same."[123] Palestinian refugee return, from this vantage point, does not jeopardize the hard-won redemption achieved by Zionism in the establishment of a sovereign, Jewish-majority state. Rather, such return is redemptive, liberating Palestinian and Israeli Jew alike from the present reality of exclusion and dispossession and pointing toward political futures of "diasporized states" in which tight bonds between the nation and the state are loosened and different peoples work to build the city together for one another.[124] Piterberg concurs, arguing that "*galut* as consciousness within a territorially oppressive reality is a prerequisite for decolonization and recognition of the binational nature of the country's history and geography."[125]

Judith Butler has rightly highlighted the "diasporic elements working within Israel to dislodge the pervasive assumptions of nationalism."[126] Raz-Krakotzkin, Piterberg, Shohat, and others marshal the resources of *galut* to undermine Zionism's negation of exile and the exclusivist nationalism to which it gives birth. They have, to use Yoder's phrase, accepted *galut* as vocation, not in the sense of abdicating or abjuring landedness or return, but as a commitment to shaping return and life in the land through the exilic commitment of seeking the peace of the cities of the land for the sake of *all* persons who dwell in those cities. A political theology of exile decenters those who live in the land, opening up a "longing for the land within the land" that might become "a new starting point of all who dwell in the land, a basis for their partnership."[127] An exilic landedness, in the felicitous phrasing of Sidra DeKoven-Ezrahi, molds "citizens and sojourners" who "touch down lightly but are never quite grounded."[128] What mappings of return such citizens and sojourners, who embrace rather than reject *galut* as their vocation, might produce will be the focus of the second half of this book.

Notes

1. The word *galut* in the phrase *shelilat ha-galut* should be underscored. What Zionism negates is not so much "diaspora" (Hebrew *golah*)—the phenomenon of Jewish communities living outside of *eretz yisrael*—as it is *galut*, an exilic state of impoverished existence that comes from living outside of the land. To be sure, life in *golah*, for Zionism, fosters a sense of *galut*. For a discussion of the distinction between *golah* and *galut*, see Gabriel Piterberg, *The Returns of Zionism: Myths, Politics, and Scholarship in Israel* (London: Verso, 2008), 95.

2. Yosef Salmon, "Zionism and Anti-Zionism in Traditional Judaism in Eastern Europe," in *Zionism and Religion*, ed. Shmuel Almog, Jehuda Reinharz, and Anita Shapira (Hanover, NH and London: Brandeis University Press and University Press of New England, 1998), 25.

3. For discussions of *shelilat ha-galut* in Zionist discourse, see Eliezer Don-Yehiya, "The Negation of Galut in Religious Zionism," *Modern Judaism* 12 (1992): 129–55 and Shalom Ratzaby, "The Polemic about the Negation of the Diaspora in the 1930s and Its Roots," *Journal of Israeli History* 16 (1995): 19–38.

4. Shlomo Avineri correctly emphasizes that "far from being a clear break with the past, national movements are essays in reinterpretations of the past and its retrieval." Zionism is no exception. See Avineri, "Zionism and the Jewish Religious Tradition: The Dialectics of Redemption and Secularization," in *Zionism and Religion*, ed. Almog, Reinharz, and Shapira, 2.

5. Amos Funkenstein, *Perceptions of Jewish History* (Berkeley: University of California Press, 1993), 20.

6. See Amnon Raz-Krakotzkin, "A National Colonial Theology: Religion, Orientalism, and the Construction of the Secular in Zionist Discourse," *Tel Aviver Jahrbuch für deutsche Geschichte* 30 (2002): 312–26. Piterberg concurs with Raz-Krakotzkin, describing the conceptual nexus of the negation of exile/the return to history/and the return to the land as part of a myth that is "inexorably national and settler-colonial, specific and comparable, shaped by European ideational currents and the reality of colonial strife." Piterberg, *The Returns of Zionism*, xiii.

7. Raz-Krakotzkin, *Exil et Souveraineté: Judaïsme, sionisme, et pensée binationale* (Paris: La Fabrique, 2007), 27. All translations from the original French are mine.

8. Raz-Krakotzkin, *Exil et Souveraineté*, 27.

9. Ella Shohat, *Taboo Memories, Diasporic Voices* (Durham, NC and London: Duke University Press, 2006), 331.

10. Ibid.

11. Laurence Silberstein, *The Postzionism Debates: Knowledge and Power in Israeli Culture* (London: Routledge, 1999), 22–23.

12. Yael Zerubavel, *Recovered Roots: Collective Memory and the Making of Israeli National Tradition* (Chicago and London: University of Chicago Press, 1995), 16, 31.

13. Ibid., 17, 19.

14. Ibid., 24.

15. Piterberg, *Returns of Zionism*, 94.

16. Shohat, *Taboo Memories*, 344. For critical studies of early Zionist historians, see David N. Myers, "Between Diaspora and Zion: History, Memory, and the Jerusalem Scholars," in *The Jewish Past Revisited: Reflections on Modern Jewish Historians*, ed. David N. Myers and David B. Ruderman (New Haven and London: Yale University Press, 1998), 88–102 and Derek J. Penslar, "Narratives of Nation-Building: Major Themes in Zionist Historiography," in *The Jewish Past Revisited*, ed. Myers and Ruderman, 104–26.

17. Shohat, *Taboo Memories*, 217. Eviatar Zerubavel echoes Shohat, describing the "highly ambitious Zionist attempt" to replace the old, weak, and feminized exilic Jew with the young, strapping, masculine *sabra*. See *Time Maps: Collective Memory and the Social Shape of the Past* (Chicago: University of Chicago Press, 2004), 90. For further discussion of the gendered dimension to the Zionist periodization of history, see Daniel Boyarin, *Unheroic Conduct: The Rise*

of Heterosexuality and the Invention of the Jewish Man (Berkeley: University of California Press, 1997). A textured discussion of the development of the *sabra* as an Israeli Jewish archetype can be found in Oz Almog, *The Sabra: The Creation of the New Jew* (Berkeley: University of California Press, 2000).

18. Yael Zerubavel, *Recovered Roots*, 190.

19. Yitzhak Laor, *The Myth of Liberal Zionism* (New York and London: Verso, 2010), 7.

20. Raz-Krakotzkin, "A National Colonial Theology," 313.

21. Shohat, *Taboo Memories*, 205–6.

22. Ibid., 331.

23. See, for example, Amal Jamal, "The Dialectics of 'Othering' in Zionist Thought—Arabs and Oriental Jews in Israel," *Tel Aviver Jahrbuch für deutsche Geschichte* 30 (2002): 283–311.

24. Laor, *The Myth of Liberal Zionism*, 6.

25. Raz-Krakotzkin, *Exil et Souveraineté*, 41. Yosef Hayim Yerushalmi concurs that only when Jews become integrated into a nation-state, either "as a result of emancipation in the diaspora" or through "national sovereignty in Israel," do they fully enter "the mainstream of history." Yerushalmi, *Zakhor: Jewish History and Jewish Memory* (Seattle and London: University of Washington Press, 1982), 99–100.

26. Raz-Krakotzkin, *Exil et Souveraineté*, 32.

27. Piterberg, *The Returns of Zionism*, 95.

28. Shohat, *Taboo Memories*, 225.

29. Raz-Krakotzkin, *Exil et Souveraineté*, 46.

30. Piterberg, *The Returns of Zionism*, 138.

31. Mendes-Flohr, "In Pursuit of Normalcy: Zionism's Ambivalence toward Israel's Election," in *Many Are Chosen*, ed. William R. Hutchison and Hartmut Lehmann (Minneapolis: Fortress Press, 1994), 206.

32. Amnon Raz-Krakotzkin, "Jewish Memory between Exile and History," *The Jewish Quarterly Review* 97, no. 4 (Fall 2007): 542.

33. Raz-Krakotzkin argues that "we must understand that 'our way of knowing the past' is imbued with the Christian attitude of superiority towards the Jews. Accordingly, we should insert the notion of exile into history, to understand 'Jewish historiography,' not only as narrating Jewish pasts but as writing history from a Jewish, exilic, perspective, challenging the notion of progress, and to take seriously Jewish perceptions of the past in order to 'brush history against the grain.'" As the final phrase makes clear, Raz-Krakotzkin's analysis is influenced by Walter Benjamin's theses on history. Ibid., 543.

34. Raz-Krakotzkin, *Exil et Souveraineté*, 39.

35. Ibid.

36. Ibid., 32.

37. See, for example, Amnon Raz-Krakotzkin, "A Peace without Arabs: The Discourse of Peace and the Limits of Israeli Consciousness," in *After Oslo: New Realities, Old Problems*, ed. George Giacaman and Dag Jørund Lønning (London: Pluto, 1998), 59–76.

38. Piterberg, *The Returns of Zionism*, 94.

39. Hannah Arendt, *The Origins of Totalitarianism* (New York: Benediction, 2009), 290. See also Idith Zertal, "Judaism and Zionism—Between the Pariah and the Parvenu," *Tel Aviver Jahrbuch für deutsche Geschichte* 30 (2002): 341–57.

40. John Howard Yoder, "Exodus and Exile: Two Faces of Liberation," *CrossCurrents* (Fall 1973): 279–309.

41. John Howard Yoder, *The Jewish-Christian Schism Revisited*, ed. Michael Cartwright and Peter Ochs (Grand Rapids: Eerdmans, 2002). To Yoder's essays, Cartwright and Ochs added a joint "Editors' Introduction"; Ochs penned brief responses to each of Yoder's chapters; and Cartwright added an extensive Afterword in which he advanced his own thinking about Jewish-Christian relations. For additional treatments by Yoder of diaspora Judaism, see John Howard

Yoder, *The War of the Lamb: The Ethics of Nonviolence and Peacemaking*, ed. Glen Stassen, Mark Thiessen Nation, and Matt Hamsher (Grand Rapids: Brazos, 2009), chapter 4; Yoder, *Christian Attitudes to War, Peace, and Revolution*, ed. Theodore J. Koontz and Andy Alexis-Baker (Grand Rapids: Brazos, 2009), chapter 10; and Yoder, *Nonviolence: A Brief History (The Warsaw Lectures)*, ed. Paul Martens, Matthew Porter, and Myles Werntz (Waco, TX: Baylor University Press, 2010), chapter 6.

42. Yoder, *The Jewish-Christian Schism Revisited*, 35. For discussions of Yoder's account of Jewish-Christian history and of his theology of Judaism, see Douglas Harink, *Paul among the Postliberals: Pauline Theology beyond Christendom and Modernity* (Grand Rapids: Brazos, 2003), 105ff.; Duane Friesen, "Yoder and the Jews: Cosmopolitan Homelessness as Ecclesial Model," in *A Mind Patient and Untamed: Assessing John Howard Yoder's Contributions to Theology, Ethics, and Peacemaking*, ed. Ben C. Ollenburger and Gayle Gerber Koontz (Telford, PA: Cascadia, 2004), 145–60; Craig Carter, *The Politics of the Cross: The Theology and Social Ethics of John Howard Yoder* (Grand Rapids: Brazos, 2001); and Paul Martens, *The Heterodox Yoder* (Eugene, OR: Cascade, 2011), 87–115.

43. Yoder, *The Jewish-Christian Schism Revisited*, 55.

44. Ibid., 152.

45. Ibid., 53.

46. For Yoder, Jeremiah's call to the exiles in Jer. 29:7 was a call to embrace "Galut as vocation." Yoder, *The Jewish-Christian Schism Revisited*, 190. Or, as Yoder put it elsewhere, "dispersion is mission." Yoder, *For the Nations: Essays Public and Evangelical* (Grand Rapids: Eerdmans, 1997), 52. Yoder characterizes the style of theopolitical witness to which Jews and Christians are both called as one of "not being in charge." Yoder, chapter 9, *The Jewish-Christian Schism Revisited*, "On Not Being in Charge."

47. Yoder, *The Jewish-Christian Schism Revisited*, 71.

48. Ibid., 243.

49. Ibid., 71.

50. Yoder noted that "both in doctrine and in sociology the king is relativized. He is at best the servant of divine righteousness, not its origin."—Ibid., 73. For Yoder, the Israelite temptation to kingship prefigures the Christian temptation of Constantinianism. Cartwright observes that for Yoder the "Davidic Project" of constituting "a monarchy in Jerusalem was prototypical of Christian forms of faithlessness."—Cartwright, "Editors' Introduction," in Yoder, *The Jewish-Christian Schism Revisited*, 20.

51. Yoder, *The Jewish-Christian Schism Revisited*, 184. Or also: "To be scattered is not a hiatus, after which normality will resume. From Jeremiah's time on . . . dispersion shall be the calling of the Jewish faith community" (183).

52. Ibid., 202n60.

53. Ibid., 97.

54. Ibid., 70.

55. "Jesus' impact in the first century added more and deeper authentically Jewish reasons, or reinforced and further validated the already expressed Jewish reasons, for the already established ethos of not being in charge and not considering any local state structure to be the primary bearer of the movement of history." Ibid., 171.

56. Ibid., 32, 33. Yoder elsewhere described diaspora Judaism's "extensive success in attracting to the synagogue community sincere seekers of non-Jewish blood" (50).

57. Yoder, *Jewish-Christian Schism Revisited*, 81–82.

58. Ibid., 86, 75.

59. See Yoder, *The Politics of Jesus: Vicit Agnus Noster*, revised edition (Grand Rapids: Eerdmans, 1994).

60. Yoder, *The Jewish-Christian Schism Revisited*, 191.

61. Ibid., 171.

62. For Yoder on "sacrament as social process" and the political character of the church's practices, see *Body Politics: Five Practices of the Christian Community before the Watching World* (Nashville: Discipleship Resources, 1992); *The Christian Witness to the State* (Newton, KS: Faith and Life, 1964); and "Sacrament as Social Process: Christ the Transformer of Culture," in *The Royal Priesthood: Essays Ecclesiastical and Ecumenical*, ed. Michael Cartwright (Grand Rapids: Eerdmans, 1994), 359–72. The phrase "with the grain of the universe" comes from Yoder, "Armaments and Eschatology," *Studies in Christian Ethics* 1 (1988): 43–61.

63. Yoder, *The Jewish-Christian Schism Revisited*, 114.

64. John Howard Yoder, "On Not Being Ashamed of the Gospel," in *A Pacifist Way of Knowing: John Howard Yoder's Nonviolent Epistemology*, ed. Christian E. Early and Ted G. Grimsrud (Eugene, OR: Cascade, 2010), 50.

65. See John Howard Yoder, "'Patience' as Method in Moral Reasoning: Is an Ethic of Discipleship 'Absolute'?" in Yoder, *A Pacifist Way of Knowing*, ed. Early and Grimsrud, 113–32.

66. "The culmination of the Constantinianism of Judaism is the development of Zionism." Yoder, *The Jewish-Christian Schism Revisited*, 86, 75.

67. Ibid., 85.

68. Ibid. "A tiny but growing number of Jews with strong roots in the theology of Jewish existence before Auschwitz," Yoder observed, "have since the beginnings of Zionism seen Israeli statehood in the same terms in which Jotham (Judg. 9) and Samuel (I Sam. 8) saw Canaanite kingship: not as an absolute evil which it should be possible to reject completely, but as an accommodation, regrettable, to the ways of the Gentiles, an innovation which will disappoint, which will not deliver on its promises." Ibid., 84–85.

69. Daniel Colucciello Barber, *On Diaspora: Christianity, Religion, and Secularity* (Eugene, OR: Cascade, 2011), 24.

70. Peter Ochs, *Another Reformation: Postliberal Christianity and the Jews* (Grand Rapids: Baker Academic, 2011), 151.

71. Cartwright and Ochs, "Editors' Introduction," in *The Jewish-Christian Schism Revisited*, 23–24, 19. Ochs concurs, arguing that Yoder's "openness to new forms of Jewish-Christian sharing is closed down when he claims already to know in advance what that sharing should be," i.e., *galut* as vocation. Ochs, "Commentary" on Chapter 1, in Yoder, *The Jewish-Christian Schism Revisited*, 68.

72. Daniel Boyarin, "Judaism as a Free Church: Footnotes to John Howard Yoder's *The Jewish-Christian Schism Revisited*," *CrossCurrents* 56, no. 4 (January 2007): 19.

73. See, for example, Daniel Boyarin, *Border Lines: The Partition of Judaeo-Christianity* (Philadelphia: University of Pennsylvania Press, 2004) and *The Ways That Never Parted: Jews and Christians in Late Antiquity and the Early Middle Ages*, ed. Adam H. Becker and Annette Yoshiko Reed (Tübingen: Mohr Siebeck, 2003).

74. Barber, *On Diaspora*, 124.

75. Gerald Schlabach, "Deuteronomic or Constantinian: What Is the Most Basic Problem for Christian Social Ethics?" in *The Wisdom of the Cross: Essays in Honor of John Howard Yoder*, ed. Stanley Hauerwas, Chris K. Huebner, Harry Huebner, and Mark Thiessen Nation (Grand Rapids: Eerdmans, 2002), 449–71.

76. Michael Cartwright, "Afterword," in Yoder, *The Jewish-Christian Schism Revisited*, 217.

77. Norman C. Habel, *The Land Is Mine: Six Biblical Land Ideologies* (Minneapolis: Fortress Press, 1995) and Walter Brueggemann, *The Land: Place as Gift, Promise, and Challenge in Biblical Theology* (Minneapolis: Fortress Press, 2002). See also Rachel Havrelock's insistence that "rather than one nation with one mythology, the literary record of ancient Israel—the Hebrew Bible—contains several national mythologies," including national mythologies that open up space to incorporate the religious, ethnic, and political Other. Havrelock, *River Jordan: The Mythology of a Dividing Line* (Chicago: University of Chicago Press, 2011), 5.

78. Brueggemann, *The Land*, xviii.

79. Ibid., 202.

80. Daniel Smith-Christopher, *A Biblical Theology of Exile* (Minneapolis: Fortress Press, 2002), 25.

81. Yoder, *The Jewish-Christian Schism Revisited*, 71.

82. Timothy J. Gorringe, *A Theology of the Built Environment: Justice, Empowerment, Redemption* (Cambridge: Cambridge University Press, 2002), 60.

83. W. D. Davies, *The Gospel and the Land: Early Christianity and Jewish Territorial Doctrine* (Sheffield, UK: JSOT Press, 1994), 375.

84. Waldemar Janzen, "Land," in *The Anchor Bible Dictionary*, ed. David Noel Freedman et al. (New York: Doubleday, 1992), IV:153.

85. Cartwright, "Afterword," in Yoder, *The Jewish-Christian Schism Revisited*, 219.

86. Ochs, *Another Reformation*, 152.

87. Ibid., 147.

88. That said, I agree with Ochs that Yoder would have been able to develop his exilic theology of land more clearly through dialogue with figures such as Mordecai Kaplan and Ahad Ha'am. These cultural Zionists who "valued corporate Jewish life, including life in the soil of Israel, but without formal nation-state self-governance," would have been "more compelling dialogue partners for Yoder than Stephan Zweig," the German-Jewish playwright and champion of diasporism. Ochs, *Another Reformation*, 153.

89. Yoder, *For the Nations: Essays Public and Evangelical*, 82.

90. Yoder, *The Jewish-Christian Schism Revisited*, 161.

91. Ibid.

92. Ibid., 162.

93. Ibid., 163.

94. Ibid., 164.

95. Peter Ochs emphasizes that "a dialectical relation between exile and landedness is therefore more representative of classical Jewish life and belief than any clear and unchanging choice *for* one against the other." Ochs, *Another Reformation*, 151. As I trust the above material makes clear, Yoder's description of true possession requiring that one use the land and build upon the land for the sake of others reflects a theology of exile that does not pit exile against return or exile against landedness. A contemporary theology of building the city for others, Rachel Havrelock suggests, will find resources within the diverse political traditions of the Hebrew Bible. While not denying the presence of exclusivist land traditions within the Hebrew Bible, Havrelock maintains that texts such as Deut. 7:1–2, with their rejectionist postures toward non-Israelites, need to be read alongside texts such as Josh. 15:63, which envisions Jerusalem "shared in perpetuity by Judah and its Jebusite neighbors." Havrelock, *River Jordan*, 16.

96. Nathan Kerr, "*Communio Missionis*: Certeau, Yoder, and the Missionary Space of the Church," in *The New Yoder*, ed. Peter Dula and Chris K. Huebner (Eugene, OR: Cascade, 2010), 335n75. Kerr's account of the dispossessive character of possession for Yoder offers a positive way to understand Yoder's claim that the church that accepts its status of living in exile among the nations does not focus on "possessing the land." As Kerr's gloss on Yoder and Yoder's reflections above on building the city for others make clear, Yoder was not here objecting to emplaced existence, but rather to a form of habitation or possession that forgets one's status as an exile whose only true home will be in God. John Howard Yoder, *The Priestly Kingdom* (Notre Dame: University of Notre Dame Press, 1984), 43.

97. Barber, *On Diaspora*, 132.

98. Julie Peteet, "Words as Interventions: Naming in the Palestine-Israel Conflict," *Third World Quarterly* 26, no. 1 (2005): 165–66.

99. Elias Sanbar, "Out of Place, Out of Time," *Mediterranean Historical Review* 16, no. 1 (2001): 90.

100. Ibid., 91.

101. Michel Warschawski, *On the Border* (Cambridge, MA: South End, 2004), x.

102. Amnon Raz-Krakotzkin trenchantly observes that the "peace discourse of the Israeli Left in fact proposes getting rid of the Arabs [through separation barriers, through a two-state solution, etc.], and therefore it sounds exactly like the talk of transfer." Quoted in Lily Galili, "A Jewish Demographic State," *Journal of Palestine Studies* 32, no. 1 (Autumn 2002): 92.

103. As'ad Ghanem, "The Bi-National Solution for the Israeli-Palestinian Crisis: Conceptual Background and Contemporary Debate," in *Palestinian-Israeli Impasse: Exploring Alternative Solutions to the Palestine-Israel Conflict*, ed. Mahdi Abdul Hadi (Jerusalem: PASSIA, 2005), 19–44.

104. Representative arguments include those advanced by Tamar Hermann, "The Bi-National Idea in Israel/Palestine: Past and Present," *Nations and Nationalism* 11, no. 3 (2005): 381–401 and Salim Tamari, "The Dubious Lure of Binationalism," in *Palestinian-Israeli Impasse*, ed. Hadi, 67–72.

105. A succinct form of this common argument can be found in Yossi Alpher, "The Palestinian Narrative Clashes with a Two-State Solution," in *The Best of Bitterlemons: Five Years of Writing from Israel and Palestine*, ed. Yossi Alpher, Ghassan Khatib, and Charmaine Seitz (Jerusalem: Bitterlemons, 2007), 51–53.

106. See, for example, Chaim Gans, "The Palestinian Right of Return and the Justice of Zionism," in *Israel and the Palestinian Refugees*, ed. Eyal Benvenisti, Chaim Gans, and Sari Hanafi (Berlin: Springer, 2007), 255–94.

107. See Michael Kagan, *Do Israeli Rights Conflict with the Palestinian Right of Return?* Working Paper No. 10 (Bethlehem: Badil Resource Center for Palestinian Residency and Refugee Rights, 2005).

108. Amnon Raz-Krakotzkin, "Binationalism and Jewish Identity: Hannah Arendt and the Question of Palestine," in *Hannah Arendt in Jerusalem*, ed. Steven E. Aschheim (Berkeley: University of California Press, 200), 168.

109. Ibid., 171.

110. Ibid., 172.

111. Laor, *The Myth of Liberal Zionism*, 11.

112. For a classic articulation of the early PLO position, see Shafiq Al-Hout, "Toward a Unitary Democratic State," *Journal of Palestine Studies* 6, no. 2 (Winter 1977): 9–11.

113. For Palestinian proponents of the one-state solution, see Mazin Qumsiyeh, *Sharing the Land of Canaan: Human Rights and the Israeli-Palestinian Struggle* (London: Pluto, 2004); Ali Abunimah, *One Country: A Bold Proposal to End the Israeli-Palestinian Impasse* (New York: Metropolitan, 2006); Jenab Tutunji and Kamal Khaldi, "A Binational State in Palestine: The Rational Choice for Palestinians and the Moral Choice for Israelis," *International Affairs* 73, no. 1 (January 1997): 31–58; and Palestine Strategy Study Group, *Regaining the Initiative: Palestinian Strategic Options to End Israeli Occupation* (August 2008), available at http://www.palestinestrategygroup.ps. Israeli Jewish defenses of the unitary democratic state model include Daniel Gavron, *The Other Side of Despair: Jews and Arabs in the Promised Land* (Lanham, MD: Rowman & Littlefield, 2004) and Uri Davis, "Whither Palestine-Israel? Political Reflections on Citizenship, Bi-Nationalism, and the One State Solution," *Holy Land Studies: A Multidisciplinary Journal* 5, no. 2 (2006): 199–210. See also Virginia Tilley, *The One-State Solution: A Breakthrough for Peace in the Israeli-Palestinian Deadlock* (Ann Arbor: University of Michigan Press, 2005) and Tony Judt, "Israel: The Alternative," *New York Review of Books* 50, no. 16 (October 2003).

114. Uri Ram, "From Nation-State to Nation—State: Nation, History, and Identity Struggle in Jewish Israel," in *The Challenge of Post-Zionism: Alternatives to Israeli Fundamentalist Politics*, ed. Ephraim Nimni (London: Zed, 2003), 20–41.

115. Shohat, *Taboo Memories*, 333.

116. Yehouda Shenhav, *The Time of the Green Line* [Hebrew] (Hakibbutz: Hameuchad, 2010). See also Shenhav, *Beyond the Two-State Solution: A Jewish Political Essay* (Malden, MA: Polity, 2013).

117. For an overview of confederation and federation models for resolving the Palestinian-Israeli conflict (with the main difference between confederation and federation models being the degree of centralized authority binding smaller units together), see Asher Susser, "Confederation Options in the Palestine-Israel Conflict," in *Palestinian-Israeli Impasse*, ed. Hadi, 217–24 and Nick Kardahji, "Dreaming of Co-Existence: A Brief History of the Bi-National Idea," in *Palestinian-Israeli Impasse*, ed. Hadi, 1–18. See also Nasser Abufarha, "Alternative Palestinian Agenda—Proposal for an Alternative Configuration in Palestine-Israel," in *Palestinian-Israeli Impasse*, ed. Hadi, 145–86; Jeff Halper, "Thinking Out of the Box: Towards a Middle East Union," in *Palestinian-Israeli Impasse*, ed. Hadi, 225–36; and Jeff Halper, *Obstacles to Peace: A Re-Framing of the Palestinian-Israeli Conflict* (Jerusalem: ICAHD, 2004).

118. Zertal, "Judaism and Zionism—Between the Pariah and the Parvenu," 356.

119. For representative writings by Magnes and Buber on binationalism, see Judah Magnes, *Dissenter in Zion: From the Writings of Judah L. Magnes* (Cambridge, MA: Harvard University Press, 1982); Judah Magnes et al., *Palestine—Divided or United? The Case for a Bi-National Palestine before the United Nations* (Westport, CT: Greenwood, 1947), and Martin Buber, *A Land of Two Peoples: Martin Buber on Jews and Arabs*, ed. Paul Mendes-Flohr (Chicago: University of Chicago Press, 2005).

120. Edward Said, *Freud and the Non-European* (London: Verso, 2003), 55.

121. Raz-Krakotzkin, "A Peace without Arabs," 75.

122. Amnon Raz-Krakotzkin, "The Zionist Return to the West and the Mizrahi Jewish Perspective," in *Orientalism and the Jews*, ed. Ivan Davidson Kalmar and Derek J. Penslar (Waltham, MA: Brandeis University Press, 2005), 180.

123. Raz-Krakotzkin, "A National Colonial Theology," 324.

124. For a discussion of "diasporized states," see the first essay in Daniel Boyarin and Jonathan Boyarin, *Powers of Diaspora: Two Essays on the Relevance of Jewish Culture* (Minneapolis: University of Minnesota Press, 2002). See also Daniel Boyarin and Jonathan Boyarin, "Diaspora: Generative Ground of Jewish Identity," *Critical Inquiry* 19, no. 4 (1993): 693–725 and Daniel Boyarin, *A Radical Jew: Paul and the Politics of Identity* (Berkeley: University of California Press, 1994), 248–55.

125. Piterberg, *The Returns of Zionism*, 122. Longtime Israeli peace activist Michel Warschawski offers a parallel analysis of how durable peace between Israeli Jews and Palestinians will require the recovery of an exilic, diasporic approach. "For Ben Gurion and his successors," Warschawski explains, "the 'return' to the Holy Land, by definition, put an end to exile. But for Orthodox Judaism, by contrast, exile is not a matter of location; it endures even after the establishment of Jewish sovereignty in Israel. It is that Diaspora identity that Israel must re-appropriate, tempering its nationalism with a strong dose of that cosmopolitanism so hated not only by the 'hooligans of the right' but also by the ideologues of Zionism. It has to moderate its obsession regarding its own security with empathy for the suffering of others, replacing its withdrawal into itself with a systematic opening to the Other." Warschawski, *On the Border*, 213.

126. Judith Butler, *Precarious Life: The Powers of Mourning and Violence* (London and New York: Verso, 2004), 119.

127. Amnon Raz-Krakotkzin, quoted in Silberstein, *The Postzionism Debates*, 182.

128. Sidra DeKoven-Ezrahi, *Booking Passage: Exile and Homecoming in the Modern Jewish Imagination* (Berkeley: University of California Press, 2000), 240.

3

Kafr Bir'im, Elias Chacour, and the Arboreal Imagination

> *They shall build houses and*
> *inhabit them;*
> *they shall plant vineyards and*
> *eat their fruit.*
> *They shall not build and another*
> *inhabit;*
> *they shall not plant and*
> *another eat;*
> *for like the days of a tree shall the*
> *days of my people be . . .*
> —Isaiah 65:21–22 (NRSV)

> *"Something in the yard stopped me. There,*
> *firmly rooted and still green with life, grew*
> *my special fig tree."*
> —Elias Chacour, Greek Catholic
> Archbishop for the Galilee[1]

The prophet Isaiah's vision of rootedness in the land and freedom from dispossession echoes the yearnings for belonging and return of millions of Palestinian refugees, both Christians and Muslims. An affirmation that one's ultimate dwelling place is in God (Ps. 90:1) does not negate human attachment to particular places, nor does it contradict Isaiah's depiction of a future of security in the land. For Samira Daou, originally from the Christian village of Kafr Bir'im in the upper Galilee, one of over five hundred Palestinian towns and villages depopulated and destroyed by the Israeli military during 1948 and its aftermath, and today a resident of the Dbayeh refugee camp outside Beirut, return represents an end to the alienation she experiences as a refugee in Lebanon: "I still feel a stranger in this country, feel that I don't belong. Even if I had lived a hundred years here I would still like to go back to Palestine, go back to Kafr Bir'im where no one can tell me that I'm a refugee and that I don't belong."[2] Displaced Bir'imites who remained within what became the State of Israel express a similar sense of estrangement. "I don't want my children and grandchildren to feel like strangers forever," states Emtanes Susan, today a resident of the village of Jish, only a few kilometers south of Kafr Bir'im's ruins. "I want them to belong to the land."[3]

In the face of an Israeli cartographic regime that seeks to erase the traces of Palestinian presence from the landscape, the displaced villagers of the nearly seven-hundred-year-old Kafr Bir'im and their descendants have over six decades been at the forefront of Palestinian refugee efforts to return.[4] Together with Abuna Elias Chacour, perhaps the village's most famous native son, who served as longtime Melkite priest of the Galilean village of I'billin and today presides as Archbishop of 'Akka, Haifa, Nazareth, and All of Galilee, Bir'imites have asked, "Am I always to be a refugee, pushed from place to place, never belonging anywhere?"[5] They have answered not only by pursuing legal and political avenues in attempts to secure their return but also by cultivating connections with the ruins of Kafr Bir'im, making regular family visits to Bir'im's demolished buildings, holding annual summer camps for the youth of Bir'im in order to pass on the village's folklore traditions, and celebrating weddings and burying the dead in the village's church and cemetery, both of which villagers won the right to renovate and use after concerted political action.

In the late 1960s, Elias Chacour, then a newly ordained priest of the Melkite (Greek Catholic) church, made his first return visit to the ruins of Kafr Bir'im, from which he, along with his fellow villagers, had been expelled by Israeli military forces at the age of six and from which he had been barred for two decades.[6] Bir'im was for centuries a Christian village in the northern Galilee. Its 1,050 inhabitants were among the hundreds of thousands of Palestinians who became refugees.[7] On November 13, 1948, the Israeli military ordered the villagers to leave Bir'im, allegedly because of security concerns, promising that they would be allowed to return after a few days. After weeks and then months passed without them being allowed to return, Bir'imites petitioned the Israeli Supreme Court, which upheld their right to return. The military responded on September 17, 1953, by placing explosive charges around the homes and bombing the village from the air while the villagers looked on from a nearby hill. Over the ensuing years, Bir'im remained off-limits as a closed military area for the expelled villagers, even as the Israeli state turned over portions of the village's land to two *kibbutzim* (Baram and Sasa) and a *moshav* (Dovev) and in the mid-1960s opened a national park and a nature reserve on top of Bir'im's ruins.

Chacour, who had entered the newly opened Baram National Park as a tourist, moved quickly through the toppled stones of the destroyed village, at first finding himself "once again a small boy rushing home through the fig trees." Then, "any illusion of the past was broken," as he surveyed the ravages of humanity and time: "The [family] orchard itself was a ruin. For some reason it had been deserted and now grew unpruned except by the straying winds of God. The house, too, was a shambles." Overcome with emotion, he began to turn away from the rubble of his family home when "Something in the yard stopped me. There, firmly rooted and still green with life, grew my special fig tree."[8]

The pivotal role played by trees in Chacour's autobiographical narrative and in his theological analysis stands as one instance of how the arboreal imagination animates Israeli and Palestinian mappings of space and landscapes of return. The planting of trees asserts connection to the land and covers over traces of prior habitation, while oak, fig, olive, and pomegranate trees become sites of memory for the imagined Palestinian refugee landscape. After recounting Bir'im's destruction, I examine Bir'imite practices and discourses around trees, with particular attention to Chacour's autobiographical-theological narrative. What cartographies can the arboreal imagination produce? Is the arboreal imagination necessarily bound up with exclusivist mappings of erasure only, mappings that encode given spaces as *either* Palestinian *or* Israeli Jewish? Or might the arboreal imagination animating the imagined landscapes of Palestinian refugees also produce cartographies of mutuality that accept, even embrace, the complex character of shared space?

THE DEPOPULATION AND DESTRUCTION OF KAFR BIR'IM

Throughout October 1948, Israeli militias moved through the Galilee as part of Operation Hiram, with tens of thousands of Palestinians expelled by or fleeing from the Zionist forces.[9] Father Yusuf Istifan Susan, Kafr Bir'im's Maronite priest, recalls the panic and misery of that month as caravans of refugees passed by the village on their march into exile in Lebanon:

Painful and sad scenes: children, women and the elderly on carts and driven by fear; rows of others walking behind beasts and carrying light belongings; cries of children who felt frightened, hungry, or cold; mothers bewailing their cruel fate, and a baffled and perplexed voice shouting: "What are you waiting for? They are coming. They are drawing nearer, so run for your lives!" A terrible sight, and words that affect one's heart. Such scenes cause conflicting reactions. On the one hand, you are pulled to join these people, while, on the other, you feel more rooted in the land on which you stand. The first reaction wants to drive you like cattle; the second shocks you, . . . makes your hair stand on end, assaults you with thoughts, and ferments in you waves of questions about the destiny of those people. . . . Every father and every mother, and indeed every sane person in Kafr Bir'im, who had seen with their own eyes those sad caravans, must have asked these questions. The people of Kafr Bir'im, however, said they were staying. "Here we stay . . . here we remain," they said. The newcomers were drawing closer and closer, but the Kafr Bir'im inhabitants said they would stay.[10]

Near the end of Operation Hiram, on October 29, 1948, the same day that Israeli forces massacred a total of nearly one hundred people in the nearby villages of Safsaf and Jish, members of the Haganah militia entered Kafr Bir'im, the sole exclusively Christian village in the Safad district of Palestine.[11] The villagers—primarily Maronites, along with two Greek Catholic families—sent their elders to greet the conquering forces.[12] "Most of us remained in our houses," recounts Elias Jacob, "but the old men and the priest received the troops at the entrance of the village with a white flag. We offered them bread and salt, the symbol of friendship and peace."[13] The villagers might have expected that they would be allowed to stay in place, given that Bir'imites had provided assistance in Zionist operations to smuggle Jews into the country from Lebanon by distracting British police officers, and given that the Maronite Patriarch in Beirut had voiced support for the establishment of a Jewish state in Palestine.[14] The arrival of an Israeli official on November 7, 1948, to take a census of the villagers spurred hope among Bir'imites that they would be permitted to remain in their homes.[15]

Less than one week later, however, on November 13, 1948, Israeli military officials ordered that villagers leave their homes, on the grounds that an expected counter-offensive in the region would jeopardize their security. Elias Chacour remembers the villagers being told by the military commander that "[o]ur intelligence sources say that Kafr Bir'im is in serious danger, but you are fortunate because my men can protect it. Your lives, however, may be in danger. Therefore, you have to close your houses, give us the keys and head to the surrounding hills for a few days. I promise you that none of your belongings will be touched."[16]

From that day forward, Bir'imites joined the ranks of "internally displaced" Palestinians (Palestinians alienated from their homes and properties by Israeli regulations and laws, but who remained within the new state of Israel); some would later become refugees in Lebanon. While Bir'imites did not qualify as "present absentees" (*nofkadim nochachim*), under the Israeli Absentee Property Law of 1950 (their expulsion from the village fell after the timeframe identified in the law), Bir'imites shared the same fate as internally displaced present absentees, in that they all shared the experience of being "present" in Israel while "absent" from their homes and properties.[17] Bir'imites quickly discovered that the Israeli military had no intention of honoring its promise to allow them back to Bir'im. As Israeli historian Benny Morris explains, the evacuation of Kafr Bir'im was part of a broader campaign following Operation Hiram in November 1948 to clear out Arab villagers from a depth of five to fifteen kilometers along the border with Lebanon.[18] After being ordered out of the village, families camped out in the hills under the olive and fig trees from which they made their living.[19] After several days, Behor Shetrit, the Israeli Minister for Minorities, visited the villagers and ordered that they be housed in nearby Jish in the empty homes of Muslim families who had already been expelled, promising that they would soon be allowed back to Bir'im.[20] Nearly 250 Bir'imites could not find room in Jish, however, and crossed the border into Lebanon for what they wrongly assumed would be a brief stay.[21] Women and men visiting the village to care for their trees or to get supplies from their homes were routinely driven off and sometimes arrested.[22] Villagers' concerns increased when in 1949 Israeli officials began surveying Bir'im's land, concerns validated later that year with the establishment of a kibbutz—Baram—on village land (fourteen years later, in 1963, an agricultural settlement, Moshav Dovev, was also built on Bir'im land).[23] [The newly founded Kibbutz Baram employed many of the displaced villagers to assist with the olive harvest, a fact that, Bir'imites were quick to observe, undercut the claim that their return to their village would constitute a security threat.[24]]

As soon as it became clear that the military authorities had no intention of allowing them to return, the Bir'im displaced began exploring a wide variety of political and legal avenues to press their case for return, including petitions to the Israeli Supreme Court.[25] When the Court ruled in July 1951 that the people of Bir'im had the right to return home, the military responded that August by declaring Bir'im a "closed area" under the 1945 Emergency Regulations drawn up by the British Mandate authorities.[26] The next month, military officials issued retroactive expulsion notices to the people of Bir'im, and two years later, on August 27, 1953, the Israeli Knesset retroactively granted ownership of Bir'im's lands to the Israel Development Authority.[27]

Then, on September 16 and 17, 1953, the Israeli military destroyed Kafr Bir'im, first placing explosives charges around the houses, then bombing the village from Israeli Air Force planes. Sami Zahra recounts that "[w]hen the planes appeared above the village, and the houses were bombed, we all went up a hill located in the high area of Jish overlooking Kafr Bir'im. Every time a bomb fell on a house, the people would mention the name of the house owner and cry, and wait for the next bomb which would destroy the next house. They were unable to intervene against the destruction. . . . Ever since that time, the hill has been called the 'Bir'imites wailing place.'"[28] The Greek Catholic Archbishop at the time observed that the village's destruction came days after the feast of the Exaltation of the Holy Cross, a celebration traditionally celebrated in Middle Eastern Christian communities by the night-time lighting of fires. "This year," Archbishop Hakim noted, "the fires of Kafr Bir'im were destroying its homes."[29]

TREES AND THE ERASURE OF PLACE

The firebombing of Kafr Bir'im was not the end of the village's erasure: through various arboreal practices, such as the neglect of trees, the uprooting of trees, and tree-planting, the Israeli state transformed the village site into a national park, as it did to scores of other destroyed villages. One can see this arboreal imagination of conquest animating the Psalmist's image of a verdant rootedness bound up with the practice of clearing out a territory in order to implant another people: "You brought a vine out of Egypt; you drove out the nations and planted it. You cleared the ground for it; it took deep root and filled the land" (Ps. 80:8–11, NRSV). Such an arboreal imagination has helped to shape the Israeli state's cartographic project of erasing Palestinian traces from the Israeli map, its designification of the Palestinian landscape, and its transformation of that landscape into a homogeneous space onto which the Zionist program of establishing Jewish hegemony within a particular territory might be realized.[30] In the Zionist imagination, argues Irus Braverman, trees stand tall as "planted flags" by which the Israeli state metaphorically and literally exerts control over space.[31] Meron Benvenisti records that the Palestinian citrus groves, olive trees, and fruit orchards covering almost one million *dunams*

(250,000 acres) in 1948 were then "neglected or destroyed outright as the Israelis destroyed" whatever could not be assimilated into the Israeli framework.[32] Through what Shaul Cohen calls an aggressive "politics of planting," the Israeli state and para-state agencies like the the Jewish National Fund (*Keren Kayemet l'Yisrael*, hereafter JNF) have exerted control over refugee land by "greening" it.[33]

Tree-planting and deracination by the JNF and the Israel Nature and Natural Parks Protection Authority (NPA) have played key roles in these attempts to cover over former Palestinian habitation, including the ruins of Bir'im. JNF afforestation at the sites of destroyed Palestinian villages, Carol Bardenstein explains, has been critical in the burial of Palestinian history, even as it asserts Jewish presence.[34] JNF tree-planting, Bardenstein argues, constitutes an "invention of tradition," the creation of "new connections and new memories in the *present*, while simultaneously invoking old memories of connection and in the process aiming to create a community of Jewish memory and collectivity." This invented tradition aims to subvert the Jewish exilic imagination captured in Isaac Deutscher's aphorism that "[t]rees have roots, Jews have legs."[35] While the JNF's image in the West is primarily associated with tree-planting, for Palestinians, including Bir'imites, it represents an agency of expropriation through surveying and mapping. JNF workers, for example, surveyed Bir'im's land prior to parts of it being turned over to Kibbutz Baram.[36]

The NPA has also been instrumental in the transformation of the destroyed Palestinian landscape into Zionist space through the ethnocratic "greening" of that space.[37] Bir'im, for example, is one of over 120 destroyed Palestinian villages over which tourism and recreation sites operated by the NPA and the JNF have been established.[38] For decades, the official signposts at the park passed over the ruins of Bir'im's homes in silence, focusing solely on the remains of a fourth-century ce synagogue at the site. The present-day sign and National Park literature are somewhat more forthcoming, yet omit more than they disclose, making no mention of the Israeli Supreme Court decision that Bir'imites should be allowed to return home, remaining mute on the bombing of the village, and failing to address why Bir'im's original inhabitants and their descendants are not permitted to return to live in the village.[39]

"I Speak with the Oak Trees, I Speak with the Olive Trees"

Trees also figure prominently within the Palestinian political imagination and in discourses and practices of internally displaced Palestinians like the villagers of Bir'im. The arboreal imagination animates not only cartographies of domination and conquest but also cartographies of memory and resistance. Alongside the grand narrative mappings of mainstream Zionism—which present a land without a people for a people without a land—and next to what Issam Aburaiya and Efrat Ben-Ze'ev term the "monumental hegemonic discourse" of the *nakba*, the grand mapping of the catastrophic destruction of Palestinian society in 1948, exist the multiple cartographies of "the miniature setting," individual refugee narratives that draw "their imagery from the locality—a specific village, the location of one's house, certain springs and trees, fences and mountain terrains."[40]

For internally displaced Palestinians like the majority of Kafr Bir'im's expellees, these individual, family, and village maps have been sustained and nurtured through regular visits to village ruins.[41] "Memory," Pierre Nora has emphasized, "takes root in the concrete, in spaces, gestures, images, and objects," with particular concrete items or locations becoming "sites of memory" (*lieux de mémoire*). The trees and ruins of destroyed Palestinian villages stand as what Nora calls "dominated" *lieux de mémoire*—"places of refuge, sanctuaries of spontaneous devotion and silent pilgrimage"—distinct from the spectacular and triumphant "dominant" sites of memory established by national authorities or other powerful interests.[42] In return visits to the ruins, trees and other vegetation (such as the resilient *sabr*, or prickly-pear cactus, often planted by Palestinians along property boundaries) stand out as such memory sites. In her visits to destroyed villages with Palestinian refugees, Bardenstein observed that "the primary way the former villager reconstructs his map and memory of the village for me is through his reading of the landscape and the trees." A strikingly tall and majestic tree, for example, helps the villager identify the former home of the village elder (*mukhtar*).[43] Fruit-bearing trees (such as olives, figs, and pomegranates) function as "other texts to be read—remains of the village's orchards, as well as configurations of individual fruit trees planted by villagers in the vicinity of where their homes once stood."[44] Bardenstein persuasively suggests that "in the face of Palestinian dispossession, deterritorialization into exile, or occupation," trees, with their longevity and rootedness, become potent sites of memory production.[45] As will surface repeatedly in the account below of Bir'imite political struggle for return, trees have been key markers on Bir'imites' mental maps of their former homes, and arboreal images spring up throughout their protests of their ongoing dispossession and their assertion of their history, identity, and right to return.

The bombing of Kafr Bir'im may have aimed to bring an end to Bir'imite appeals to be allowed to return to the village by demolishing its physical structures, but Bir'imite determination to return persisted. An open letter to the government from the villagers following the bombardment stressed that "[t]he bombing of the houses will not make the owners cede their rights."[46] Bir'imites consistently refused government offers of different land in exchange for relinquishing their claims to Kafr Bir'im's lands. "We neither want to be absorbed nor belong to another place," Kamel Yacoub stated.[47] Fr. Susan stressed that "[w]e are not citizens who came to beg you for charity or ask you to give us a piece of land. We have been the owners of the place for hundreds of years." Noting that the government proposed to give Bir'imites refugee land that had been taken over by the State of Israel's Custodian of Absentee Property, Susan insisted that "[w]e are not in need of the land of strangers and do not want to settle on the land of refugees, who are still hoping to return in the future. We do not want them to say that we stole their land in violation of logic and conscience. We have enough land, our own property inherited from our fathers and forefathers, and we will not cede it. We are pleased with our rocks and will not move away. Kafr Bir'im is ours and will be ours forever."[48]

The displaced of Kafr Bir'im continued to mobilize as a community even after the village's demolition. Beginning on September 26, 1954, villagers staged annual marches from Jish to the "Hill of Tears" from which they had witnessed Bir'im's destruction. In addition to keeping their demand to return in the public eye, Bir'imites also put forward creative proposals to the Israeli government. For example, in 1965 the villagers, taking the State of Israel at its word that only security concerns along the Lebanon border prevented their return, asked that their names be included in Israel's official Land Register as owners of the land, in return for the villagers agreeing not to return until a peace treaty between Israel and Lebanon had been concluded. The government's rejection of the proposal exposed the hollow pretense of the security rationale for the denial of return.[49] Such creative proposals and communal action were particularly noteworthy in the context of Israel in the 1950s and 1960s, a time when Israel's Palestinian citizens lived under the restrictions of emergency military rule. Even amidst prohibitions on political organization, press censorship, and curtailed freedom of movement, the people of Kafr Bir'im were successful, as Riyadh Ghantous, a member of the village's al-'Awda [Return] Movement, notes, in being "among the first to launch the struggle for return in the country, and the only community who raised the issue of return widely."[50]

Israel lifted military rule over its Palestinian citizens in 1966, and the years following Israel's victory in the 1967 war and its conquest of the West Bank and the Gaza Strip (among other territories) witnessed increasingly visible protests by Bir'imites for return. Under the leadership of Greek Catholic Archbishop for the Galilee Joseph Raya, a Lebanese-American appointed to the position in 1968, Kafr Bir'im's political struggle was joined to that of the villagers of Iqrit, a Greek Catholic town in the 'Akka district whose depopulation and destruction mirrored that of Bir'im. Raya, an early and active participant in civil rights protests while serving as pastor of St. George Greek Catholic Church in Birmingham, Alabama in the 1950s and 1960s, was a passionate advocate of nonviolent struggle and rallied many Israeli Jews to join the people of Bir'im and Iqrit in protests against their denied return.[51]

Large-scale public protests began in 1970, reflecting a broader shift among Palestinians inside Israel from quiescence to activism, with Bir'imites, joined by sympathetic Israeli Jews, defying the enduring military closure on Kafr Bir'im and staging a six-month-long protest camp in the ruins of the village.[52] As will be described in greater detail below, trees played a prominent role in some of these protests and continue to play a striking role in memories of these protests. In these early protests, as Baruch Kimmerling observes, Iqrit and Bir'im were represented as "*special* and *deviant*" cases of destroyed villages, given the promises made by the military commanders that the villagers should be allowed to return and given the subsequent Supreme Court rulings in the villagers' favor. Within little more than a decade, however, Bir'imites were actively linking their local struggle to the broader political campaign by Palestinian citizens of Israel for equality.[53]

The largest demonstrations came in 1972, generating widespread publicity not only within Israel but also internationally.[54] Archbishop Raya issued a call to "all our clergy, sons and daughters, to ring the church bells in mourning over the absence of justice in Israel and in protest, because the government has made for itself a golden calf called 'land,' which replaces real justice. In the name of this calf the most horrible atrocities are committed. Where is Prophet Moses to deal with you, golden calf?"[55] Raya and leaders of the Bir'im and Iqrit communities mobilized solidarity marches on May 8 of that year to the two towns, marches in which over one thousand Israeli Jews joined the villagers. Later that month, nearly 3,000 Palestinians and Israeli Jews marched in Jerusalem waving banners with biblically resonant slogans such as "Let my people go to Kafr Bir'im" and, in modification of Ps. 137:5, "If I forget thee, Bir'im, may my right hand lose its cunning."[56] Golda Meir was presented as a modern-day Jezebel who recapitulated the crime of Naboth's vineyard (1 Kings 21), dispossessing the people of Bir'im and Iqrit by not allowing them to return home.[57] Baruch Kimmerling argues that such biblical slogans and allusions, along with others adapted from the Zionist mythos (including "Our hope is not yet lost," from the Israeli national anthem, *Hatikva*, and "If there be justice—let it appear immediately," from a 1903 verse by the Zionist poet Bialik about a pogrom against the Kishniev Jewish community), established a parallelism "between the Jewish people and the territory of the state and the evacuees and the territory of their villages." This parallelism, Kimmerling contends, had the inadvertent effect of causing many in the Israeli Jewish public to understand the demand for return in zero-sum terms, evoking fears that the return of any refugees would entail Jewish displacement, just as Zionist return had meant the displacement of Palestinians.[58]

The protests of the 1970s did not secure return to Bir'im and Iqrit, with the Israeli government, stepping out from behind the dubious security rationale, arguing that allowing the inhabitants of the two villages to return would establish a negative precedent that could threaten the Zionist character of Israeli space.[59] The protests did result, however, in the Israeli military relaxing restrictions on visits to the village and in villagers receiving permission to use the church on feast days and to bury their dead in the village cemetery.[60]

Arboreal memories and practices have been interwoven in the account above of Bir'imites' decades-long campaign to secure return to the village site. Bir'im is not unique in this regard: as Randa Farah notes, "the symbols of roots, trees, and seeds punctuate the life histories, symbols of belonging, and historical depth for those forcefully displaced."[61] Imagery of rootedness, furthermore, occurs frequently within Palestinian Christian self-description. Arboreal discourse and practices are most evident in efforts by the villagers to transmit memories of Bir'im from one generation to the next. A primary form of memory transmission laden with arboreal discourse is the return visit to Bir'im's ruins. Given that many of Bir'im's displaced lived in nearby Jish, with many others relatively close by in other Galilee towns, the majority of Bir'im's families began making frequent trips to the ruins following the easing of military restrictions on access to the site. Riyadh Ghantous estimates that today the typical family visits Bir'im around ten times per year, not only celebrating Easter and Christmas in the village church and gathering for weddings and burials, but also making personal trips.[62] Such visits by internally displaced persons to their ruined villages, Efrat Ben-Ze'ev claims, are marked by "rites of return," such as the preparation and serving of traditional foods under village trees and picking and eating wild herbs and fruit from specific trees, "sensual experiences, whereby taste and smell play a major role, assisting in the retrieval of memories through embodiment."[63] Through these rites of return, Ilan Magat observes, villagers carry on a dual struggle, both against the Israeli state and its institutions that deny their rights to the land and against sedentary tendencies and forgetfulness. The rites of return become means of memory production in which the past continuously infiltrates the present, and vice-versa, with the village ruins becoming what Magat terms a site of the "continuous present."[64] Another key way in which Bir'imites have sought to mobilize and transmit memories of Kafr Bir'im has been to organize summer camps for young children and youth descended from the original inhabitants. The first such "roots and belonging summer camps" (*mukhayamaat al-intima' wa al-judhur*)—note the arboreal expression of connection—were staged in the 1970s, and have been held annually since the mid-1980s. Other groups of internally displaced Palestinians in Israel have since followed suit.[65] The camps serve to transmit memories of the village from one generation to the next, to generate continued political commitment to working for return, and to assert rootedness in the face of uprooting.[66] In these camps, community elders lead children in cooking traditional foods, signing folkloric songs, and performing mock wedding ceremonies in a resurrection of village life in the present aimed at transmitting communal memories in order to strengthen local and Palestinian national identity.[67] Frequent locations for camp activities include two favored sites of memory: in and around the village church and under trees.[68] The young camp participants are described as *bara'im*, an Arabic word meaning "buds" (and sharing the same root as the village name, *Bir'im*), another vegetative metaphor deployed to emphasize the organic connection of the villagers to the land and of generation to generation.[69] The summer camp, for Zahra and for other organizers, functions as "a means of struggle for return. We spend a whole week in Kafr Bir'im, although we were prevented from spending even one day there in the past. All of the inhabitants of the village, old and young, meet during that week. This generates a feeling of family and strong attachment to everything related to the village."[70]

At the summer camps—as well as at other community events, such as weddings—members of the community recite poems composed in honor of Kafr Bir'im, poems suffused with arboreal imagery. Through poetry, Bir'imites teach their youth the geography of the village, passing on the names of springs and hills in a versified oral tradition. Deborah Tall highlights the "symbiotic relationship between the landscape and the oral tradition": "without the land the stories will fade; without the stories, land becomes less meaningful."[71] The relative proximity of internally displaced persons to Kafr Bir'im's ruins allows for the embodied transmission of oral history, be it through return visions or poetry. For example, in the poem below, 'Issa Chacour includes the names of a local spring (al-Safra) and of local hills (al-Bayad and Ghazzal), geographical markers associated with the fruitful bounty of Bir'im's trees and vines:

Your beauty is God-given

Your beauty is God-given
A human being strains to describe it.
North, south, east, west
Vistas of hills and valleys.
When you tire along the way and feel thirsty
You may drink from the well of al-Safra
And on a dessert of figs you may feast.
Feast on a dessert of figs, of Bayad and Ghazzal.
Tarry as you near the grapes
And when you approach the vine,
Give thanks, and lift up your voice.
Your people, Bir'im, have not died,
And will not forsake a grain of sand from you.[72]

Other Bir'imite poetry celebrates the village's arboreal heritage. Bir'imite Ibrahim 'Issa portrays the village's trees as a living source of historical memory: "I speak with the oak trees. I speak with the olive trees," he states. Expelled at the age of fourteen from Kafr Bir'im, today 'Issa spends his retirement volunteering in the village cemetery. "We speak to Bir'im, with its trees, with its rocks, with the destroyed and ruined homes."[73] For 'Issa, the oak tree represents a nurturing presence under whose branches he sat as a child: "When we were little kids we used to come and sit right under her." Thanks to its antiquity, however, the oak tree also functions as "the living witness," its "ground the true document" that can "tell the truth to the invader" and "the occupier," the truth that "This homeland is ours/And the truth shall not be concealed."[74] Then, in praise of the olive tree, 'Issa declares:

You old olive tree
With roots so deep,
You are the origin
You are the goal
You are the truth.
I come today to pick your fruit
The way I picked it centuries ago.
I come today to pick your fruit,
Fruit after fruit providing testimony.
They believed the years had killed your branches
And hoped that your death would conceal the truth.
They believed the years had killed your branches
And that neglect had withered your vigilant eyes.

I am returning to prune your branches and relieve

You from the burden of your emaciated limbs.[75]

Arboreal imagery thus not only testifies in 'Issa's spoken-word poetry to the rights of Bir'imites, but also functions as a metaphor for a community that has weathered attempts to obliterate it yet has nevertheless survived, maintaining its attachment to its land. As in the case of the Psalmist's declaration of rootedness in God ("I am like a green olive tree in the house of God. I trust in the steadfast love of God forever and ever"—Ps. 52:8), 'Issa proclaims his community's attachment to Kafr Bir'im and its land.

Trees also populate poetic visions of future return. In an ode to the village, 'Issa concludes with an invocation: "May its descendants return to erect its buildings and churches, to plant its figs, olives, and pomegranates." This poetic plea not only names the fruit-bearing trees that served as the mainstay for Kafr Bir'im's economy, but also evokes God's promise to the people Israel that God will bring them into "a land of wheat and barley, of vines and fig trees and pomegranates, a land of olive trees and honey" (Deut. 8:8). Kafr Bir'im, remembered as a lost paradise, thus also becomes the promised land of Bir'imite hopes and dreams, a land conceptualized through an arboreal imagination.

The decades-long struggle by the internally displaced village of Kafr Bir'im (and Iqrit) has pioneered and in turn inspired activism on the part of other internally displaced persons (IDP) inside Israel, with Palestinian IDP communities and the Palestinian Arab citizenry of Israel at large not only building upon Bir'imite activism but also deploying arboreal imagery for the struggle. While some Bir'imites have in the past sought to distinguish their case from the fate of other internally displaced Palestinians, repeated legal and political setbacks to the Bir'imite return cause has pushed most Bir'imites to view their situation as part and parcel of the broader Palestinian refugee struggle.[76] As IDP activism has gained traction in the post-Oslo era, fueled by the conviction that the PLO cannot be counted upon as a defender of IDP rights, Bir'imite experiences in creative protests and practices of return have served as a resource for local village committees and nationwide IDP campaigns. Numerous IDP communities have organized "roots and belonging" summer camps for village youth modeled after the Bir'im example.[77] The revived IDP struggle, meanwhile, has become part of the broader political campaign by Palestinian civil society organizations inside Israel to combat discriminatory Israeli land practices and transform the Israeli state into a state of all of its citizens. This campaign, in turn, stresses the "historic roots" of the Palestinian Arab citizens of Israel.[78]

THE ARBOREAL THEOLOGY OF ELIAS CHACOUR

Our roots are entrenched
Deep in the earth.
Like twenty impossibles
We shall remain.

—TAWFIQ ZAYYAD[79]

How should the arboreal discourse of Bir'imites and other Palestinian refugees, with its emphasis on roots and rootedness, be understood theologically? If Zionist arboreal practices have been bound up with the erasure of Palestinian presence on the land, are Palestinian arboreal practices doomed simply to mirror Zionist tree-plantings and tree-commemorations, with Palestinian and Israeli Jew locked once more into a winner-take-all competition of who has deeper roots? Put another way: Must arboreal discourse and practice be centered on metaphors of rootedness, metaphors that Liisa Malkki has shown assume and perpetuate ahistorical and naturalized conceptions of the relationship between people and land?[80] A careful reading of the role played by trees in Archbishop Elias Chacour's theological autobiographies will help provide tentative answers to these questions.

In the autobiographical mappings of Bir'im offered by Chacour, trees also form a central part of the remembered landscape. Furthermore, trees offer Chacour his key theological metaphor for reconciliation between Palestinians and Israeli Jews and secure existence for all peoples in the land. Greek Catholic theologian and erstwhile politician Geries Khoury has compared Palestinian contextual theology to an olive tree, able to "grow on dry and stony ground" and produce fruit under hard conditions, but unable to flourish when uprooted from its context.[81] If all Palestinian contextual theology is arboreal in that sense, Chacour's theology is arboreal in the additional sense that reflection on and interpretation of particular trees serve as the means for advancing broader theological claims.

In his first book, *Blood Brothers*, Chacour begins his narration as a six-year-old boy shirking his chores in the field, ensconced in the boughs of a fig tree, his special hideaway as a child. Described by Chacour as warm and nurturing, the fig tree, planted by Chacour's father, operates as a synecdochic metaphor for the Chacour family house and property. Gaston Bachelard defines the house as "space that is supposed to condense and defend intimacy," space that "shelters daydreaming," "protects the dreamer," and "allows one to dream in peace" by giving "proofs or illusions of stability."[82] Yi-Fu Tuan builds on Bachelard, explaining that the "enchanted images of the past" evoked by the house have less to do with the house's physical structures and more to do with the "components and furnishings" in and around the house.[83] If, as Bachelard claims, "the house we were born in is physically inscribed in us," so has Chacour's childhood fig tree shaped his life.[84] The rhythm of work, play, and meals in and around the childhood house, and especially in and around the family's orchard, fostered what Tuan has called "attachment of a deep though subconscious sort" that comes "simply with familiarity and ease, with the assurance of nurture and security, with the memory of sounds and smells, of communal activities and homely pleasures accumulated over time."[85] Chacour's narrative account of familiarity and homeliness is characteristic of memory books that portray "the village as a site for the folkloric and the traditional, a place where life was pleasant, satisfying, and idyllic, and marked and circumscribed by the natural world around it."[86]

The nurturing warmth of familiarity and home, however, is about to be disrupted as Chacour's account begins. Elias's elder brother Atallah arrives to tell him that the boys' father, Mikhail, is buying a lamb, news of which sets off fevered speculation as to possible reasons for celebration, for typically the family only bartered for a lamb to roast for the Easter celebrations.[87] The remainder of the chapter, told from the perspective of an excited child, has the young Chacour scampering through the village to find his father in order to discover the reason for this unexpected feast.[88] When the father eventually returns home that evening with lamb in tow, he gathers the children to tell them the village will be welcoming Jewish soldiers for up to a week. The lamb, he continues, will be slaughtered in order to welcome the soldiers into the village. The chapter offers only fleeting narrative foreshadowing of Bir'im's fate, as Chacour describes his older brothers sitting "stiffly quiet," his sister's face "a mixture of emotions," the "strange chill mood" that descends when the father tells them that soldiers with guns will be staying in their homes, the "surface calmness" with which Chacour's parents prepare for the soldiers' arrival.[89]

The fig tree in which Chacour begins the chapter was sheltering an innocence about to be shattered, and stands in Chacour's memory as a paradise lost. The soldiers' stay, as Chacour and the reader soon discover, will not be brief, and the villagers' hospitable gestures of surrender (perceived by the young Chacour as a celebration) fail to save Bir'im from the fate of nearby villages. The soldiers order the villagers to leave, offering what turn out to be empty promises of future return. After the family has found shelter in the abandoned homes of refugees from the neighboring village of Jish, Chacour's father and older brothers are rounded up on trucks and forced across the border into the Jordanian-controlled West Bank (only to infiltrate back across the border a few weeks later).[90]

The devastation and loss of the months and years that follow the arrival of the army in the village are encapsulated for Chacour's father (as for the young Chacour) by the loss of the family's fig orchard. Upon hearing that the trees, expropriated along with all of Bir'im's land by the state, had been purchased by a settler as an investment, "Father's face furrowed with grief. I was terrified that he would weep. He was still, his eyes shut, his mustache drooping above a faintly trembling lip. He had planted those fig trees himself one by one, straining with heavy clay jars of water up the steep slopes, caring for each sapling until it was strong enough to survive on its own. They were almost like children to him."[91] The trees that the elder Chacour had tended formed part of a Palestinian cultural landscape now shattered. As Simon Schama observes, "Landscapes are culture before they are nature; constructs of the imagination projected onto wood and water and rock."[92] While some of the trees from Chacour's orchard remained after Bir'im's destruction, they no longer functioned as part of a cultural landscape that presented itself as "natural" to Bir'imites: the destroyed cultural landscape had to be consciously pieced back together through interpretation of the arboreal and architectural traces that remained.

After overcoming the initial shock from the news that the family land had been bought by an outside investor, Mikhail, like many of his fellow villagers, agreed to work as a day laborer in Bir'im's former orchards:

> Father persuaded us that we, the true owners, would care properly for our beautiful trees and keep them safe and healthy for the next year. Foreigners with no relation to the trees would break the branches, take the fruit, and kill the trees. Some of our trees were more than a thousand years old. Chacour forefathers had planted them, tended them, and passed them on to us. Other trees in our village were closer to two thousand years old. People in our generation plant trees for their children's children. It was too much to think of these precious trees being neglected or even destroyed by uncaring strangers.[93]

Mikhail Chacour's insistence that only the "true owners" could properly care for the trees sounds a common theme of Palestinian refugee memory and writing.[94] After three years as a day laborer in the orchards, however, Mikhail quit, finding the experience of becoming a "hewer of wood" and "drawer of water" (Josh. 9:21-27) on his own land humiliating. "We were becoming slaves," he told his children, "and our personal dignity, our very soul, was too much to sacrifice. If the trees were destroyed when we returned, Father said, we would plant new ones and begin all over."[95]

The Chacour family connection to Bir'im's ancient trees serves as proof, for the elder Chacour, of the family's rightful place on the land: just as the trees' roots run deep, so do the roots of the Chacour family. In more than one place in *Blood Brothers* and *We Belong to the Land*, Chacour describes the antiquity of Kafr Bir'im and his family's presence in the village in ways that, if interpreted in literalistic terms, run up against the historical record. Thus, for example, any thousand-year-old olive trees in Kafr Bir'im would not have been planted by the ancestors of contemporary Bir'imites, for the village's founding, Palestinian sources report, dates back six to seven hundred years. Furthermore, Chacour's family, one of the two Greek Catholic families in the predominantly Maronite Christian village, came to Kafr Bir'im in the eighteenth century ce from the village of Hurfeish, and so would not have planted Kafr Bir'im's oldest trees. That said, the families in Kafr Bir'im intermarried, and so Chacour could certainly have ancestors from the founding of the village. Another account in *We Belong to the Land*, in which Chacour, asked by an Israeli security official at the airport how many generations his family goes back in Bir'im, tells of one of his forefathers welcoming the "stranger" Abraham to the village, also cannot be interpreted in literalistic terms.[96]

Such passages, however, should not be interpreted in a baldly literal fashion, but instead represent assertions of rootedness in the face of a Zionist ideology that deploys claims of antiquity in the land in order to justify its acts of colonization and dispossession. Chacour's insistence on ancient roots is commonplace among Palestinian Christian clergy (and laity): for example, Anglican priest Naim Ateek claims that "[t]he Palestinian Christians of today are the descendants of those early Christians," even as he hurries to stress that this genealogy is "not cause for *hubris*," but instead "carries with it a responsibility for service."[97] While some, perhaps many, Palestinian Christian families may be able to trace their ancestry back to the early church, others arrived in Palestine during the intervening centuries, including during the fluid years of the Ottoman Empire. Claims to trace ancestral roots back to the first century ce, while understandable as a reaction to Zionist discourse and practice that erase Palestinian traces from the landscape, obscure and fail to acknowledge that Palestinian national identity, like all national identities, is a modern construction.

Palestinian Christian assertions of antiquity participate in the broader dynamic within the mythos of Palestinian nationalism of claiming ancient roots, for example, "Canaanite" progenitors who pre-date Jewish presence in the land. Cartographer Abu-Sitta is representative of this tendency within Palestinian nationalism when he claims that "taken as a whole," Palestinians "are the modern representatives of those old tribes which the Israelites found settled in the country, such as the Canaanites, Hittites, Jebusites, Amorites, Philistines, Edomites, etc."[98] Eviatar Zerubavel describes Palestinians and Zionists as being caught up in a competition to "out-past" one another, with Zionists stressing the Jewish presence in *eretz yisrael* prior to the Arab conquest and Palestinians highlighting their claimed Philistine or Canaanite heritage.[99] One implication of this chapter's argument is that instead of adjudicating between competing discourses of indigeneity and autochthony, in which one people's antiquity in the land can be used to exclude or dispossess another people, the theological challenge is to articulate a vision in which all of God's children are "rooted" in the land. Chacour, I argue, is a proponent of such a vision. His appeals to ancient roots are not deployed to serve a cause of dispossession or exclusion but to insist on his rightful place in the land.

For Mikhail, the geography of *al-'awda* was intimately intertwined with Bir'im's trees. "Will the government allow us to go back soon?" the aged Mikhail asks his son Elias. "Will they help us rebuild our houses and regain our olive and fig trees? Will I be able to die in Biram where I was born?"[100] Return for Mikhail meant being able to live in a rebuilt Bir'im: "If my fondest wish could be granted," he tells Elias, "I would go back to Biram alive and rebuild our house, the house I inherited from my forefathers. I would sit under the fig tree in front of our house, and even if it were for only one day, I would die a happy man."[101]

For Chacour, as for his father, arboreal and other vegetative metaphors stressing the "rootedness" of Bir'imites serve to counter Zionism's ideological portrayals of Palestine as an "empty land" or a "wasteland."[102] "We were not like some weed newly sprung up after rain," Chacour insists, "but our spiritual heritage was firmly rooted in the first century."[103] From his father, Chacour learned that "we should love and respect our Galilean soil, for our people had long struggled to survive here. We were rooted like the poppies and wild, blue irises that thrust up among the rocks. Our family had tilled this land, had worshiped here longer than anyone could remember."[104] To claim, as Chacour and other Bir'imites do, that "we belong to the land," is thus to assert one's presence in the face of an exclusionary ideology.[105]

However, arboreal claims to rootedness can be and are deployed in the service of nationalist cartographies that envision a homogeneous space in which the nation might be implanted, even at the violent expense of other peoples. Are the landscapes and maps produced by the Palestinian arboreal imagination simply the mirror of the "flawless Hebrew map" of Zionism, as Israeli analyst Meron Benvenisti suspects, with the Zionist map and the Palestinian map trapped in a winner-take-all cartographic battle?[106] Or might visions of the shared rootedness of Palestinians and Israelis in the land spring forth from the arboreal imagination?

One can begin to answer this question by considering the role of trees in efforts led by Chacour and other Bir'imites to press for return. On February 17, 1979, Chacour, in concert with the Committee for the Uprooted of Kafr Bir'im (CUB), attempted to plant trees on Bir'im land, a concrete way to demonstrate the villagers' rooted attachment to their land. Chacour led a march of Bir'im's children from Jish to the Kafr Bir'im site, with marchers carrying olive saplings—the olive tree being a common Palestinian symbol for *sumud*, or steadfastness—to plant.[107] The protest coincided with the Jewish holiday of Tu B'Shvat (often called the Jewish "Arbor Day"), a day on which the JNF plants trees bought with donations from the Jewish diaspora. The Israeli military turned the march back, declaring the area to be a closed military zone. In protest, the CUB sent the saplings by mail to the Prime Minister's Office and to Knesset members.[108]

This protest action admits of at least two interpretations. First, it can be understood in the broader context of efforts to affirm Palestinian ownership of land and protect land from state expropriation through the planting of trees. As such, tree-planting protests can be viewed as part of a battle for control over territory (e.g., covering over destroyed Palestinian villages with JNF forests and creating "Green Zones" to inhibit Palestinian building, bringing land into cultivation in an attempt to keep Israel from confiscating it).[109] A second interpretation, however, is offered by Chacour, who presents the 1979 planting action as a peace witness. "Children of Biram, are you ready to bring life and peace to your village?" Chacour asked the marchers as they prepared to walk to the village to plant the olive saplings.[110] The two interpretations, to be sure, are not necessarily in conflict, for one can persuasively argue that an indispensable element to a robust peace witness is advocacy to ensure the rights of the dispossessed and displaced to secure dwelling in the land.

From Chacour's vantage point, Bir'imite demonstrations at the village site functioned both to advance the villagers' claims to the land and to present a vision of future reconciliation with Israeli Jews. Bir'im's trees play a key role in both Chacour's descriptions of Bir'imite connection to the land and in his vision of Palestinian-Israeli Jewish reconciliation. Reflecting on the half-year demonstration at the village site in the early 1970s, Chacour writes: "I felt unearthly, as if I were living in a vision. The hot summer morning stretched into a cool evening, and I rushed about, helping volunteers to settle amid the fallen stones and timbers. The sky darkened, and still a vibrance drove me: voices mixed with laughter; women cooked over blazing wood fires; boys and girls played beneath the olive trees again."[111] The protestors renovated the Maronite church that had been damaged in the bombing of the village, but for Chacour the true rebuilding of the church was "not with mortar and rock but with living stones."[112] The gathering also stood for Chacour as the fulfillment of a vision he had had of Palestinian-Israeli Jewish reconciliation as a minor seminarian in Haifa in 1952: "An image of Biram resurrected beneath the ancient olive trees, of all the ransacked homes restored and the women safe within. Palestinian and Jew—sipping coffee together again in tranquil conversation."[113]

To understand Chacour's theological interpretation of this reconciliation, let us return to the fig tree that captured Chacour's gaze upon his return to Bir'im's ruins in the late sixties. The tree, Chacour remembers, was the product of his father having grafted branches from five different varieties of figs into the trunk of a sixth variety. "Beneath the rough bark where my hand rested, I knew that the living wood had fused together so perfectly that, should I cut the tree down, I could never see where one variety stopped and the other began."[114] Standing under his childhood fig tree, Chacour engages in his most sustained biblical exposition and explicit theological analysis. The tree's grafted branches not only exhibit the practical, historical lesson Chacour learned from his father that Palestinian Arab "lives were bound together with the other people who inhabited Palestine—the Jews. We had suffered together under the Romans, Persians, Crusaders, and Turks, and had learned to share the simple elements of human existence—faith, reverence for life, hospitality."[115] The tree also drives home for Chacour the meaning of Paul's proclamation that Jew and Gentile have been reconciled through Jesus Christ, the dividing wall between them broken down (Eph. 2:10-20). For Chacour, Paul's message of reconciliation in Ephesians, Galatians 3:28-29, and Romans 9–11, where the grafting metaphor takes center stage, means that "[w]e Gentiles had been 'grafted in' among God's chosen people of faith, just as Father had grafted six different kinds of fig trees together to make a delightful new tree."[116] Palestinians, including the people of Kafr Bir'im, may "have been cut off like unwanted branches" by Israeli policies and laws of dispossession and exclusion, but in God's vision, Chacour discovers, Palestinians and Israeli Jews are intertwined with one another in one body.[117]

Chacour's appeal to the arboreal imagery of Romans 9–11 necessarily raises the question of whether or not his theology negates ongoing Jewish election, a question that hovers over Paul's complicated reflections in that epistle. Elsewhere, Chacour addresses Jewish election by bluntly claiming that Jewish chosenness has been replaced by a new vision of election. "We have been taught for centuries that the Jews are the Chosen People of God," says Chacour. "We do not believe anymore that they are the Chosen People of God, since now we have a new understanding of the Chosenness. Who is chosen? Man and Woman—every man and every woman—are invited to take part in the divine banquet."[118] Such a statement, I would argue, fails to do justice to Chacour's nuance at other points in his writings on the question of election. For example, Chacour's translation of Rom. 9:8 in *Blood Brothers*—"It is not only the natural children who are God's children, but also the children of the promise who are regarded as Abraham's offspring"—actually mitigates standard translations of that verse, for example, "it is not the children of the flesh who are the children of God, but the children of the promise are counted as descendants" (Rom. 9:8, NRSV).[119] In Chacour's reading of Romans 9–11, Gentiles are not grafted in at the expense of Jews, a reading that fits well with Paul's hopeful insistence that the "natural [Jewish] branches" will be "grafted back into" God's cultivated olive tree alongside grafted-in Gentile branches (11:24).

To be sure, Chacour opposes any theology of election that would underwrite an exclusivist politics, including any form of Zionism tied to the creation and maintenance of homogeneous national space, for such a politics requires the cutting off of Palestinians as unwanted branches. Yet, as Chacour intimates in *Blood Brothers*, without fully developing the insight, a different understanding of election is possible. "God's true purpose in regathering Israel" in the Hebrew Scriptures, Chacour contends, citing Ezek. 36:23b, "was to demonstrate to the world that He is holy and He leads a holy nation." Prophets such as Isaiah insist that God's deliverance of the people Israel from persecution requires them "to live up to a high calling."[120] The people Israel's election is not a matter of pride or boasting, but, properly understood, demands openness to God's surprising action of incorporating the foreigner and the eunuch into God's people.[121] For Chacour, taking his cue from Isa. 56:1-8, an integral part of God's intention "to hold up His new Israel as a banner of justice before all the nations of the world" is the joining of the "foreigner" to the people Israel: "God's Israel included 'foreigners,' those who were not of the fleshly tribes of Israel, but who had been grafted into his family—just as the branches had been grafted into this fig tree."[122] Chacour certainly affirms Jewish rootedness in the land, but simply rejects the idea that such rootedness should come at the expense of Palestinians: "Come, let us be brothers and sisters together in this beautiful land in which all of us have history and roots," he presents his father and fellow Bir'imites saying to Israeli Jews. "There is room enough for all of us. Aren't we the co-persecuted brothers and sisters?"[123] Chacour's theology thus draws on arboreal and other vegetative imagery in the service of a theopolitical vision of common belonging in the land.

Mapping Return to Kafr Bir'im: The Possibility of Shared Space

Bardenstein asks whether Palestinian nostalgic representation of village trees is "merely a reactionary, escapist response to the 'real world in the present' which merely lulls people into passivity, or if it is also capable of playing an enabling role in the construction of collective memory that can be mobilized for resistance or other forms of engagement with the immediate present."[124] That Chacour's theological mapping of the landscape of Israel-Palestine does not negate but indeed affirms Jewish rootedness in the land reveals that Meron Benvenisti's claim that Palestinian mappings simply mirror the exclusions of Zionist cartography fails to account for at least one case. In this final section, through an examination of Bir'imite maps and proposals of return, I contend that the mappings of return produced by Bir'imites' arboreal imagination do not exhibit what Gilles Deleuze and Félix Guattari have called arborescent thought, a form of thought structured by hierarchical binarisms that can thus only map a given space as *either* Palestinian *or* Israeli Jewish.[125] Instead, these mappings of return point to the possibility of shared, heterogeneous space, a rhizomatic cartography of interconnections.[126]

"We've told the government that Kafr Bir'am is like a house of three rooms," states Bir'imite Elias Jacob. "One is now the kibbutz. One is the moshav. One is empty. We don't ask much. But that we must have."[127] Jacob's statement describes the CUB's map and statement of principles submitted to the Liba'i Commission in 1995, a body established by the Israeli government in an attempt to resolve the cases of Kafr Bir'im and Iqrit. In its submissions, the CUB charted a proposal for the villagers' return to Kafr Bir'im and for a space shared by the reconstructed village and the Israeli kibbutzim (Baram and Sasa) and the moshav (Dovev) partially built on Bir'im's land.[128] The CUB's February 1, 1995 statement to the commission emerged from the CUB's principles for a just solution that would rectify the injustice of their forced displacement:

> *The recognition of the ownership of our land, as well as our right to return to it and to our homes, and the recognition of all that this process entails.
>
> *We are not claiming back, to our use, the portion of our land used by the settlements.
>
> *We wish to live in peace, harmony, and co-operation with the inhabitants of the settlements in the area.[129]

The map that the CUB presented to the Liba'i Commission reflected these principles, a cartographic representation of a return that would not erase Israeli Jewish presence.[130] The CUB map thus not only asserted Bir'imite knowledge of the site but also embodied the promise and possibility of shared space.[131]

Two Bir'imites—one architect and one artist—have since drawn on CUB principles for return in order to construct models of what the rebuilt village might look like. In the mid-1990s, Deeb Maron, a graduate of Israel's prestigious Technion Institute in Haifa who lives in Jish, used British Mandate maps of the Safad region and CUB maps of land ownership and potential return to build a scale model of a rebuilt Kafr Bir'im that would at first house four thousand returnees.[132] Several years later, Hanna Farah, a Wizo Institute art graduate who adds "Kafr Bir'im" to his signature "as a second family name, like a code and a key to Palestinian familial and communal memory," built another model of the reconstructed village.[133] Farah's reconstruction tackles the reality that "return" cannot be a simple re-creation of the past, the recapturing of a lost paradise: the simple fact, Farah notes, that "we have ten or more people who want to return to the house of their grandparents in Kafr Bir'im" makes such a return impossible. Instead, any cartographic projection of return, Farah insists, must seek to integrate elements of the old (the ruins of the destroyed homes) with contemporary realities, "to create coexistence between the old and the new," thus enabling memory to "become part of the present."[134]

An even more recent vision for return emerged from a 2004 initiative organized by the Zochrot Association, an Israeli organization dedicated to "remembering the *Nakba* in Hebrew."[135] For several months in 2004, Israeli Jewish residents of Kibbutz Baram and displaced persons from Kafr Bir'im met with two Zochrot facilitators (one an Israeli Jew, one a Palestinian citizen of

Israel), first separately and then together, to discuss what had happened to Kafr Bir'im and its inhabitants in 1948 and to consider what steps should be taken in the future. After several sessions of facilitated meetings, the kibbutz residents and Bir'imites agreed that "[w]ith great sorrow for the injustice done in 1948, throughout the military regime and until today, we wish to tell the story of what happened and act for the return of the displaced people of Bir'im and their descendants to their village." The group then delineated specific principles to guide the practical implementation of future return:

> 1. Kafr Bir'im will be reestablished on the land and forest not currently cultivated by Kibbutz *Bar'am*, Kibbutz *Sasa*, and Moshav *Dovev*;
> 2. Land built up and cultivated by the kibbutzim will not be returned to the original owners, unless the members of the kibbutzim agree otherwise;
> 3. Palestinian owners of the above land will be compensated;
> 4. Kafr Bir'im displaced who choose not to return will also be compensated;
> 5. Kafr Bir'im displaced who live in exile are considered rights-holders just like those present in the country as internally displaced;
> 6. All members of the group, Kafr Bir'im displaced and members of Kibbutz *Bar'am*, will work together in order to prevent further confiscation of land.[136]

To be sure, the members of Kibbutz Baram in the group that produced this joint statement did not represent the dominant perspective on the kibbutz. However, that some kibbutzniks could envision a place for a rebuilt Kafr Bir'im on land it now uses, and that Bir'imites could accept a place for the kibbutz on the land they once held, shows that mappings of return are not necessarily acts of cartographic erasure and that cartographies are possible that incorporate both Palestinian and Israeli Jewish space.

Dan Rabinowitz has argued that the demands of villagers from Bir'im and Iqrit—along with the claims raised by other internally displaced Palestinians, not to mention Palestinian refugees from outside Israel—are perceived by Israeli Jews as a "Palestinian onslaught" against "Israeli sovereignty." The movement of Palestinian citizens of Israel into spaces previously conceptualized as purely Jewish, such as Natzerat Illit (Upper Nazareth), is also experienced as part of this broader "onslaught." These perceptions, Rabinowitz contends, point to a twofold reality: a) that Palestinians, for mainstream Zionist ideology, function as a threat to the integrity of Israeli space; and b) that mainstream Zionism thus is "inherently insecure regarding the durability of its achievements."[137] Palestinian cartographies of return will thus inevitably threaten the integrity of constructed Zionist spaces, because the creation of those spaces required the uprooting and then the conceptual erasure of prior Palestinian presence.[138] Yet not all Israeli Jews understand Palestinian refugee mappings of return to be a threat, charting cartographic futures of binational accommodation instead of creating landscapes of separation. It is to a close examination of one such Israeli Jewish group—the Zochrot Association—that I now turn.

Notes

1. Elias Chacour, *Blood Brothers*, with David Hazard (Grand Rapids: Chosen Books, 2003), 144.

2. Quoted in William Dalrymple, *From the Holy Mountain: A Journey among the Christians of the Middle East* (New York: Henry Holt, 1997), 275. I use the standard transliteration of Kafr Bir'im. The reader will observe, however, that different authors transliterate the village's name in a variety of ways.

3. Quoted in Ilan Magat, *Bir'am: A Conscripted Community of Memory* [Hebrew] (Giv'at Haviva: ha-Makhon le-heker ha-shalom, 2000), 42. Quoted in Nihad Boqai, *Returning to Kafr Bir'im* (Bethlehem: Badil Resource Center for Palestinian Residency and Refugee Rights, 2006), 77.

4. For information on Bir'im's history, see *The Palestinian Encyclopedia* [Arabic], vol. 3 (Damascus: Hayat al- Filistiniyyah, 1984), 648.

5. Elias Chacour, *We Belong to the Land: The Story of a Palestinian Israeli Who Lives for Peace and Reconciliation*, with Mary E. Jensen (Notre Dame: University of Notre Dame Press, 2001), 74.

6. For accounts of Kafr Bir'im's history, its depopulation, and the struggle of Bir'imites to return, see Yusuf Istifan Susan, *My Testimony: Bir'im Days, 1948–1968* [Arabic] (n.p.: self-published, 1986); Sharif Kana'nah and Muhammad Ishtayyah, *The Destroyed Palestinian Villages: Kafr Bir'im* [Arabic], no. 13 (Bir Zeit: Bir Zeit University Press, 1991); Nihad Boqai, *Returning to Kafr Bir'im*; Joseph Ryan, S.J., "Refugees within Israel: The Case of the Villagers of Kafr Bir'im and Iqrit," *Journal of Palestine Studies* 2, no. 4 (Summer 1973): 55–81; Ilan Magat, *Bir'am: A Conscripted Community of Memory*; and Sarah Ozacky-Lazar, Ikrit and Bir'am [Hebrew] (Giv'at Havivah: ha-Makhon le-limudim 'Arviyim, 1993).

7. For a critical analysis and overview of historical and contemporary Palestinian Christian presence in the Galilee, see Una McGahern, *Palestinian Christians in Israel: State Attitudes towards Non-Muslims in a Jewish State* (London and New York: Routledge, 2011) and Samir Geraisy, "Who Are the Christians in Galilee?" in *Jerusalem: What Makes for Peace! A Palestinian Christian Contribution to Peacemaking*, ed. Naim Ateek, Cedar Duaybis, and Marla Schrader (London: Melisende, 1997), 213–16.

8. Chacour, *Blood Brothers*, 144.

9. For a description of Operation Hiram, see Benny Morris, *The Birth of the Palestinian Refugee Problem, 1947–1949* (Cambridge: Cambridge University Press, 1987), chapter 7. See also Ghazi Falah, "Israeli 'Judaization' Policy in the Galilee," *Journal of Palestine Studies* 20, no. 4 (Summer 1991): 69–85 and Nafez Nazzal, *The Palestinian Exodus from Galilee* (Beirut: Institute for Palestine Studies, 1978).

10. Susan, *My Testimony*, 10–11. Quoted in Boqai, *Returning to Kafr Bir'im*, 17.

11. On the Safad district, see Mustafa 'Abbasi, *Safad during the British Mandate, 1917–1948* [Arabic] (Beirut: Institute for Palestine Studies, 2005). For an analysis of massacres carried out by Israeli forces during the 1948 war, see Abdel Jawad Saleh, "Zionist Massacres: The Creation of the Palestinian Refugee Problem, in the 1948 War," in *Israel and the Palestinian Refugees*, ed. Eyal Benvenisti, Chaim Gans, and Sari Hanafi (Berlin: Springer, 2007), 59–127. The Jish massacre surfaces in Chacour's autobiographical narration of the early days of his family's exile from Kafr Bir'im in Jish, as the young Chacour discovers two dozen buried corpses in shallow graves while playing soccer. See *Blood Brothers*, 56–57.

12. See Kana'nah and Ishtayyah, *The Destroyed Palestinian Villages: Kafr Bir'im*, for a breakdown of the religious affiliation of Bir'im's families. The Chacour and Badeen families are Greek Catholic, whereas the remaining families are Maronite. All worshiped at the Maronite church, al-Sayyidah (The Virgin Mary). Baruch Kimmerling wrongly identifies Bir'im as a Greek Orthodox village. See Kimmerling, "Sovereignty, Ownership, and 'Presence' in the Jewish-Arab Territorial Conflict: The Case of Bir'im and Ikrit," *Comparative Political Studies* 10, no. 2 (July 1977): 159.

13. Quoted in Dalrymple, *From the Holy Mountain*, 366. Some families took refuge in the church. See Boqai, *Returning to Kafr Bir'im*, 21–22.

14. Aaron Becher describes the relatively friendly relations between Kafr Bir'im and Zionist settlers in Mandate Palestine in his "Hill of Tears of Bar'am," *Yediot Aharonot* (28 July 1972), quoted in Joseph Ryan, S.J., "Refugees within Israel," 57–58. Ryan notes that the Maronite Patriarch of Beirut Ignatius Mubarak "had submitted to the UN Special Committee on Palestine a Memorandum in favour of a Jewish home in Palestine and a Christian home in Lebanon" (58).

15. "The inhabitants of Kafr Bir'im interpreted the fact that they were not expelled like the inhabitants of neighboring villages, and the fact that the census was conducted, as indicators of the Israeli army's intention to permit their stay." Boqai, *Returning to Kafr Bir'im*, 22.

16. Quoted in Kana'nah and Ishtayyah, *The Destroyed Palestinian Villages: Kafr Bir'im*, 27–28. Quoted in Boqai, *Returning to Kafr Bir'im*, 23.

17. The legal mechanisms deployed by the Israeli state to formalize the expropriation of land from Palestinian refugees and internally displaced persons are extensive and complex. For descriptions and analyses of the numerous strategies to legalize Palestinian dispossession, see: Alexandre Kedar, "The Legal Transformation of Ethnic Geography: Israeli Law and the Palestinian Landholder, 1948–1967," *New York Journal of International Law and Politics* 33, no. 4 (2001): 923–1000; Geremy Forman and Alexandre Kedar, "From Arab Land to 'Israel Lands': The Legal Dispossession of the Palestinians Displaced by Israel in the Wake of 1948," *Environment and Planning D: Society and Space* 22 (2004): 809–30; Hanna Dib Nakkara, "Israeli Land Seizure under Various Defense and Emergency Regulations," *Journal of Palestine Studies* 14, no. 2 (Winter 1985): 13–34; Wakim Wakim, "The 'Internally Displaced' Seeking Return within One's Own Land," *Journal of Palestine Studies* 31, no. 1 (Autumn 2001): 32–38; Hussein Abu Hussein and Fiona McKay, *Access Denied: Palestinian Land Rights in Israel* (London: Zed, 2003); Sabri Jiryis, "The Legal Structure for the Expropriation and Absorption of Arab Lands in Israel," *Journal of Palestine Studies* 2, no. 4 (Summer 1973): 82–104; Tovia Fenster, "Belonging, Memory, and the Politics of Planning in Israel," *Social and Cultural Geography* 5, no. 3 (September 2004): 403–17; and *Ruling Palestine: A History of the Legally Sanctioned Jewish-Israeli Seizure of Land and Housing in Palestine* (Geneva: Centre on Housing Rights and Evictions and Bethlehem: Badil Resource Center for Palestinian Residency and Refugee Rights, 2005).

18. Morris, *The Birth of the Palestinian Refugee Problem*, 237. Nur Masalha contends that the expulsion of Christians during Operation Hiram foreshadowed the ongoing efforts by Yosef Weitz of the Jewish National Fund to persuade and coerce Arab Christians to emigrate. See Masalha, "A Galilee without Christians? Yosef Weitz and 'Operation Yohanan' 1949–1954," in *Palestinian Christians: Religion, Politics, and Society in the Holy Land*, ed. Anthony O'Mahony (London: Melisende, 1999), 200–201, 205.

19. Kafr Bir'im's economy relied on the production and local export of figs, tobacco, and olives. See Kana'nah and Ishtayyah, *The Destroyed Palestinian Villages: Kafr Bir'im*, 10.

20. Dalrymple, *From the Holy Mountain*, 366–67. Fr. Susan records Shitrit telling the villagers, "Don't take with you to Jish anything not needed during this short period of time" (Susan, *My Testimony*, 14). Quoted in Boqai, *Returning to Kafr Bir'im*, 27.

21. Ryan, "Refugees within Israel," 60.

22. Riyadh Ghantous observes that during the first weeks of exile from Bir'im, villagers routinely managed to enter the village, sometimes with the military's permission, to care for chickens and to gather tobacco leaves for sale that had been drying in their homes: "We used to keep the keys to our homes in our pockets. My mother used to send me to our home in Kafr Bir'im to bring the necessary supplies." Such returns to the village were not always accepted by the military, however, and were sometimes punished—for example, on February 22, 1949 the military arrested sixty-five villagers who were renovating rain-damaged homes (Boqai, *Returning to Kafr Bir'im*, 28).

23. Dalrymple, *From the Holy Mountain*, 369.

24. Fr. Susan, for example, in an August 9, 1951 letter to the Military Governor of Nazareth, Na'man Stavi, protested the ongoing denial of the villagers' return, ironically observing that "[i]f we work at the Kibbutz, we are not considered Arabs and a threat to security, but if we pick our olives for ourselves, we are considered Arabs and a threat to security. Is this logical?" (Susan, *My Testimony*, 41–42). Quoted in Boqai, *Returning to Kafr Bir'im*, 59.

25. For a discussion of Bir'imite activism for return within the broader context of Palestinian activism and discourse within the new state of Israel around the right of return, see Maha Nassar, "Palestinian Citizens of Israel and the Discourse on the Right of Return, 1948–1959," *Journal of Palestine Studies* 40, no. 4 (Summer 2011): 45–60.

26. Boqai, *Returning to Kafr Bir'im*, 44.

27. Ryan, "Refugees within Israel," 63.

28. Boqai, *Returning to Kafr Bir'im*, 35.

29. Ryan, "Refugees within Israel," 63. The destruction of Kafr Bir'im's homes represented part of a broader campaign by the Israeli military during the 1950s and the 1960s to destroy the structures of depopulated Palestinian villages. See Meron Rapaport, "History Erased: The IDF and the Post-1948 Destruction of Palestinian Monuments," *Journal of Palestine Studies* 37, no. 2 (Winter 2008): 82–88 and Aron Shai, "The Fate of Abandoned Arab Villages in Israel, 1965–1969," *History and Memory* 18, no. 2 (Fall/Winter 2006): 86–106.

30. Ghazi Falah, "The 1948 Israeli-Palestinian War and Its Aftermath: The Transformation and De-Signification of Palestine's Cultural Landscape," *Annals of the Association of American Geographers* 86, no. 2 (June 1996): 256–85.

31. Irus Braverman, *Planted Flags: Trees, Land, and Law in Israel/Palestine* (Cambridge: Cambridge University Press, 2009). See also Irus Braverman, "'The Tree Is the Enemy Soldier': A Sociolegal Making of War Landscapes in the Occupied West Bank," *Law & Society Review* 42, no. 3 (2008): 449–82.

32. Meron Benvenisti, *Sacred Landscape: The Buried History of the Holy Land since 1948*, trans. Maxine Kaufman-Lacusta (Berkeley: University of California Press, 2000), 7.

33. "A clear function of Israeli planting which is visible in the landscape . . . is to prevent the spread of Palestinian land use to areas heretofore unused. Forests are also used in those areas that may have been, or in the future might be, used by Palestinians, but that are currently vulnerable to the application of Israeli control." Shaul Ephraim Cohen, *The Politics of Planting: Israeli-Palestinian Competition for Control of Land in the Jerusalem Periphery* University of Chicago Geography Research Paper No. 236 (Chicago: University of Chicago Press, 1993), 188.

34. "The planted forest asserts Jewish presence, implicitly both past and present," Bardenstein claims, "and simultaneously effaces Palestinian memory of the site." Carol B. Bardenstein, "Threads of Memory and Discourses of Rootedness: Of Trees, Oranges, and the Prickly-Pear Cactus in Israel/Palestine," *Edebiyat* 8, no. 1 (March 1998): 9. See also Nasser

Abufarha, "Land of Symbols: Cactus, Poppies, Orange and Olive Trees in Palestine," *Identities* 15, no. 3 (May 2008): 343–68.

35. Quoted in Bardenstein, "Threads of Memory," 8, 2.

36. For a critical analysis of the JNF, see Walter Lehn and Uri Davis, *The Jewish National Fund* (London and New York: Kegan Paul, 1988) and Lehn and Davis, "And the Fund Still Lives: The Role of the Jewish National Fund in the Determination of Israel's Land Policies," *Journal of Palestine Studies* 7, no. 4 (Summer 1978): 3–33. Bir'imites exiled in Jish reacted with shock and concern upon finding "employees of the Keren Kayemet surveying our land in the same way as the abandoned neighbour-villages." "The activities of the Keren Kayemet are causing confusion while we are trying to rest assured based on your promises that we will return to our village as soon as the temporary military need comes to an end," the village elders protested in an April 29, 1949 cable sent to the Israeli Minister of Minorities and the Military Governor for the Eastern Galilee. "We hope that this time will arrive very soon." The villagers correctly suspected that such surveying represented the first step to the land's expropriation and its being turned over to Jewish development. Indeed, Kibbutz Baram occupied Bir'im's land on June 5, 1949. See Susan, *My Testimony*, 49, 18. Quoted in Boqai, *Returning to Kafr Bir'im*, 55.

37. See Naama Meishar, "Fragile Guardians: Nature Reserves and Forests Facing Arab Villages," in *Constructing a Sense of Place: Architecture and the Zionist Discourse*, ed. Haim Yacobi (Aldershot, UK and Burlington, VT: Ashgate, 2004), 303–32, esp. 304–10.

38. In 1965, the State of Israel created Baram National Park and the Baram Oaks Nature Reserve on Bir'im and its land. For a list of destroyed Palestinian villages over which Israeli national parks and nature reserves have been established, see Noga Kadman, *Erased from Space and Consciousness: Depopulated Palestinian Villages in the Israeli-Zionist Discourse* [Hebrew] (Jerusalem: November Books, 2008), 140–68.

39. While highlighting the synagogue's ruins, the webpage for Bar'am National Park does note that "[t]he park also contains remains of the Maronite village of Bir'am, whose inhabitants were required to leave by the Israel Defense Forces in 1948 for security reasons. The village church is still the spiritual center of that community." See http://www.parks.org.il/parks/ ParksAndReserves/baram/Pages/default.aspx. While admitting that the park is located over a Maronite village, park managers obfuscate by invoking "security" as the rationale for the villagers being ordered to leave, a claim that removes Bir'im's depopulation from the wider context of the depopulation and destruction of hundreds of Palestinian villages in 1948 and 1949. The NPA also neglects to mention that Bir'imites continue to demand to return to the village. Noga Kadman underscores that the "practices of touristic signing and information distribution in sites that used to be Arab villages can be seen as another arena—a symbolic one—in the Israeli Palestinian conflict . . . . The marginalization of the depopulated Arab villages in tourist sites in Israel can be seen as a victory of Israel in this arena, which was enabled by and followed the military victory of Israel in 1948." Kadman, "Roots Tourism—Whose Roots? The Marginalization of Palestinian Heritage Sites, in Official Israeli Tourism Sites," *TÉOROS* 29, no. 1 (2010): 65.

40. Efrat Ben-Ze'ev and Issam Aburaiya, "'Middle-Ground' Politics and the Re-Palestinianization of Places in Israel," *International Journal of Middle East Studies* 36 (2004): 640.

41. Kafr Bir'im was one of eleven destroyed villages the majority of whose population remained in what became Israel; more than 2,000 Bir'imites live in the country today. Boqai, *Returning to Kafr Bir'im*, 39.

42. Pierre Nora, "Between Memory and History: Les Lieux de Mémoire," *Representations* 26 (Spring 1989): 9, 23. Samera Esmeir underscores that the absence of national institutions to support memory production stands as "an obstacle in the face of memory itself." Samera Esmeir, "1948: Law, History, Memory," *Social Text* 21, no. 2 (Summer 2003): 27–47.

43. Bardenstein, "Threads of Memory," 9.

44. Ibid., 10. Ben-Ze'ev concurs, observing that "[f]ruit trees for the fallahin (the peasants) signify their land, be it the garden surrounding home (al-hakura) or the trees of one's distant plots." Efrat Ben-Ze'ev, "The Politics of Taste and Smell: Palestinian Rites of Return," in *The*

Politics of Food, ed. Marianne Elisabeth Lien and Brigitte Nerlich (Oxford and New York: Berg, 2004), 148.

45. Bardenstein also notes that "Israeli collective memory fixates on trees at the time of implementation and enactment of the Zionist narrative of Jewish return to Zion." Bardenstein, "Trees, Forests, and the Shaping of Palestinian and Israeli Collective Memory," in *Acts of Memory: Cultural Recall in the Present*, ed. Mieke Bal, Jonathan Crewe, and Leo Spitzer (Hanover, NH and London: University Press of New England, 1999), 166.

46. Quoted in Susan, *My Testimony*, 71. Quoted in Boqai, *Returning to Kafr Bir'im*, 36.

47. Quoted in Magat, *Bir'am: A Conscripted Community of Memory*, 13. Quoted in Boqai, *Returning to Kafr Bir'im*, 87.

48. Susan, *My Testimony*, 81. Quoted in Boqai, *Returning to Kafr Bir'im*, 62.

49. Boqai, *Returning to Kafr Bir'im*, 88.

50. Ibid., 60.

51. Afif Ibrahim of Bir'im reports that "Bishop Raya played a lead role in the campaign until he was declared persona non grata and forced to leave the country: the Israeli authorities were not keen on having a clergyman lead a national battle. The Bishop was inspired by the role of Christian clergy in South American revolutionary movements; he was convinced that there can be no church without the people. The fact that he was also a supporter of non-violent struggle made many Jews stand with him as well." Boqai, *Returning to Kafr Bir'im*, 71. Raya resigned his post in 1974, attributing his decision partly to the Catholic Church hierarchy, although given the unwanted negative publicity that the Bir'im and Iqrit campaigns had caused, Israeli pressures on the church undoubtedly played a role as well. For a biography of Raya, who wrote extensively on the Byzantine liturgy, see Lesya Sabada, *Go to the Deep: The Life of Archbishop Joseph Raya* (Newton, MA: Sophia, 2006). While Palestinian Christian political activism is not limited to the Greek Catholic communion, Andrea Pacini is also undoubtedly correct in her observation that a "strong sense of Arab identity" marks the Melkite church in Palestine, Jordan, Lebanon, and Syria, an identity often "expressed in practical initiatives of a prominently political nature." See Pacini, "Socio-Political and Community Dynamics of Arab Christians in Jordan, Israel, and the Autonomous Palestinian Territories," in *Christian Communities in the Arab Middle East: The Challenge of the Future* (Oxford and New York: Clarendon, 1998), 280.

52. Not all Israeli Jews, of course, were sympathetic with the Bir'imite campaign to return. In an extreme form of opposition, for instance, in September 1987 activists of Meir Kahane's Kach party entered the village site, destroyed crosses on the church, demolished rebuilding work on the one-time schoolhouse, and wrote slogans such as "We shall teach you, people of Biram, you have no right to return," on the ruins. Chacour, *We Belong to the Land*, 182. For an account of the dynamics of Palestinian political activity under conditions of military rule during the 1950s until the mid-1960s and of the emergence of more public activism in the late 1960s onwards, see David Mark Neuhaus, "Between Quiescence and Arousal: The Political Functions of Religion, A Case Study of the Arab Minority in Israel, 1948–1990," Ph.D. dissertation, Hebrew University (Jerusalem, 1991); As'ad Ghanem, *The Palestinian-Arab Minority in Israel, 1948–2000: A Political Study* (Albany: State University of New York Press, 2001); and Sabri Jiryis, *The Arabs in Israel*, trans. Inea Bushnaq (New York: Monthly Review, 1976).

53. Kimmerling, "Sovereignty, Ownership, and 'Presence,'" 166–67. Afif Ibrahim, secretary of the Committee for the Uprooted of Bir'im, explains that "[a]fter 1984, the Committee took a different approach. We worked more than our parents to connect the case of Kafr Bir'im with the wider Palestinian Arab society, and not the Christian community only. The authorities always try to isolate us, but we will not accept that. Our work has been guided by the belief that our case is of importance for all Arabs in Israel, and that it is in fact the case of all Arab citizens in Israel." Boqai, *Returning to Kafr Bir'im*, 52.

54. See, for example, Amos Elon, "Two Arab Towns That Plumb Israel's Conscience," *New York Times Magazine*, October 22, 1972, 44. Unwelcome publicity for the villages' cause came when the Palestinian militant group Black September named its Munich Olympics action—the

kidnapping and subsequent murder of eleven Israeli athletes—"Operation Kafr Bir'im and Iqrit." See Ryan, "Refugees within Israel," 69.

55. Quoted in Kana'nah and Ishtayyah, *The Destroyed Palestinian Villages: Kafr Bir'im*, 34. The use of Christian symbols in the 1972 protests sometimes proved to be a point of contention. For example, some Israeli Jews sympathetic to the protests objected to Raya's idea of ringing church bells, arguing that such an action would evoke the ringing of church bells in some European communities as a call for attacks on Jews. Another suggestion put forward by Raya, to stage a march with a large cross down the Via Dolorosa in lament of the plight of Bir'im and Iqrit, was criticized for inadvertently echoing anti-Jewish Christian charges of deicide. See Edwin M. Wright, *A Tale of Two Hamlets: Berem and Iqrit, Symbols of Israel's Intentions for Its Christian Citizens*, Position Paper #4 (Cleveland: Northeast Ohio Committee on Middle East Understanding, Inc., 1973), 6. For Raya, these proposed actions simply mirrored ways that African-American churches had appropriated Christian tropes in the midst of the civil rights struggle in the United States.

56. Ryan, "Refugees within Israel," 69.

57. Chacour, *We Belong to the Land*, 88–89.

58. Kimmerling, "Sovereignty, Ownership, and 'Presence,'" 167.

59. Kimmerling explains that "Two types of precedents were feared: (a) the claims of Arabs from villages which remained within Israel's boundaries after the cease-fire agreements of 1949; (b) the creation of a precedent contrary to Israel's position that even when a peace agreement or any other arrangement is arrived at with the Arabs, the refugees will not be allowed to return to their places, but will rather be settled in the Arab Countries." Golda Meir, Israeli Prime Minister at the time of the protests, expressed this fear of a precedent being set: "I do not make light of the feelings of the people of Bir'im and Ikrit. I understand them, and I do not envy them. But I do not accept the argument that states that their case will not set a precedent. I have already received letters and telegrams from other villages whose people wish to return to their lands, and in the Galilee there are 22 such villages whose inhabitants either abandoned them or were evacuated." Kimmerling, "Sovereignty, Ownership, and 'Presence,'" 164–65.

60. The focal point the church plays in the Bir'imite imagination reflects the central role that churches and mosques perform in the memories of other internally displaced Palestinians. For a study of the fate of pre-1948 Palestinian Christian and Muslim shrines inside Israel and of Palestinian attempts to renovate those shrines, see Alexander Key, *Sanctity Denied: The Destruction and Abuse of Muslim and Christian Holy Places in Israel* (Nazareth: Arab Association for Human Rights, 2004). The remains of churches and mosques become key sites around which village, clan, regional, and national identities are shaped. See Tamir Sorek, "Cautious Commemoration: Localism, Communalism, and Nationalism in Palestinian Memorial Monuments in Israel," *Comparative Studies in Society and History* 50, no. 2 (April 2008): 337–68.

61. Randa Farah, "Palestinian Refugees: Dethroning the Nation at the Crowning of the 'Statelet'?" *interventions* 8, no. 2 (July 2006): 228–52.

62. Boqai, *Returning to Kafr Bir'im*, 89.

63. Ben-Ze'ev, "The Politics of Taste and Smell," 155.

64. Magat, *Bir'am: A Conscripted Community of Memory*, 9.

65. Ben-Ze'ev and Aburaiya, "'Middle-Ground' Politics," 648.

66. In 1978, at one of the first of these camps, Fr. Chacour led the campers in an oath of commitment to the cause of return: "I swear in the name of God and the ruins of Biram never to forget this is our village. I swear I shall rebuild these ruined stones and raise them from death to life. I swear never, ever to use the insane methods of violence to retaliate and regain our rights. I swear I will do everything to convince those who have deprived us of our homes that they cannot enjoy peace and security unless we return home. I swear that if we are not allowed to come back alive, we will come back dead, but that we will return to Biram. I swear we shall be united in our cause and never abandon Biram." Chacour, *We Belong to the Land*, 123.

67. Magat, *Bir'am: A Conscripted Community of Memory*, 49. Sami Zahra, expelled from Kafr Bir'im in 1948, explains that "[t]hey invite me every year to meet with groups of children and youth and tell them about our lives before the Nakba, our habits and traditions, and about the occupation of the village." Boqai, *Returning to Kafr Bir'im*, 97.

68. Boqai, *Returning to Kafr Bir'im*, 86. The focus on immersion in nature as a way of gaining experiential knowledge of one's heritage not only is a common feature of Palestinian summer camps, but also arguably mirrors the Zionist emphasis on the importance of a peripatetic encounter with nature for shaping proper Jewish identity. See Orit Ben-David, "Tiyul (Hike) as an Act of Consecration of Space," in *Grasping Land: Space and Place in Contemporary Israeli Discourse and Experience*, ed. Eyal Ben-Ari and Yoram Bilu (Albany: State University of New York, 1997), 129–45 and Rachel Havrelock, *River Jordan: Mythology of a Dividing Line* (Chicago: University of Chicago Press, 2011), 258ff.

69. Boqai, *Returning to Kafr Bir'im*, 97.

70. Ibid.

71. Deborah Tall, *From Where We Stand: Recovering a Sense of Place* (Baltimore: Johns Hopkins University Press, 1993), 207.

72. For video of 'Issa Chacour reciting this poem, see http://palestineremembered.com/Safad/Kafr-Bir'im/Story9903.html.

73. All quotations and translations from Ibrahim 'Issa are taken from John Halaka, director, *The Presence of Absence in the Ruins of Kafr Bir'im*, film (Sitting Crow Productions, 2007).

74. Ibid.

75. Ibid.

76. Amal Jamal, "The Palestinian IDPs in Israel and the Predicament of Return: Between Imagining the Impossible and Enabling the Imaginative," in *Exile and Return: Predicaments of Palestinians and Jews*, ed. Ann M. Lesch and Ian S. Lustick (Philadelphia: University of Pennsylvania Press, 2005), 153.

77. See Isabelle Humphries, "Palestinian Internal Refugees in the Galilee: From the Struggle to Survive to the New Narrative of Return (1948–2005)," *Holy Land Studies: A Multidisciplinary Journal* 3, no. 2 (2004): 213–31.

78. "The Palestinian Arab citizens of the State of Israel have lived in their homeland for innumerable generations. Here they were born, here their historic roots have grown, and here their national and cultural life has developed and flourished." See *The Democratic Constitution* (Shafa'amr: Adalah, the Legal Center for Arab Minority Rights in Israel, 2007), point 5. For contemporary Palestinian political activism within Israel for greater equality and aimed at contesting the state's ethnocratic character, see Nadim Rouhana, "The Political Transformation of the Palestinians in Israel: From Acquiescence to Challenge," *Journal of Palestine Studies* 18, no. 3 (Spring 1989): 38–59; Nadim Rouhana, *Palestinian Citizens in an Ethnic Jewish State: Identities in Conflict* (New Haven: Yale University Press, 1997); Oren Yiftachel, "The Shrinking Space of Citizenship: Ethnocratic Politics in Israel," in *The Struggle for Sovereignty: Palestine and Israel, 1993–2005*, ed. Joel Beinin and Rebecca L. Stein (Stanford: Stanford University Press, 2006), 162–74; and Ilan Peleg, "Jewish-Palestinian Relations in Israel: From Hegemony to Equality?" *International Journal of Politics, Culture, and Society* 17, no. 3 (Spring 2004): 415–37. For discussions of the rise of IDP activism and Palestinian political organization inside Israel, see: Ilan Pappé, *The Forgotten Palestinians: A History of the Palestinians inside Israel* (New Haven: Yale University Press, 2011); Ilan Peleg and Dov Waxman, *Israel's Palestinians: The Conflict Within* (Cambridge: Cambridge University Press, 2011); Hillel Frisch, "Ethnicity or Nationalism? Comparing the *Nakba* Narrative among Israeli Arabs and Palestinians in the West Bank and Gaza," in *The Israeli Palestinians: An Arab Minority in the Jewish State*, ed. Alexander Bligh (London and Portland, OR: Frank Cass, 2003), 165–84; As'ad Ghanem and Sarah Ozacky-Lazar, "The Status of the Palestinians in Israel in an Era of Peace: Part of the Problem but Not Part of the Solution," in *The Israeli Palestinians: An Arab Minority in the Jewish State*, ed. Bligh, 263–89; Shany Payes, "Palestinian

NGOs in Israel: A Campaign for Civic Equality in a Non-Civic State," *Israel Studies* 8, no. 1 (Spring 2003): 60–90; Oded Haklai, "Palestinian NGOs in Israel: A Campaign for Civil Equality or 'Ethnic Civil Society?" *Israel Studies* 9, no. 3 (Autumn 2004): 157–68; and Oren Yiftachel, "Regionalism among Palestinian-Arabs in Israel," in *Nested Identities: Nationalism, Territory, and Scale*, ed. Guntram H. Herb and David H. Kaplan (Lanham, MD: Rowman & Littlefield, 1999), 237–66.

79. Long-time mayor of Nazareth, Zayyad was also one of the most prominent Palestinian poets inside Israel. Quoted in Edward Said, *The Question of Palestine* (New York: Times Books, 1979), 130.

80. Liisa Malkki, "National Geographic: The Rooting of Peoples and the Territorialization of National Identity among Scholars and Refugees," *Cultural Anthropology* 7, no. 1 (February 1992): 24–44 and Malkki, "Refugees and Exile: From 'Refugee Studies' to the National Order of Things," *Annual Review of Anthropology* 24 (1995): 495–523.

81. Quoted in Uwe Gräbe, *Kontextuelle Palästinensische Theologie: Streitbare und Umstrittene Beiträge zum Ökumenischen und Interreligiösen Gespräch* (Erlangen: Erlangen Verlag für Mission und Ökumene, 1999), 181.

82. Gaston Bachelard, *The Poetics of Space*, trans. Maria Jolas (Boston: Beacon, 1958), 48, 6, 17.

83. Yi-Fu Tuan, *Space and Place: The Perspective of Experience* (Minneapolis: University of Minnesota Press, 1977), 144.

84. Bachelard, *The Poetics of Space*, 14. The Palestinian Christian poet and novelist Anton Shammas, native of Fassouta in the northern Galilee, echoes Bachelard when he asserts that people's understandings of place are not fundamentally about abstract conceptions of the nation, but are rather much more localized—about particular buildings, rooms, plants, etc. A fighter, Shammas contends, does not struggle on behalf of the abstract map of the nation, but for "the map of a favorite room in that house. And now that the house is gone, it's probably the remembered room that he is fighting for, the room whose lingering space defines that fragile presence that we call identity, forever humming in our internal ear." Anton Shammas, "Autocartography: The Case of Palestine, Michigan," in *The Geography of Identity*, ed. Patricia Yeager (Ann Arbor: University of Michigan Press, 1994), 468.

85. Tuan, *Space and Place*, 159.

86. Rochelle A. Davis, *Palestinian Village Histories: Geographies of the Displaced* (Stanford: Stanford University Press, 2011), 168.

87. In *Blood Brothers*, Chacour uses the Anglicized version of his father's name, Michael, whereas in *We Belong to the Land* he employs the more faithful transliteration, Mikhail.

88. Chacour, *Blood Brothers*, chapter 1, "News in the Wind," 19–30.

89. Ibid., 28–29.

90. Ibid., 67–68.

91. Ibid., 70.

92. Simon Schama, *Landscape and Memory* (New York: Vintage, 1996), 61.

93. Chacour, *We Belong to the Land*, 79.

94. Carol Bardenstein explains that "[t]he notion of the land and its trees remaining 'loyal' (i.e., healthy, alive, and fruitful) only to its 'rightful' tenders, and shriveling up as if in protest when tended to by strangers is a recurring theme in Palestinian writing." Bardenstein, "Threads of Memory," 19.

95. Chacour, *We Belong to the Land*, 79.

96. For background on the Chacour family's history in Kafr Bir'im, see Kana'nah and Ishtayyah, *The Destroyed Palestinian Villages: Kafr Bir'im*, 10 and Ibrahim 'Issa in Halaka, *The Presence of Absence*.

97. Naim Ateek, *Justice, and Only Justice: A Palestinian Theology of Liberation* (Maryknoll, NY: Orbis, 1989), 113.

98. Abu-Sitta, *The Return Journey: Guide to Destroyed and Remaining Villages and Holy Places in Palestine* (London: Palestine Land Society, 2007), E17.

99. Eviatar Zerubavel, *Time Maps: Collective Memory and the Social Shape of the Past* (Chicago and London: University of Chicago Press, 2003), 106.

100. Chacour, *We Belong to the Land*, 5.

101. Ibid., 6.

102. Ibid., 80.

103. Chacour, *Blood Brothers*, 39.

104. Ibid., 40.

105. "Mobile Western people have difficulty comprehending the significance of the land for Palestinians. We belong to the land. We identify with the land, which has been treasured, cultivated, and nurtured by countless generations of ancestors. . . . The land is so holy, so sacred, to us because we have given it our sweat and blood." Chacour, *We Belong to the Land*, 80.

106. Meron Benvenisti, *Sacred Landscape*, 43.

107. "Long a major element of the local economy, the olive tree has taken on symbolic characteristics, which the Palestinians present as an image of themselves." Shaul Cohen, *The Politics of Planting*, 186. John Collins explains that for Palestinians "the olive tree—a powerful and poetic symbol of rootedness in the milieu, of fertility, of stubborn habitation—is a holistic source of emotional, financial and political sustenance." Collins, "Global Palestine: A Collision for Our Time," *Critique: Critical Middle Eastern Studies* 16, no. 1 (Spring 2007): 17. Together with other objects like oranges, large iron keys, and embroidered dresses, olive trees during the 1960s came to symbolize "prelapsarian life in Palestine," invoked by the reemergent nationalist movement "as signifiers of Palestinianness."—Laleh Khalili, *Heroes and Martyrs: The Politics of National Commemoration* (Cambridge: Cambridge University Press, 2007), 6.

108. Chacour, *We Belong to the Land*, 114–17.

109. See Cohen, *The Politics of Planting*.

110. Chacour, *We Belong to the Land*, 114.

111. Chacour, *Blood Brothers*, 193.

112. Ibid., 179. The metaphorical description of Palestinian Christians as living stones, drawn from 1 Peter 2:5, surfaces repeatedly within Palestinian Christian discourse, often as a judgment against European and North American Christians whose Holy Land pilgrimages focus on the ancient stones of the holy places while turning a blind eye to the travails of the Palestinian church. As "living stones," Palestinian Christians bring the ancient stones to life. The trope of refugees bringing the stones of destroyed villages back to life also runs throughout much contemporary Palestinian literature. See Barbara McKean Parmenter, *Giving Voice to Stones: Place and Identity in Palestinian Literature* (Austin: University of Texas Press, 1994).

113. Chacour, *Blood Brothers*, 94–95.

114. Ibid., 145.

115. Ibid., 40.

116. Ibid., 145.

117. Ibid., 150.

118. Chacour, "Reconciliation and Justice: Living with the Memory," in *Holy Land—Hollow Jubilee: God, Justice, and the Palestinians*, ed. Naim Ateek and Michael Prior (London: Melisende, 1999), 112.

119. Chacour, *Blood Brothers*, 145.

120. Ibid., 148.

121. Chacour points in this direction when he claims that through Isaiah "God was requiring a true change of heart in the Jewish people, a change in their traditional exclusiveness which caused them to believe that they alone were God's favored ones. All the prophets had made it clear that such thinking led to pride and error and wrongdoing." Chacour, *Blood Brothers*, 149. Chacour's argument, unfortunately, is marred by the phrase "traditional exclusiveness," which falls into the rhetorical trap of contrasting "traditional" Jewish "exclusiveness" with the "inclusiveness"

of Christianity. The substantive point that can be recovered from Chacour's claim, I believe, is that when election becomes a matter of boasting or self-congratulation, God's people lose sight of the task of living as a paradigm nation in the land, instead engaging in the exclusivist politics practiced by nations the world over.

122. Chacour, *Blood Brothers*, 149–50.

123. Chacour, *We Belong to the Land*, 68. See also Chacour, "Reconciliation and Justice," 111–15.

124. Bardenstein, "Threads of Memory," 20.

125. "Binary logic is the spiritual reality of the root-tree." Gilles Deleuze and Félix Guattari, *A Thousand Plateaus: Capitalism and Schizophrenia*, trans. Brian Massumi (Minneapolis: University of Minnesota Press, 1987), 5.

126. Trees need not be "arborescent," Guattari and Deleuze stress: "Trees may correspond to the rhizome, or they may burgeon into a rhizome." *A Thousand Plateaus*, 17. Similarly, actual rhizomes, like vines, can be used to display arborescent thought: the logic of Psalm 80, with the vine spreading across the land, uprooting other vines as it expands, certainly exhibits the binary logic of arborescent thought, the vine metaphor notwithstanding.

127. Quoted in Dalrymple, *From the Holy Mountain*, 372.

128. Nihad Boqai provides a breakdown of the present-day use of Kafr Bir'im's former land: "As of today, the land of Kafr Bir'im is held and used by: Kibbutz Bar'am (2,587 dunums, including 90 dunums for housing 569 dunums for cultivation and 1,928 dunums for grazing); Kibbutz Sa'sa (1,000 dunums, including 70 dunums for agriculture and 930 dunums for grazing); and, Moshav Dovev (5,250 dunums, of which 265 dunums are built-up, 1,010 used for agriculture and 3,975 for grazing). The 'Nature Reserve' covers an area of 2,783 dunums of Kafr Bir'im land, with the 'National Park' established on 80 dunums. In addition, there are 514 dunums of land which have not been reallocated, including 70 dunums cultivated by Kafr Bir'im displaced, and 439 dunums of forest held by the Jewish National Fund and used by Kibbutz Bar'am for grazing" no more than fifty cows. Boqai, *Returning to Kafr Bir'im*, 39. One dunum equals one thousand square meters, or approximately one-quarter of an acre.

129. The CUB's submission to the Liba'i Commission stated the following principles (Boqai, *Returning to Kafr Bir'im*, 75):

• Property rights of the people of Kafr Bir'im will be restored as they were before 1948;
• Kafr Bir'im landowners will not demand use of the built-up areas and the agricultural land currently used by *Kibbutz Bar'am* and *Moshav Dovev*;
• The return of the Kafr Bir'im displaced will not lead to the displacement of the Jewish residents of *Kibbutz Bar'am* and *Moshav Dovev*;
• All land currently used by Kibbutz Bar'am for grazing will be returned for use by the owners of Kafr Bir'im;
• All former inhabitants of Kafr Bir'im and their descendants can return to the village;
• The village will be rebuilt on the site of the original village, which will be expanded, and land currently allocated for forests and the national park will be reallocated.

130. The Liba'i Commission eventually recommended that, while no security grounds prevented the return of villagers to the site of Kafr Bir'im, village land should stay confiscated. The commission agreed that 600 dunums of the expropriated land could be set aside to allow for construction by the villagers. The commission's recommendations were roundly rejected by CUB. Afif Ibrahim explains the reasons behind this rejection: "First, the recommendations did not allow return of all Kafr Bir'im displaced and their descendants to their homes and properties; second, it was recommended that those who would return would rent their properties and not own them; third, the returnees would have to waive claims to their original land; and fourth, the villagers would not be allowed to expand and develop in the future." Quoted in Boqai, *Returning to Kafr Bir'im*, 75–77.

131. Denis Wood claims that "[t]he very point of the map [is] to present us not with the world we can *see*, but to point *toward* a world we might *know*." Wood, *The Power of Maps* (New York and London: Guilford, 1992), 12. The CUB map points toward a world presently known by the internally displaced of Kafr Bir'im *and* to a shared place that Palestinians and Israeli Jews might come to know as equals.

132. Boqai, *Returning to Kafr Bir'im*, 104–5.

133. For an essay about Hanna Farah's photographic art about Kafr Bir'im, see Tal Ben-Zvi, "Biographies," in *Six Solo Exhibitions at Hagar Art Gallery* (Jaffa: Kal, 2006), 14.

134. Quoted in Boqai, *Returning to Kafr Bir'im*, 106. See also Norma Musih, "Hanna Farah—Kufr Bir'im," in Solution 196–213: United States of Palestine-Israel, ed. Joshua Simon (Berlin: Sternberg, 2011), 66–73.

135. Zochrot's enacted mappings of return will be explained in greater depth in chapter 4.

136. Quoted in Boqai, *Returning to Kafr Bir'im*, 80.

137. Dan Rabinowitz, *Overlooking Nazareth: The Ethnography of Exclusion in Galilee* (Cambridge: Cambridge University Press, 1997), 78–79.

138. The demands of IDPs to return to the sites of their destroyed villages form one part of the broader critique by Palestinians inside Israel concerning the ethnocratic nature of the state. See As'ad Ghanem, "Zionism, Post-Zionism, and Anti-Zionism in Israel: Jews and Arabs in the Conflict over the Nature of the State," in *The Challenge of Post-Zionism: Alternatives to Israeli Fundamentalist Politics*, ed. Ephraim Nimni (London: Zed, 2003), 98–116.

4

Return Visits to 'Imwas and the Liturgical Subversion of Ethnocratic Topology

"A specter haunts the Middle East, the daunting specter of Palestinian-Jewish binationalism."

——UDI ALONI[1]

"Haunted places are the only ones people can live in."

——MICHEL DE CERTEAU[2]

"Then their eyes were opened, and they recognized him; and he vanished from their sight."

——LUKE 24:31 (NRSV)

In this book I have examined competing political theologies of exile, considering how a political theology of exilic landedness (as articulated in different, yet I would argue complementary, ways by Yoder, Raz-Krakotzkin, and others) might counter Zionism's political theology of negation of exile. I have also analyzed what mapping practices these political theologies support. Questions that have driven this investigation include: What forms of counter-mapping might not only oppose Zionist practices of dispossession and cartographic erasure, but also subvert the exclusivist, nationalist logic that animates so many mapping and counter-mapping projects, charting instead alternative forms of political organization? What forms of political life might be shaped by an acceptance of exile as vocation and an acknowledgment of divine extraterritoriality (Yoder)? What types of practices and actions flow from a commitment to live in exile within the land (Raz-Krakotzkin)? Previous chapters have offered tentative answers to these questions, in particular the Bir'imite mappings of return discussed in chapter 3. To deepen and develop these tentative answers further, I will describe and analyze the counter-mappings produced and performed by the Zochrot Association, a decade-old Israeli organization dedicated to "remembering the *Nakba* in Hebrew," giving particular attention to its alternative mapping practices at the site of the depopulated village of 'Imwas on the western edge of the West Bank. Zochrot's cartographic performances, I argue, should properly be understood as *liturgical* actions in the sense of liturgy advanced by political theorist Vincent Lloyd as a practice that creates a space in which the hegemony of social norms is suspended, thus pointing to new political possibilities. More specifically, following Lloyd and Catholic theologian Jean-Yves Lacoste, I contend that Zochrot's mappings and at least some cartographic practices of Palestinian refugees should be viewed as *exilic vigils*, actions in which return is shaped by the exilic commitment to building the city for others and that anticipate a coming, binational future.

Byzantine and Crusader-era remains within 'Imwas' ruins commemorate the biblical account of the encounter between the resurrected Jesus and two of his disciples as they walked along the road to Emmaus (Luke 24:13-35).[3] To visit the ruins of 'Imwas today within the park created by the Jewish National Fund on the village's lands is to walk within a haunted place. Michel de Certeau has observed how all places are haunted, haunted in the sense that they become *places* rather than coordinates on a Cartesian plane thanks to the memories, stories, and legends individuals and communities attach to them. Certeau's observation certainly rings true for what Zali Gurevitch has called "the double site of Israel": while Zionist cartography seeks to construct and portray an exclusively Israeli Jewish landscape, the landscape remains haunted by traces of the prior, never completely effaced Palestinian habitation.[4] Zochrot's counter-mapping practices call attention to those traces, and in doing so arouse and invoke a specter that appears threatening to many Israeli Jews, namely, the specter of binationalism. "Zionism's significant Other—the intolerable one that mustn't be seen—is the Palestinian *Nakba*," Zochrot founder Eitan Bronstein asserts. "It is kept a secret, like a fantasma, a ghost that continues to walk through our space and time and continues to interfere in strange, sometimes uncontrollable ways."[5] By highlighting the palimpsest character of the Israeli landscape, Zochrot provokes a conversation within the Israeli Jewish public about the binational specter uncovered by mapping Palestinian refugee return back onto the landscape, a conversation about whether that specter must be encountered as a threat, or if it might instead herald a future way of living in the land.

But Zochrot does not simply instigate argument and debate over the future of binationalism. Through its counter-mappings, I argue, Zochrot *performs* the promise of binationalism in the present through enacted rememberings of the past. These alternative cartographic performances are *liturgical* actions, in the sense of liturgy developed by Lloyd and Lacoste. Specifically, by building on Paul Virilio's account of dromocracy, I argue that the return visits and other forms of counter-mapping undertaken by Zochrot can be fruitfully interpreted as *exilic vigils* that uncover the landscape as always already binational in character, vigils that by embodying patient counter-habitation within the ethnocratic landscape oppose the regime of speed by which the Israeli military seeks to police internal borders and thus to maintain the illusion of homogeneous Israeli Jewish space. Through a close examination of Zochrot's counter-mapping at the ruins of 'Imwas, I contend that these exilic vigils offer a theopolitical vision of life in the land in which acknowledgment of the landscape as a palimpsest points to the promise of a binational topology. Just as the risen Christ cannot be constrained or controlled by his disciples when they recognize him as they break bread together at Emmaus, so exilic vigils reveal the land not as a space to be grasped or claimed exclusively, but rather as the place in which Palestinians and Israeli Jews alike might together build and anticipate new futures as they recognize themselves as exiles who must seek refuge with one another.

REMEMBERING THE *NAKBA* IN HEBREW: ZOCHROT'S PRACTICES OF COUNTER-MAPPING

For Zochrot, the memory of Palestinian towns and villages before 1948 and the Israeli role in their destruction need not be feared as a curse but can instead be embraced as a sign of hope. With the mission "to commemorate, witness, acknowledge, and repair" by making the *nakba* part of Israeli Jewish discourse and memory, Zochrot was founded in 2002 by a small group of Israeli Jews led by Eitan Bronstein: several Palestinians with Israeli citizenship soon joined them in the endeavor. Zochrot's genesis can be found in Bronstein's previous work as a conflict resolution trainer at the School for Peace operated by Neve Shalom/ Wahat as-Salam (NSWAS), the only intentionally mixed Palestinian/Israeli Jewish community in Israel-Palestine.[6] As a conflict resolution coordinator, Bronstein regularly led workshops about Palestinian-Israeli reconciliation. In the course of his work Bronstein became interested in the ruins within the Jewish National Fund–operated Canada Park near NSWAS. A little bit of research led Bronstein to discover that the ruins were the remains of three Palestinian villages—Yalu, Beit Nuba, and 'Imwas—that had been part of the so-called Latrun salient on the westernmost edge of the West Bank. Shortly after Israel conquered the West Bank in 1967, Israeli troops expelled the inhabitants of the three villages, sending them eastward to Ramallah (with others continuing on to Jordan), and then proceeded to bulldoze the buildings. The Jewish National Fund then took control of the land and planted a forest over the ruins with financial support from Jewish communities in Canada—hence the present-day name of Canada Park. Bronstein was struck by the fact that none of the historical signs in the park referred to the prior Palestinian presence. Given this absence, an average visitor to the park would undoubtedly assume that the village ruins belonged to one of the earlier eras (Hasmonean, Byzantine, etc.) mentioned on the park's historical markers. How, Bronstein wondered, could the goal of Palestinian-Israeli reconciliation ever hope to be achieved so long as Palestinian history and geography—especially Palestinian stories and landscapes of dispossession—went ignored and denied?

The failure to identify the ruins of destroyed Palestinian villages is not limited to Canada Park, but is rather representative of what Meron Benvenisti describes as "intentional disregard for the Arab stratum of the landscape."[7] This disregard takes many forms. So, for example, even when roadmaps or street signs include Arabic alongside Hebrew script (by no means most of the time), the place names in Arabic are typically transliterations of the Hebrew, rather than the Palestinian names for the places. The most striking example of such misidentification by transliteration can be seen on signs marking *yerushalayim* (Hebrew for Jerusalem) in Arabic script, rather than *al-quds*.[8] Israeli archaeological surveys and digs, meanwhile, have historically perpetuated this disregard, bypassing and ignoring as inconsequential Ottoman-era findings, focusing instead on trying to uncover traces of prior Jewish life in the land that could be used as part of Zionism's national colonial theology of return to origins and indigeneity.[9] And, as was discussed in chapter 3, state and para-state institutions such as the Jewish National Fund, the Israel Lands Administration, and the National Parks Authority have actively perpetuated public disregard for Palestinian land by afforesting the sites of destroyed villages and then leaving the architectural traces of those villages unmarked.

In the face of such intentional disregard, it should come as no surprise that most Israeli Jews fail to recognize the palimpsest character of the Israeli landscape, with "a three-dimensional Jewish space underlain by an equally three-dimensional Arab space."[10] Israel, in Hassan Jabareen's turn of phrase, is a "place with no Palestinian memory."[11] The Israeli Jewish public, Rebecca Stein concurs, is captive to "spatial fantasies" that seek "to preserve the myth of Israel as a Euro-Jewish space."[12] Within such spatial fantasies, the remains of destroyed Palestinian villages appear as "primitive and ancient features of the landscape," as "anonymous creations from the ancient past and never the work of named, known, often living Palestinian stonemasons and masterbuilders."[13] Zochrot founder Bronstein recounts precisely such a fantasy shaping his boyhood years as a young immigrant to Israel from Argentina. Bronstein lived on Kibbutz Bahan and regularly played amidst the remains of what he assumed were from a Crusader-era castle. Only as an adult did he discover that alongside the ruins of a Crusader fort were the detritus of the destroyed village of Qaqun.[14] Drawing on the work of Ann Laura Stoler, the Israeli political theorist Ariella Azoulay identifies this Israeli Jewish misperception of Palestinian places as an example of *colonial aphasia*: Israeli Jews experience "difficulty retrieving an available vocabulary" to name and acknowledge the traces of the destruction carried out by Israeli forces.[15] Zochrot's efforts to "Hebrewise the *nakba*" seek to treat this aphasia by enabling Israeli Jews correctly to identify the remains of dispossession created by the State of Israel's formation through the return of Palestinian names to the mental and physical maps used by Israeli Jews to construct and navigate their landscapes.[16]

Zionist cartography operates with the binary understanding of place characteristic of nationalist imaginings of territory more generally. So, for example, if a particular map location is marked Zippori, Israel, then those same coordinates, it is assumed, cannot also denote Saffuriya, Palestine. Responding to such binary cartographic thinking, a form of thinking it identifies with the masculine logic of nationalism, Zochrot, whose name is the third-person feminine plural participle of the Hebrew verb "to remember" (*zachar*), counters with a cartographic imagination that embraces the heterogeneous character of places. Zochrot program manager Norma Musih explains: "We decided to call it Zochrot because we wanted to promote a different kind of memory. It is not just the memory of wars and the memory of men. It is also a memory of a place that tells other stories."[17]

Musih and her colleagues are not promoting some form of gender essentialism in their choice of name for Zochrot, juxtaposing a supposedly "feminine" understanding of "place" to an inherently "masculine," nationalist logic of place. The claim is not that women naturally experience space and place in a different manner than men. Rather, the gendered naming of Zochrot serves to highlight and call into question the gendered assumptions of Zionism which, as examined in chapter 2, disparage diaspora as weak and feminine while extolling return to a supposedly exclusive Jewish space as the opportunity for a revitalized, masculine Judaism. Zochrot's name is a call for a different way to map and remember place, a way that is different from exclusivist, nationalist cartographies that are encoded as masculine. The work of the feminist geographer Doreen Massey helps to clarify the significance of Zochrot's name. Massey notes that nationalist conceptualizations that present themselves as masculine represent "attempts to fix the meaning of places, to enclose and defend them: they construct singular, fixed, and static identities for places, and they interpret places and bounded enclosed spaces defined through counter-position against the Other who is outside."[18] Such nationalist construals of place, Massey contends, fail to do justice to the complex and fluid character of place. Massey explains that "what is specific about a place, its identity, is always formed by the juxtaposition and co-presence there of particular sets of social interrelations, and by the effects which that juxtaposition and co-presence produce."[19] This alternative understanding of place being formed by juxtaposition and co-presence is no more essentially "feminine" than nationalist portrayals of place are necessarily "masculine": by naming themselves "the women who remember," the men and women of Zochrot are thus not affirming gender essentialism, but are instead seeking to disrupt it, pointing to the possibility of new mappings of space that affirm co-presence and reject binary depictions of territory. "We live on these legends that it's either them or us, that there's not enough space here for both Jews and Palestinians," explains Musih. "I think that part of what we're doing is trying to open up these negative binary understandings, to say that it's not either them or us. It can be both."[20]

Zochrot's main counter-mapping strategy is simple.[21] Several times a year it organizes trips open to all Israelis, be they Jewish or Palestinian, to the sites of destroyed Palestinian villages and to formerly Palestinian neighborhoods and villages now part of mixed Palestinian-Israeli Jewish cities such as Ramleh, Lydda, and Haifa. The Palestinian participants are typically what the State of Israel designates as "present absentees," persons who remained inside Israel but who were absent from their homes during the fighting of 1948, either because they had been expelled or had fled for safety from the conflict, and whose property had thus been subject to confiscation under Israel's Absentee Property Law of 1950. Zochrot is certainly not unique in organizing return visits. As examined at length in chapter 3, internally displaced Palestinians inside Israel have been organizing return visits to the remains of demolished villages as individuals, families, and extended communities.[22] In addition, Palestinian civil society organizations have arisen inside Israel like the Association for the Defense of the Rights of the Internally Displaced and the Al-Aqsa Foundation of the Islamic Movement in Israel that dedicate themselves to documenting and preserving remains from destroyed villages, and these organizations often organize return visits.

Zochrot's return trips, however, are distinctive for their binational composition. Visit participants board a bus departing from Tel Aviv with the number 194, named after United Nations General Assembly Resolution 194 guaranteeing Palestinian refugees the right of return. At the village site internally displaced Palestinian refugees act as hosts, share their memories of the village, and offer testimonies regarding its depopulation and destruction.[23] Sometimes they speak in Hebrew, sometimes in Arabic with Hebrew translation provided. Zochrot distributes memory books telling the story of the village, with both Arabic and Hebrew text and often with Mandate-era, Israeli, and Palestinian maps of the village and its environs.[24] Finally, Israeli Jews and Palestinians together erect signs in both Hebrew and Arabic, identifying trees and other plants pre-dating 1948, naming ruined buildings (identifying them as churches, mosques, schoolhouses, private residences, etc.) and, in places where Israeli cities now stand, like Ashqelon (Arabic al-Majdal) or Beersheva (Arabic Bir al-Saba'), posting street signs with the pre-1948 names.[25] So, for example, under the contemporary street sign in Ashkelon for Rehov Herzl (Herzl Street), one Zochrot group placed a sign in Hebrew and Arabic reading Shari' al-Ustaaz (the Teacher's Street).[26] If Maoz Azaryahu and Rebecca Kook are correct that typically the posting of street signs "is part of the ongoing process of mapping the nation," then Zochrot's signposting actions should be interpreted as attempts to map a post-national geography.[27]

As noted in earlier chapters, through the mapping of and return visits to the sites of destroyed Palestinian villages, those locations and remains become what Pierre Nora has called dominated *lieux de mémoire* (in contrast to the dominating memory sites established by governmental and para-state institutions). A key function of these memory sites "is to stop time, to block the work of forgetting to establish a state of things, to immortalize death, to materialize the immaterial."[28] Gathered amidst the crumbling remains of mosques, churches, schools, and private residences, Zochrot participants mourn and memorialize the dead.

Yet the objective of Zochrot's signposting actions is not simply commemorative, but also performative. By posting signs identifying the ruins, Zochrot, according to founder and director Eitan Bronstein, works to reconstruct "the 'space' in which Jews and Arabs operate." As forms of spatial protest, Zochrot's signposting maps a binational landscape and charts new political possibilities.[29] Through its signposting activities, Bronstein asserts, Zochrot opens up "heterogeneous space" within the Israeli landscape, or what Michel Foucault called *heterotopias*. These bilingual signs add "to the space a reminder of what had been taken away, and the people who take down the signs seek to maintain the illusion of transparency, the purely Jewish-Israeli nature of the space." The signs "represent a challenge to written history inscribed on the landscape" and work, through aesthetic-political means, to reshape Israeli topology. "This is taking action upon the landscape in the hope of rediscovering and remodeling it, creating a renewed landscape that will reveal the traces of what has refused to be wiped out."[30] Zochrot's mapping activities create "subversive maps of the borders" that separate Palestinians from Israeli Jews, its cartographic practices representative of the type of mapping the Hackitectura collective called for when it proposed maps that "create space of mutual contagion of the post-national multitude."[31]

Zochrot has undertaken several additional counter-mapping ventures to supplement its monthly return visits. Examples of such alternative cartographic performances include:

- Developing an interactive, online database in Hebrew of destroyed Palestinian villages: The user accesses the database by clicking on part of a map of Israel-Palestine (with the borders for the West Bank and the Gaza Strip marked), which leads her to a list of destroyed villages within that quadrant of the map where she clicked. She can then select the name of a particular village in order to learn more details about it: its population before it was destroyed; the date it was occupied; the military operation of which its depopulation was a part; the Israeli military brigade that occupied the village and (if applicable) expelled its inhabitants; and the name of Jewish settlements constructed after 1948 on the village's built-up areas as well as its agricultural and public lands. The database is searchable by Palestinian village name, but also by contemporary Israeli districts and by Israeli city and town names, so that the user can see what Palestinian locales once existed near one's own home.[32] Comparable in some ways to online databases like Palestine Remembered and AlNakba.org, Zochrot's database is distinctive for its primary focus on the Israeli Jewish public.[33]

- The placement of life-size photograph cut-outs of Palestinian refugees living in the United Nations–run Ein al-Hilweh camp in southern Lebanon at the ruins of the destroyed village of Ras al-Ahmar from which they were expelled and within the Israeli moshav of Keren Ben Zimra built over Ras al-Ahmar's village lands, a way of visually restoring Palestinian presence on the landscape and of spurring discussion within the moshav about what it would mean for the expelled residents of Ras al-Ahmar to return.[34]

- The laying out of a grid map of Israel-Palestine in Tel Aviv's Rabin Square, with passersby invited to return destroyed Palestinian villages to the map by placing cards with village names in the corresponding grid boxes. Since it first carried out this action in 2004, Zochrot has placed instructions online for this "We're On the Map" activity for groups around the world wishing to construct their own versions of the map as part of protests and educational workshops.[35]

- Although the *nakba* is not a "secret event that only few know of" (given how much has been written by Israeli historians and others about the dispossession of Palestinians during and after the 1948 war), it nevertheless remains a topic that is not "taught out in the open," and that has yet to "become an integral part of the school curriculum or the political discourse in Israel."[36] To combat this lacuna in the Israeli education system, Zochrot developed a curriculum ("How Do We Say Nakba in Hebrew?"), complete with maps and refugee testimonials, that high school educators can use to introduce Israeli Jewish teenagers to the *nakba* and to spur conversation about how to relate to refugees in the future. Zochrot has also organized teacher-training events to discuss how the curriculum might be used most effectively.[37] Disturbed by this challenge to the dominant mode of history education in Israel, the Israeli Ministry of Education has threatened to punish schools that use Zochrot's curriculum.[38]

- Zochrot initiates and joins in legal actions to contest Israeli building and development plans on the sites of destroyed villages that do not address the claims of Palestinian refugees. Most significantly, Zochrot has challenged plan 2351, the master plan for the reconstruction of the ruins of Lifta, which would incorporate the destroyed village's tress, spring, terraces, olive oil processing structures, and damaged and undamaged houses into a high-scale housing development that would become part of Jerusalem's western suburbs. On the one hand, the master plan displays a preservationist intent: the "larger, newer,

Lifta" the plan proposes "will be a kind of duplication of the preserved kernel of Lifta's original houses." On the other hand, while the plan promises to preserve the buildings (the better to give the development an "authentic" feel), the plan simultaneously excludes the Palestinian presence. "The original Palestinian inhabitants are nowhere to be found in the plans," note Bronstein and architect Malkit Shoshan. "Those who created and cultivated this space, their memories of the village, their exile and longing to return are not mentioned at all. Only a deconstruction of the plan reveals how they were removed."[39]

- Recognizing that the *nakba* names an ongoing phenomenon of Palestinian dispossession, in addition to the uprooting of Palestinians in 1948, Zochrot organizes protests at the sites of Palestinian locales in Israel threatened with destruction. For example, Zochrot leads solidarity visits to contemporary sites of dispossession and destruction within Israel, such as the Bedouin town of Al-Araqib demolished by Israeli authorities in 2010.[40]

- Finally, Zochrot has brought together internally displaced Palestinians from the villages of Miska and Kafr Bir'im to meet and work with Israeli Jewish residents of kibbutzim built on the ruins of those villages to map practical strategies of return. Counter-mapping activities make memory practical by creating cartographic palimpsests in which the erased Palestinian presence is reinscribed onto the map. From these conversations Ahmad Barclay has developed a proposal for four stages of return to Miska, an "architecture composed of a dialogue among the layers of memory, erasure, and presence" that adapts and reuses remains of the ruined village.[41] Einat Manoff, meanwhile, reports how the Zochrot-sponsored dialogue group consisting of displaced Miskawis and moshav residents adopted a cartographic strategy of resistance that treated state maps as "critical frameworks open to reconsideration," within which they then mapped out practical steps for Miskawi return. The Miska group discovered that focusing on the local level, rather than on questions of the borders of future Palestinian or Israeli states, allowed them to "discuss the practical aspects of creating common space." Counter-mapping for the group became "an exercise in the practical space of utopia: we looked at the future in order to create the space for a discourse of change in the present as part of a strategy of movement through time and space in opposition to segregation and the ongoing policy of occupation."[42] These alternative cartographies developed by the Zochrot-sponsored study groups represent an example of what Israeli architects Eyal Weizman,

Sandi Hilal, and Alessandro Petti call "decolonizing architecture," a practice not of erasing the colonial landscape and colonial architecture, but instead of repurposing colonial structures so that "what the colonial order had separated and divided" will be restored to common use.[43]

Zochrot's commemorative practices are not, as Ronit Lentin accuses, simply melancholic rituals that remain silent about Palestinian refugee rights of return, compensation, and restitution.[44] Zochrot's founders also vigorously affirm the right of Palestinian refugees to return. "We support the right of return for Palestinians," insists Bronstein, "those still living in Israel-Palestine and those outside."[45] Palestinian refugee return, meanwhile, is championed by Zochrot not only for its own sake, but for the sake of Israeli Jews: "Our humanity is bound up with your right to return," Bronstein claims in an open letter to Palestinian refugees. "The day we expelled you from your land you carried a part of it [our humanity] with you. Only when you can return will we be able to restore our humanity."[46] Zochrot's logo matches this vision—a keyhole awaiting the key that has become one of the most common symbols of Palestinian refugee identity. Whereas mainstream Zionist discourse presents Palestinian refugee return as an existential threat to the Jewish character of the Israeli state, Zochrot counters that Palestinian refugee return will free Israel from its discriminatory, colonial character.[47]

Through these and other forms of counter-mapping, Zochrot names that which should be unnamable within Zionist discourse and subverts the map of empty space charted by the Zionist project by returning Palestinian places to the landscape and by creating heterotopias in which the rigid, exclusivist division between Palestinians and Israeli Jews becomes permeable, while not being completely effaced.

The way in which Zochrot's counter-mapping practices undermine and challenge the dominant cartographies established by the Israeli state and para-state institutions such as the JNF can be seen clearly in the actions it has organized at the ruins of 'Imwas.[48] Israeli troops evacuated 'Imwas and the other villages in the Latrun salient early in the 1967 war, after which they demolished the village's buildings. The bulldozers that set about destroying these three villages had already been busy at work in the mid-1960s, as Aron Shai has documented, deconstructing the remains of Palestinian villages inside Israel evacuated in 1948.[49]

Visiting the ruins of 'Imwas today takes one to Canada/Ayalon Park, a nature reserve created in the 1970s over the ruins of two villages—'Imwas and Yalu—destroyed in the wake of the 1967 Israeli conquest of the West Bank.

The Canadian Jewish community donated $15 million (Cdn.) through the JNF to plant thousands of pine and cypress trees on the remains of these villages in the Occupied West Bank. As Noga Kadman and Naama Meishar have documented, Canada Park is one of scores of Israeli national parks and nature reserves built on the ruins of Palestinian villages through the combined efforts of the Israel Lands Administration, which administers the bulk of Palestinian refugee property confiscated under the terms of the Absentee Property Law, and the JNF, which raises funds worldwide with the aims of "making the desert bloom" and of "greening Israel."[50] JNF tree-planting gradually "greened" 'Imwas' ruins, turning the area into an "Israelised" landscape.[51] An everyday visitor to the park today will encounter remains of the village, including the shrine (*maqam*) commemorating Abu Ubayda (one of Muhammad's companions), prickly-pear cactus stands that would have demarcated property boundaries, and old trees pre-dating the forest planted by the JNF. These remains stand unmarked, mute traces of and testimonies to the effaced Palestinian presence.[52]

In 2003 Zochrot began organizing return visits to the remains of 'Imwas and Yalu. One such visit featured testimony not only from Palestinian refugees from the villages but also from a teacher from a nearby kibbutz who had participated in the expulsion of 'Imwas' residents and the destruction of their homes. The razing of the village was proceeding systematically, the former soldier recalled, when his company

> came to a building with an old man inside. He told us that for him to leave would be like dying, and he preferred to die inside his home. At that moment the coin dropped. In that second I realized the significance of what I and the others were doing here. I knew that demolishing the buildings was intended to prevent the area from ever being returned to Jordan or to the Palestinians. I also knew that the destruction was revenge for Israel's defeat here in 1948. But none of that was worth destroying the life of that old man and the lives of thousands who were expelled. I demanded that my commander stop the action. They refused to listen to me, of course. We removed the old man and demolished his home. I shouldn't have done it.[53]

In addition to organizing these tours, Zochrot wrote to the JNF, the body in charge of maintaining the park and posting signs around it, asking that signs be erected in the park noting and naming the ruins of the destroyed villages. The JNF responded that it did "not deal with topics having political significance, and therefore we suggest you address your request to the appropriate official bodies."[54] Zochrot responded by posting signs of its own in Hebrew in the park, together with representatives from the displaced communities and from nearby Neve Shalom/Wahat al-Salam. A couple of days after Zochrot erected the signs, the maintenance supervisor of Canada Park called Bronstein, noting that the signs Zochrot had erected were illegal. When Bronstein observed that Canada Park, along with other parks in Israel, was cluttered with advertisements signs posted without permits, the park supervisor replied that the problem with Zochrot's signs was their political character. "And yours," Bronstein asked in turn, "those that describe the Romans, the Hasmoneans, the Byzantines, the Ottomans, but don't say a word about centuries of Palestinian settlement—they aren't political?"[55] The park supervisor was not persuaded, and had the Zochrot signs taken down. When Bronstein contacted the Jewish National Fund to inquire what had happened to the signs, JNF officials referred to the signs as "the Muslim Brotherhood signs" and insisted, in a counterfactual rewriting of history, that in any case there was nothing to memorialize, as the villages in question had not been destroyed in 1967, with its residents expelled, but had instead been abandoned in 1948.[56]

Undeterred, Zochrot proceeded to write to the Civil Administration of the Israeli military government (given the fact that the park is located in the Occupied West Bank), asking that signs be erected that mentioned the destroyed Palestinian villages. The JNF, Zochrot stressed, "hopes to educate the public about the country we live in. We believe that it is appropriate that the information provided in Canada Park, as well as that provided elsewhere, should not selectively ignore the Palestinians who have lived here for hundreds of years."[57] The Civil Administration did not reply, leading Zochrot in 2005 to initiate legal proceedings in Israel's High Court against the military government and the Jewish National Fund, arguing that failure to mention the destroyed villages was arbitrary and undermined the state's values. The legal action led the JNF to reverse its stance about erecting a sign, and after negotiations Zochrot agreed to suspend its legal action if a sign had been erected prior to the court date. The JNF and the Civil Administration then placed two signs in the park in Hebrew with the following anodyne text, scrubbed of all words such as *refugees*, *destruction*, or *occupation*:

> The villages of 'Imwas and Yalu existed in the area of the park until 1967. 'Imwas had 2,000 inhabitants, who now live in Jordan and in Ramallah. A cemetery is located next to the ruins of the village. Yalu

had 1,700 inhabitants, who now live in Jordan and Ramallah. A well and a number of cisterns can be found there.[58]

Bronstein notes that, on the one hand, the posting of the signs represented a breakthrough achievement, one that could set a precedent for other parks and nature reserves. On the other hand, he conceded, the wording of the signs was "so euphemistic that it could create the impression that the disappearance of the villages was the result of some natural evolutionary process rather than of the Zionist project of conquest."[59]

Two weeks after the signs were erected one of them was uprooted from the ground and disappeared. When Zochrot contacted the JNF to enquire what had happened, a JNF official suggested that metal thieves had taken it, an explanation rendered dubious by the fact that only three meters away another metal JNF sign about the Hasmonean period stood undisturbed.[60] The other Zochrot sign was left in place, but with the text covered over in black paint. This act of vandalism, Bronstein suggests, can be viewed as a recapitulation of the original destruction of the villages, an only partially successful erasure. "The black paint is incontrovertible evidence of the erasure of the villages, as well as erasing the fact of their erasure. Someone either doesn't want us to know what happened, or prefers that such knowledge not be exposed in a public space." "The very act of erasure leaves its traces," he notes, "and makes the reader of the sign curious to know what was deleted."[61]

RETURN VISITS AS LITURGICAL ACTIONS

Bronstein and his collaborators describe Zochrot's actions in different (yet arguably compatible) ways. As discussed above, one language Zochrot uses to talk about its work is that of cartography. Another common vocabulary Zochrot deploys to explain its work is therapeutic, with its signposting actions described as surfacing the *nakba* reality that the Zionist political body represses. Drawing on Lacanian psychoanalytical thought, Bronstein contends that the *nakba* "is a mirror that, at this stage, Israeli Jews cannot look straight at."[62] Zochrot's actions aim to foreground the "ghost" of the *nakba* that interferes and disturbs the Israeli political body "in strange, sometimes uncontrollable ways."[63] Zochrot's actions combat the repression of this *nakba* specter by speaking that which Zionist discourse silences in the Modern Hebrew created to speak only Zionist nationalism. Not surprising, then, that Zochrot's actions are often (but certainly not always) met with hostility by Israeli Jews.

The repression of the *nakba* within Israeli political life is linked, several Israeli Jewish commentators have argued, to Jewish trauma in Europe. As Ilan Gur Ze'ev has argued, "The fear of a new Holocaust and the fear of acknowledging responsibility for the *Nakbah* became inseparable."[64] Bronstein highlights the irony that through the *nakba* "the Palestinians became the Jews' successors to refugee status; they actually confiscated the refugee status from us." As an exiled people, Palestinians present Israeli Jews with a disconcerting mirror in which to see themselves and their past.[65] Zionism was to have addressed and cured the supposed disease of exile, to have provided a "land without a people for a people without a land." Such a mapping of return practically requires denial of the violence needed to make the mapped future a reality. As Bronstein explains, "Constructing the *Nakba* as a 'non-event' goes along with the common Zionist notion that 'a people without a land returned to a land without a people.'"[66] To acknowledge that Zionism created a new exile is to arouse fears that Jewish exile has not been overcome and that the landed security Zionism was to have guaranteed is tenuous. "The Zionist subject stands on somewhat shaky ground," Bronstein emphasizes. "It established itself by means of a violent process that is denied as an event that did not happen. When the ghostly spirit of this process is risen (by Zochrot, for example), it triggers astonishment and anger."[67]

Israeli anthropologist Dan Rabinowitz has observed "a tendency within mainstream Zionism to evaluate its own territorial advent as tentative and fragile."[68] Rabinowitz continues, saying that "mixed settlement" (of Palestinians and Israeli Jews) on territory viewed by Israeli Jews as "Judaized" becomes "abominable for Israelis as it signifies the ultimate evil they dread so deeply: the deterioration of collective achievements through rapid dissolution of control over the territory."[69] Bronstein concurs, stating that "the relationship of the Jews in Israel to the Palestinian refugees is founded on this axis between closeness and the sense of threat."[70] Zochrot's signposting actions thus not only stoke Israeli Jewish fears by evoking memories of Jewish exile in Europe and the Holocaust through the mirror of Palestinian exile, but also by embodying, if only for a fleeting moment, a binational reality in a purportedly purely Jewish space. By confronting the repressed *nakba* specter, Bronstein argues, Israeli Jews can also confront the fears aroused by memories of the Holocaust and of binational co-presence with Palestinians, thus freeing them "from the automatic violence and/or the victimhood that Israeli Jews are taught to feel."[71] With such freedom will come the recognition that "the Israeli Jews and the refugee belong here," with Palestinians and Israelis often sharing a sense of belonging to "the very same geographical site."[72]

Critical cartography as therapeutic practice, meanwhile, is not an end in itself for Zochrot, but is for the sake of a future reconciliation. Accordingly, Zochrot activists also often depict their actions in testimonial language, with the sharing of testimonies by internally displaced Palestinians and the recognition of those testimonies by Israeli Jews functioning as a small-scale Palestinian-Israeli version of the South African Truth and Reconciliation Commission, with injustices named and acknowledged and forward-looking joint actions of commemoration taken. Bronstein observes that during these visits "we organize the time and space for Palestinians to tell their stories in their own places of origin. Usually, but not always, their reaction is positive, with lots of emotions reacting to all the Israelis and Jews who want to hear their stories. Usually, this acknowledgement is accepted as a really great experience, a healing experience in a way—for both sides."[73]

Understood as historical truth-telling within a broader effort at reconciliation, Zochrot's mapping actions enact in concrete fashion Edward Said's call for Palestinians and Israeli Jews to "confront each's experience in light of the other" for the sake of "reconciliation."[74] Ilan Pappé makes the link between Zochrot and Said, claiming that Zochrot's signposting actions embody Said's proposal that rememberings of the *nakba* be creatively situated in the context of Palestinian-Israeli Jewish reconciliation.[75] For Palestinians subjected to dispossession and other forms of violence carried out by the Israeli state, political acts of commemoration are forms of protest that demand acknowledgment from the state.[76] In the face of the state's silence, a civil society organization like Zochrot offers uprooted Palestinians acknowledgment, response, and commitment to some form of resolution. While such actions do not resolve Palestinian refugee claims, they present a foretaste of how acknowledgment of the *nakba* and refugee return will necessarily be part of such a resolution.[77]

Interpretations of Zochrot's mapping actions as therapeutic or testimonial capture some dimensions of Zochrot's work. Yet I would suggest that understanding Zochrot's memory performances as *liturgical* actions will shed light on some aspects of Zochrot's work not explained by therapeutic or testimonial language. Specifically, an account of Zochrot's memory mappings as liturgical will complicate and rebut critiques of memory discourse that assume that memory actions are necessarily bound to reactionary politics. Kerwin Lee Klein has vigorously criticized the "religious" character of much memory discourse, with its attempt "to re-enchant our relation to the world and pour presence back into the past" and its "celebration of a new ritualism under the cover of historical skepticism."[78] If one accepts Klein's reading of memory work, Palestinian refugee memory production and the memorial actions of a group like Zochrot are captive to a restorationist imagination, reflecting atavistic attempts to recapture and recreate a pristine vision of the remembered past. However, I contend that Klein's critique betrays an impoverished understanding of the "religious." While I agree with Klein that there is something "religious"—in the sense of "liturgical"—about Zochrot's memory performances, those actions are not "religious" in the narrow sense presented by Klein, as an atavistic and reactionary attempt to replicate the past, to embody the past's presence in the present. Instead, as liturgical actions, Zochrot's counter-mapping activities are much more directed toward the future, pointing beyond themselves to a coming future that disrupts nationalist topologies with the promise of heterogeneous spaces.

Bronstein contends that "posting signs at villages integrates the past, present, and future."[79] As such, I would argue, these actions might properly be called *liturgical*, in that present-day performed memories of the past point toward a hope and vision for the future. While memory discourses and practices may well often be bound up with primitivist, nationalist, and essentialist construals of identity, they need not be. Zochrot's memory performances are not reactionary, but instead disrupt nationalist essentialisms by creating binational spaces in which, for a fleeting moment, the violent conjunction of demographic hegemony and territorial control no longer holds sway, leaving traces and animating hopes for a binational Palestinian-Israeli future of mutuality and equality.

A brief examination of Vincent Lloyd's account of liturgy as a theopolitical strategy will help to illuminate why Zochrot's counter-mapping performances can be fruitfully designated as liturgical. For Lloyd, liturgy "presents a means of refusing the hegemony of the visible, of refusing to be limited by the options that present themselves."[80] Liturgy is a "practice that does not aspire to match norms," a practice that, when employed, "has the potential to alter a certain set of norms."[81] This liturgical practice, Lloyd explains, must be differentiated from ritual practice. "Ritual reinforces social norms," argues Lloyd, "and calling something a ritual is a bid to reinforce particular norms. In contrast, *liturgy* refers to moments when it is as if social norms do not hold sway, and these movements may inflect the social norms that do hold sway."[82] By creating a "space where social norms are suspended," liturgy loosens the always already present pull that social norms have on us, thereby broadening our political imaginations.[83]

Liturgical practices, as defined by Lloyd, need not deploy explicitly "religious" or "theological" language. To be sure, some liturgical practices

Lloyd cites would clearly appear to be religious, such as the Sebastian Acevedo Movement in Chile that held regular public celebrations of the Eucharist in order to call attention to persons who had been "disappeared" by the Pinochet regime. By highlighting this example, Lloyd's definition of liturgy as protest might seem to converge with William Cavanaugh's description of liturgy as protest and protest as liturgy in his study of the Sebastian Acevedo Movement. One of the participants in the Chilean protests articulated a rationale for joining in the liturgical protest that certainly fits Lloyd's definition of "refusing the hegemony of the visible": "They can beat us or attack with water and gases, but there we are to anticipate this new society."[84] Lloyd's account of liturgy, however, is broader than Cavanaugh's, broad enough to encompass seemingly "secular" actions as the annual bicycle protests staged by the Critical Mass movement. Both the Sebastian Acevedo Movement and Critical Mass have created spaces in which particular norms (silence in the face of an oppressive regime; confining the Eucharist to church buildings; being trapped in the typical congestion of vehicular traffic) are upended through specific practices (celebrating the Eucharist in public spaces; riding bikes *en masse* to provide a counterweight to car traffic) that in turn broaden political imaginations. In so doing, both movements, Lloyd insists, "understand themselves as offering a momentary glimpse of what an alternative society might look like."[85]

Lloyd recognizes that liturgical theologians like William Cavanaugh, Aidan Kavanagh, and Geoffrey Wainwright "attribute the authority of liturgy to its status as a foretaste of the world to come," something that Lloyd rejects as a "supersessionist" conviction that the modern world needs to be "redeemed" by a coming future.[86] So, for example, Philip Sheldrake presents the Eucharist as "a practice of resistance to any attempt to homogenize human place," a practice carried out against an eschatological horizon "that judges radically all human systems of exclusion." Viewed from this angle, the Eucharist "makes space for a new history that tells a different story beyond the selectivities of tribalism or sectarianism," subverts all topologies that maintain "hard boundaries between inside and outside, centre and periphery," and proleptically anticipates a new future.[87] Just as Bronstein points to the ghost of the *nakba* that haunts the Israeli Jewish political landscape, so Sheldrake observes that those whom "we prefer to exclude from communion with us in the world of public place are already uncomfortable ghosts at our eucharistic feastings": the work of the eucharistic liturgy is to anticipate in the present a future when such exclusions will be no more.[88] Lloyd acknowledges that the eschatological horizon animating the liturgical political theology of someone like Sheldrake is not present in, say, the protest rallies organized by Critical Mass, yet he nevertheless contends that the description of liturgy offering a foretaste of a coming future can be "bracketed as a rhetorical flourish," leaving the political theorist with a practice that expands political horizons by momentarily upending social norms.[89]

A Christian theologian may well interpret Zochrot's signposting within an eschatological horizon, as proleptically anticipating and embodying in the present a coming future—and that is indeed how I understand Zochrot's actions. That the majority of Zochrot activists would not use theological language to describe their own actions and would not view their work within an eschatological framework does not detract from how Zochrot's cartographic practices create spaces in which Israel's ethnocratic norms of separation and dispossession do not, at least for a moment, hold sway, and are thus liturgical in Lloyd's sense. Through posting bilingual signs at the ruins of destroyed Palestinian villages, Zochrot works to broaden the political imaginations of those who participate in and witness its performances. By embodying binational places of mutuality, Zochrot's actions expand political horizons, demonstrating that the current binational reality of exclusion and dispossession can be transformed into a binational reality of equality and co-presence.

THE EXILIC VIGIL AGAINST DROMOCRATIC ETHNOCRACY

Zochrot's counter-mapping actions can therefore be identified as liturgical in the sense advanced by Lloyd. More specifically, I would argue that Zochrot's cartographic performances can be promisingly interpreted as a specific type of liturgical action, namely, as *exilic vigils*. Drawing on the work of the Roman Catholic theologian Jean-Yves Lacoste, Lloyd defines the vigil as "a practice that one can bring about but cannot determine the outcome of."[90] A closer examination of Lacoste's discussion of liturgy and vigil will illuminate my decision to call Zochrot's spatial protests exilic vigils.

Human beings, according to Lacoste, seek to possess, appropriate, and grasp place, yet liturgy "exceeds being-in-the-world and the relation to the earth."[91] Even as I seek to possess a place and to define it as mine, "the world constantly indicates the limit of every 'here' by indicating the 'there' beyond it."[92] Liturgy "opens up a space in the world where appropriation loses its importance," with "eschatological anticipation" subverting the topological insistence that persons fundamentally belong to particular places.[93] Through liturgical practices, the human being discovers that she is not fundamentally defined by place, but that she is at root a "foreigner" (or exile), even though she "neither comes from elsewhere nor is going anywhere else."[94] As a foreigner dwelling amidst places she would grasp or attempt to possess, the human being discovers that "only the Kingdom" can be a suitable homeland and that against that eschatological horizon one can "neither have anything nor can take possession of anything."[95]

The community gathered in liturgical celebration (the church) thus embodies a particular spatial politics, living within the world and amidst particular places, yet foreign, or in exile, to those places. The church, explains Lacoste, "does not thus put itself forward as a space established for definitive existence, and its narthex does not separate the unhappiness of history from the happiness of the *eschaton*. It puts itself forward as something else: the place of a fragile anticipation."[96] The liturgy the church celebrates "thwarts all the laws of topology; place would no longer be defined in terms of inherence, or more precisely, inherence would define man only secondarily. Man could 'be in a place' ['*avoir lieu*'] without his being-in-the-world providing the coordinates of this place, which is thinkable evidently only on account of a grace that suspends the authority the world exercises over our being."[97] Liturgy as exilic vigil, as a work in which participants come to understand themselves as not completely determined by ties to particular locations, but rather as foreigners and exiles in the places in which they dwell, thus suggests a "redefinition of place" not as "being-there but as being-toward."[98] This redefinition of place does not, it should be stressed, mean rootlessness or an escape from place, but a new way of dwelling in place.

Liturgy upends any notion of place as that which can be grasped and fully possessed, offering instead an eschatological understanding of place as the coming, future site of new relations. The biblical narrative of the encounter of two disciples with the risen Jesus as they walk together on the road to Emmaus (Luke 24:13-35) unfolds this understanding of place as "being-toward." The two disciples walking toward Emmaus are grieving and perplexed, mourning Jesus' death by crucifixion only a few days before, and bewildered by reports that Jesus' tomb was empty and that some disciples had encountered him. As they walk, they are joined by Jesus, who appears as a stranger to them. They continue on their journey, with Jesus commenting upon the scriptures and explaining his death to them according to scriptural prophecy. Upon arrival at Emmaus, the two disciples insist that the stranger whom they still do not recognize as Jesus stay and have supper with them. Then, as they sit down and Jesus breaks bread with them, the disciples' eyes are opened; they recognize the stranger as Jesus, and he then vanishes from their sight.

The disciples' encounter with Jesus, the stranger, on the road to Emmaus represents an exilic vigil. Their breaking of bread together takes place within a context of (admittedly confused and bewildered) eschatological anticipation, and it is as the bread is broken that Jesus, whose memories had been haunting the disciples' conversation, becomes present to the disciples' sight. Yet even as the disciples recognize the stranger as Jesus, the one whom they had hoped would be "the one to redeem Israel" (Luke 24:21), he vanishes from their sight. The disciples had anticipated a messiah who would redeem Israel's landed existence, a messiah who would solidify and defend the people Israel's inherence, or "being-there," in the land. Yet the risen Jesus does not submit himself to their grasp and control, but disappears, going on as he was going to do before the disciples entreated him to eat with them. Jesus' vanishing, his going on, reflects how place has now been reconfigured in eschatological perspective in terms of "being-toward," rather than "being-there." Jesus' vanishing from the disciples' sight underscores that from now on the disciples' calling is not so much to "see" Jesus as to "show" Jesus as they observe exilic vigils. In such vigils they break bread with strangers; land and particular places become significant as sites in which the "being-toward" of a future of communion and reconciliation might be unveiled.[99] This future communion cannot be controlled or determined and will always, short of the *eschaton*, remain incomplete—yet the exilic vigils held in our present reality point toward and offer foretastes of that future communion.

The memory performances of Zochrot are thus not only *liturgical* actions, as defined by Lloyd, but can also be understood to be exilic vigils, as presented by Lloyd in conversation with Lacoste. The return visits organized by Zochrot, including the return visits to 'Imwas/Emmaus, need not be solely about the "being-there" of inherence, the assertion of Palestinian presence in a particular place (important as that is in the face of the erasure of the Palestinian landscape), but should much more fundamentally be understood to be about the "being toward" of that place, with place so reconfigured gesturing in hopeful anticipation toward a future of heterogeneous places, a future of binational equality and mutuality to overcome the present ethnocratic regime of inequality and dispossession marked by walls, electrified fences, checkpoints, land confiscations, and biometric passcards. Like the disciples on the road to Emmaus, Israeli Jews and Palestinians are often prevented from recognizing the promise of a binational future because the separatist and exclusivist assumptions grounding nationalist cartographies "leave them petrified within a matrix of irrefutable prejudices."[100] Zochrot's exilic vigils work to suspend these norms shaping the nationalist mapping of space, allowing new political visions shaped by the "being-toward" of place to emerge.

As exilic vigils, Zochrot's counter-mapping actions operate according to a different sense of time than does the Israeli regime that maps and enforces ethnocratic separations. As several architectural and political theorists have argued, the Israeli ethnocratic regime is an example of what the French theorist Paul Virilio has called "dromocracy," a regime in which the rule of speed attains strategic value as a means of territorial control.[101] Electrified fences that can trigger rapid response by Israeli jeeps and tanks, aerial drones that police the air, the "wall and tower" architecture of Israeli colonies, and checkpoints and roadblocks that restrict and reroute Palestinian movement all reflect Israeli control over time.[102] To the extent that the Occupied Palestinian Territories can be viewed as being subject to a perpetual state of emergency, this can be traced to Israeli control over time. As Virilio observes, "the state of emergency, the age of intensiveness, is linked to the primacy of speed."[103] Building on Virilio's notion of dromocracy, John Collins explains that it is not "just speed that produces confinement; rather, the one whose hand is on the throttle, and who has the option of speeding things up or slowing things down at will, is the one who controls confinement."[104] Israel's weaponizing of time gives it "the ability to regulate the pace of daily life in the battlespace," permitting it to act "at times of its own choosing, while Palestinians are made to wait . . . and wait . . . and wait."[105]

In the face of the Israeli dromocratic regime, a politicizing of speed and time is required in order to resist its rule. Forms of Palestinian resistance like suicide bombing that engage "the Israeli state on the level of the dromos" are bound to fail.[106] Virilio warns against an arms race for the control of time and speed: what is needed is disarmament as deceleration, a defusing of "the race toward the end."[107] Dromocracy must be opposed by another conception of time—for example, by the politics of patient anticipation advanced by Yoder, a patience born out of eschatological anticipation. Precisely such an alternative conception of time is offered by the exilic vigils conducted by Zochrot.[108] Within the colonized landscape, Zochrot return visits-as-exilic vigils embody what Virilio (and Said) calls *counter-habitation*, an exilic existence within public spaces.[109] These exilic vigils bracket the spatial norms of separation enforced by Israeli ethnocracy, opening up new political possibilities by mapping binational landscapes that "transgress spaces of segregation."[110] By "presencing the past in order to create the possibility for a different kind of participation and cooperation in the future," Zochrot's exilic vigils create fragile and tenuous sites of counter-habitation. Zochrot's return visits and the Palestinian refugee return for which it advocates are thus not about "a nostalgic, impossible return that restores everything to its original location" (and thus not about a form of return tied, in Lacoste's terms, to an understanding of place as inherence, or "being-there").[111] Rather, Palestinian refugee return, if it is not to be a mirror of Zionist return, must reconfigure place as "being-toward" a future in which Palestinians and Israeli Jews might discover one another as exiles in the land, seeking refuge with one another. Return visits as exilic vigils thus take place within an eschatological horizon of a coming community of mutual co-presence. Or, put another way, return visits as mappings and remembrances of the horrors of the *nakba* that pile up at the feet of the angel of history unfold within the "time of the now," which "is shot through with chips of Messianic time."[112] Suspending the norms of the present ethnocratic rule, Zochrot's exilic vigils thus allow participants to glimpse the binational reality that, in the words of Udi Aloni, is "always already."[113]

MAPPING THE FUTURE: THE PROMISE OF PALIMPSESTS

To describe return journeys as exilic vigils is to understand return not as the replication of a lost past or the reclaiming of a pristine, homogeneous space for the rebirth or revitalization of the nation, but rather as an acceptance of particular places as always already heterogeneous in character and an embrace of the promise such places hold for a future politics of co-presence. Colonial apparatuses—such as the JNF and the Israel Lands Authority—have unwittingly created palimpsests across the colonized landscape, with efforts to efface traces of prior habitation and to superimpose a new colonial landscape proving incomplete and ineffective, "because the underlying picture seeps through."[114] Palestinians, like other colonized peoples, Susan Slyomovics explains, "have developed the capacity to see palimpsests," to identify the Palestinian landscape covered over by the Israeli Jewish landscape through interpretation of plants and ruins.[115]

Zochrot's counter-mapping actions combat the colonial aphasia that prevents Israeli Jews from seeing the landscape as a palimpsest. Revealing the landscape to be a palimpsest is to reveal the landscape as a site of "contentious experience."[116] As such, Zochrot's performances of alternative cartographies are often initially experienced as threats by the Israeli Jewish public. Given the partisan political assumption that only one "time map" (to use Eviatar Zerubavel's felicitous expression) can hold sway, Zochrot's initiatives to highlight how the Zionist time map has covered over the Palestinian time map register as a wholesale delegitimizing of the Israeli Jewish map. Such a reaction relies on the assumption that there can only be one true map: the Palestinian map bleeding through the Israeli Jewish map is thus the "true map," and so the lines and the marks of the Israeli Jewish map must be scraped away to reveal the real, original territory.[117] Yet Zerubavel contests this assumption, insisting on the need to cultivate "a pronouncedly multiperspectival" outlook that acknowledges that only by reading multiple time maps *together* can one appreciate the "inevitably multilayered, multifaceted social topography of the past."[118]

While Zerubavel's focus is on charting richer and denser time maps of past landscapes, my aim throughout this study has been on what possible futures cartographies of return open up: In the palimpsest-style maps created by Salman Abu-Sitta or by the Committee for the Uprooted of Kafr Bir'im, do we find a cartographic call to arms, a roadmap for restoring the precolonial landscape and effacing the colonial map, or might we instead find maps of exilic vigils that unveil and embrace the always already pluralized landscape? Bir'imite cartographies and Zochrot's counter-mappings, I have argued, suggest that cartography need not be bound to the homogeneous logic of colonialist and nationalist mapping, but can instead reflect and guide patient journeys into exilic forms of landedness and political organization. In this concluding section, I reflect on what possible futures a theopolitics of exilic vigils might uncover for Palestinians and Israelis.

The musings of the Italian philosopher Giorgio Agamben on the figure of the refugee are particularly suggestive of a politics of exile in which exile is not only a state to be overcome and remedied but also a signpost pointing to new political forms.[119] Taking Hannah Arendt's compact meditation on the significance of mass refugee movements for contemporary politics as his starting point, Agamben contends that "the refugee is perhaps the only thinkable figure for the people of our time and the only category in which one may see today—at least until the process of dissolution of the nation-state and of its sovereignty has achieved its completion—the forms and limits of a coming political community."[120] The refugee, according to Agamben, represents "a disquieting element in the order of the nation-state," in that "by breaking the identity between the human and the citizen and that between nativity and nationality, it brings the originary fiction of sovereignty to crisis."[121] The intrusion of the refugee disrupts the nationalist attempt to collapse nation and territory into one another. The refugee thus stands either as a threat or as the harbinger of a new form of political community (or both: the new form of political community for which the refugee is a harbinger is a threat to the post-Westphalian order of nation-states). For Agamben, it is clearly the latter, as the refugee confronts nation-states with the necessity of finding "the courage to question the very principle of the inscription of nativity as well as the trinity of state-nation-territory that is founded on that principle" and of discovering new political modes of organization.[122]

Agamben's writings on the concrete shape of such new political communities are for the most part elusive and cryptic.[123] His vision begins to achieve specificity, however, in his discussion of Jerusalem and Israel-Palestine. Agamben begins by noting that "one of the options taken into consideration for solving the problem of Jerusalem is that it become—simultaneously and without any territorial partition—the capital of two different states." Taken by itself, this observation might initially seem compatible with visions of a two-state solution to the Palestinian-Israeli conflict that remain tied to nationalist politics: while Jerusalem might be shared by the Palestinian and Israeli states, the underlying logic of separate nation-states would remain uncontested. However, Agamben then proceeds to extrapolate from the proposal of a shared, undivided Jerusalem to a broader vision of Israel-Palestine shaped by what he calls "the paradoxical condition of reciprocal extraterritoriality (or, better yet, aterritoriality)."[124] In the case of Israel-Palestine, such a politics of reciprocal extraterritoriality would represent an abandonment of political programs wedded to the form of the nation-state (be they mainstream Zionist or Palestinian nationalist), with their drive to secure demographic hegemony or even exclusivity within policed borders, programs that in Israel-Palestine have, through a series of legal and physical exclusions, reduced Palestinian existence to "bare life."[125] An Israel-Palestine shaped by the politics of reciprocal extraterritoriality would be a binational polity, a polity that does not dissolve communal identities but in which Palestinians and Israelis come to understand themselves as living as refugees within the land, seeking refuge with one another. "Instead of two national states separated by uncertain and threatening boundaries," Agamben explains, "one could imagine two political communities dwelling in the same region and in exodus one into the other, divided from each other by a series of reciprocal extraterritorialities, in which the guiding concept would no longer be the *ius* [right] of the citizen but rather the *refugium* [refuge] of the individual."[126]

Such a politics of reciprocal extraterritoriality acts to "perforate" "homogeneous national territories," turning them into spaces in which all who dwell within them stand "in a position of exodus or refuge" into one other.[127] In the case of Israel-Palestine, such perforation means the disruption of geographies of exclusivist possession, and the uncovering of a binational geography shaped by exile. Taking up Arendt's description of refugees as "the vanguard of their people," Agamben applies the phrase to the 425 Palestinians whom Israel expelled to the hills of southern Lebanon in December 1992. These displaced persons represent a "vanguard" not necessarily or not merely in the sense that they might form the originary nucleus of a future national state, or in the sense that they might solve the Palestinian question in a way just as insufficient as the way in which Israel has solved the Jewish question. Rather, the no-man's-land in which they are refugees has already started from this very moment to act back onto the territory of the state of Israel by perforating it and altering it in such a way that the image of that snowy mountain has become more internal to it than any other region of Eretz Israel. Only in a world in which the spaces of states have been thus perforated and topologically deformed and in which the citizen has been able to recognize the refugee that he or she is—only in such a world is the political survival of humankind today thinkable.[128]

Agamben's argument here can and should be fruitfully extended to all Palestinian refugees and internally displaced persons. While Palestinian refugee return is often presented as a mirror to Zionist return, such return, Agamben emphasizes, would "solve the Palestinian question in a way just as insufficient as the way in which Israel has solved the Jewish question." But Palestinian return from the "nonplace" of the refugee camp does not have to be a restorationist retrieval of place, but can instead be a return to a "perforated and topologically deformed" place that subverts the circumscribed and exclusivist logic of the nation-state, with return shaped by exile and with all persons and communities in the land discovering themselves as refugees who seek refuge in one another.[129]

Agamben's brief proposal for a future, shared Israel-Palestine marked by "reciprocal extraterritorialities" in which the rigid boundaries of the nation-state are broken down has been fleshed out in greater detail in parallel efforts by Palestinian and Israeli Jewish political theorists. "While the territorial image rests on the longing for wholeness, always attained through establishing borders and erecting fences, the exterritorial image consists of differences that are not defined through a binary," argue Maayan Amir, Ruti Sela, and Raji Bathish.[130] Palestinians and Israeli Jews must relinquish fantasies of homogeneous space where "territory presents itself as a complete and ostensibly natural continuum," accepting instead the fragmented and fluid nature of place.[131] The failed peace processes of the past two (and more) decades have been predicated upon politics of separation and "modernist nation-state logic."[132] Reciprocal extraterritoriality as a model will push for new models of shared life. Sari Hanafi, for example, proposes the formation of a confederation between Israel and

Palestine as "two extraterritorial nation-states, with Jerusalem as their shared capital, contemporaneously forming two different states without a territorial division," with "flexible borders, flexible citizenship, and some kind of separation between nation and state" marking this polity.[133] David Newman offers a similar vision to Hanafi's, stressing the importance of "more permeable, more inclusive" borders of national identity, with a delinking of rigid ties among nation, state, and territory, while also leaving room for the acknowledgment of differences between (and within) Palestinian and Israeli national identities.[134] Tired efforts at partition, efforts that monitor and enforce separations, must give way to practices that foster, create, and celebrate shared places, places in which Palestinians and Israeli Jews might find refuge with one another (while not erasing differences between them).[135]

Nurturing this politics of shared places that affirms co-presence while not effacing distinctions between Palestinians and Israeli Jews (as unitary, "state-of-all-its-citizens" proposals threaten to do) calls for a revised understanding of sovereignty and self-determination. Political theorist Iris Marion Young offers such a revision, opposing self-determination as "nondomination" to standard accounts of self-determination as "noninterference." Self-determination as nondomination, Young explains, implies "relationships between self-determining units and the joint regulation of such relationships," a form of "federalism as a mode of being together with other self-determining units," with federal relations as "local, plural, and horizontal."[136]

Through its counter-mapping actions, Zochrot unveils the always already heterogeneous nature of the land and its places. Its alternative cartographic performances, or what I have termed exilic vigils, embody in the present a foretaste of a coming politics that embraces binationalism as a promise rather than as a threat. Zochrot's mapping practices thus reveal that return need not be about grasping land and erecting and defending the rigid borders of the nation-state, but that return can instead be a form of living restlessly within the land. By coming to understand themselves as exilic communities, Palestinians and Israeli Jews might in turn seek the peace of the shared communities in which they dwell—and by building the city (and the village) for one another, Palestinians and Israeli Jews truly return. Zochrot's counter-mapping performs and heralds a form of return shaped by a coming future that promises to reconfigure a landscape torn apart by war and the violence of partition, a return that is both about the concrete realities of how to live together in the same land without physical and legal walls that uproot and exclude and about liturgical anticipation. The current geography of Palestine-Israel is scarred by the walls and fences of partition and the violence upon which such strategies of separation inevitably depend. Zochrot's performative mappings—like the cartographic performances of Bir'imites pressing for return to their village—embody and gesture toward a political theology for a shared future, a political theology for a binational future of Palestinian-Israeli mutuality in the land that replaces today's warped binationalism of violent partition. Such a political theology promises that while "the place itself"—the remembered homes and villages of Palestinian refugees like Taha Muhammad Ali, Edward Said, and Elias Chacour—can never be recovered in its fullness, the places of Palestine-Israel nevertheless carry traces of the erased past, traces that gesture toward new possibilities of shared existence.

Notes

1. Udi Aloni, *What Does a Jew Want? On Binationalism and Other Specters* (New York: Columbia University Press, 2011), 13.

2. Michel de Certeau, *The Practice of Everyday Life*, 3rd edition (Berkeley: University of California Press, 2011), 108.

3. Other locations identified by tradition and archaeologists as possible locations for the biblical Emmaus are al-Qubeibeh (also in the West Bank); Abu Ghosh (a Palestinian town inside of Israel—and the only Palestinian town or village in the corridor leading up to Jerusalem not depopulated in 1948, because of an alliance the Abu Ghosh clan had made with Zionist forces); and the ruins of Colonia on the Kiryat Yearim ridge route on the road up to Jerusalem. For a poignant account of the last Christian family in al-Qubeibeh, see Charles Sennott, *The Body and the Blood: The Holy Land at the Turn of a New Millennium, A Reporter's Journey* (New York: PublicAffairs, 2001), chapter 15.

4. Zali Gurevitch, "The Double Site of Israel," in *Grasping Land: Space and Place in Contemporary Israeli Discourse and Experience*, ed. Eyal Ben-Ari and Yoram Bilu (Albany: State University of New York, 1997), 203–16.

5. Eitan Bronstein, *Studying the Nakba and Reconstructing Space in the Palestinian Village of Lifta* (Florence: European University Institute, 2005), 11.

6. For more on the community of Neve Shalom/Wahat as-Salam, see www.nswas.org.

7. Meron Benvenisti, *Sacred Landscape: The Buried History of the Holy Land since 1948* (Berkeley: University of California Press, 2000), 339.

8. For a study of how particular naming choices on maps assert ownership and control (and provoke counter-namings and counter-claims), see Mark Monmonier, *From Squaw Tit to Whorehouse Meadow: How Maps Name, Claim, and Inflame* (Chicago: University of Chicago Press, 2006).

9. See Raz Kletter, *Just Past? The Making of Israeli Archaeology* (London: Equinox, 2005) and Nadia Abu al-Haj, *Facts on the Ground: Archaeological Practice and Territorial Self-Fashioning in Israel* (Chicago: University of Chicago Press, 2001).

10. Benvenisti, *Sacred Landscape*, 1.

11. Hassan Jabareen, "The Future of Arab Citizenship in Israel: Jewish-Zionist Time in a Place with no Palestinian Memory," *Hagar: International Social Science Review* 4, no. 1–2 (2003): 113–19.

12. Rebecca L. Stein, "The Oslo Process, Israeli Popular Culture, and the Remaking of National Space," in *The Struggle for Sovereignty: Palestine and Israel, 1993–2005*, ed. Joel Beinin and Rebecca L. Stein (Stanford: Stanford University Press, 2006), 236. As noted in chapter 2, the

Zionist construction of Israel as a nation like other (European) nations not only displaces Palestinians, but also marginalizes *mizrahim* (i.e., Jews from Arab countries).

13. Susan Slyomovics, *The Object of Memory: Arab and Jew Narrate the Palestinian Village* (Philadelphia: University of Pennsylvania Press, 1998), 52.

14. See http://afsc.org/story/eitan-bronstein.

15. Ann Laura Stoler, quoted in Ariella Azoulay, *From Palestine to Israel: A Photographic Record of Destruction and State Formation, 1947–1950* (London: Pluto, 2011), 14. See also Ann Laura Stoler, "Colonial Aphasia: Race and Disabled Histories in France," *Public Culture* 23, no. 1 (2011): 121–56.

16. Eitan Bronstein, "The *Nakba* in Hebrew: Israeli-Jewish Awareness of the Palestinian Catastrophe and Internal Refugees," in *Catastrophe Remembered: Palestine, Israel and the Internal Refugees*, ed. Nur Masalha (London: Zed, 2005), 214–41. See also Azoulay, *From Palestine to Israel*, 14–15 and her argument that the *nakba* should be understood as a catastrophe for Israeli Jews as well as for Palestinians.

17. Quoted in Meera Shah, "'A Different Kind of Memory': An Interview with Zochrot," *Middle East Report* 244 (Fall 2007): 35. See also Eitan Bronstein, "The Nakba in Hebrew," 221.

18. Doreen Massey, *Space, Place, and Gender* (Minneapolis: University of Minnesota Press, 1994), 168. For Massey, accounts of place in terms of "the security of boundaries" and the "defensive and counterpositional definition of identity" that such boundaries aim to secure are "culturally masculine" (7). This claim does not depend on any notion of an essentialist account of gender. One can recognize gender as fluid and constructed, even as one observes how nationalist attempts to shore up identity through the policing of boundaries against others regularly present themselves using the language of masculinity.

19. Ibid., 168.

20. Quoted in Meera Shah, "'A Different Kind of Memory,'" 37.

21. For a journalistic account of Zochrot's earliest signposting actions, see Aviv Lavie, "Right of Remembrance," *Haaretz Magazine*, 12 August 2004, 6–8.

22. See also Lila Abu-Lughod, "Return to Half-Ruins: Memory, Postmemory, and Living History in Palestine," in *Nakba: Palestine, 1948, and the Claims of Memory*, ed. Ahmad H. Sa'di and Lila Abu-Lughod (New York: Columbia University Press, 2007), 77–104.

23. Having the internally displaced Palestinians host the visiting Zochrot group is one way that Zochrot seeks to address the power imbalance in mixed groups between Israeli Jews, on the one hand, and Palestinians from inside Israel, on the other. For a discussion of the power of hospitality in the Palestinian-Israeli conflict, see Rabinowitz, "In and Out of Territory," in *Grasping Land*, ed. Ben-Ari and Bilu, 195.

24. Electronic versions of the nearly fifty village memory books produced by Zochrot can be downloaded at http://www.zochrot.org/.

25. The stories told by the internally displaced participants are often interactive, with their narratives becoming "more tangible through the encounter with the relics—stone fences still erect, fruit trees, graveyards, or remnants of houses." Efrat Ben-Ze'ev, "Transmission and Transformation: The Palestinian Second Generation and the Commemoration of the Homeland," in *Homelands and Diasporas: Holy Lands and Other Places*, ed. André Levy and Alex Weingrod (Stanford: Stanford University Press, 2005), 123.

26. Maoz Azaryahu and Rebecca Kook, "Mapping the Nation: Street Names and Arab-Palestinian Identity: Three Case Studies," *Nations and Nationalism* 8, no. 2 (2002): 195–213.

27. Ibid., 195.

28. Pierre Nora, "Between Memory and History: Les Lieux de Mémoir," *Representations* 26 (Spring 1989): 19.

29. For a discussion of the spatial character of protests in "mixed" cities inside Israel, see Haim Yacobi, "In-Between Surveillance and Spatial Protest: The Production of Space of the 'Mixed City' of Lod," *Surveillance and Society* 2, no. 1 (2004): 55.

30. Eitan Bronstein, "The *Nakba* in Hebrew," 237. For Foucault on heterotopias, see Foucault, "Of Other Spaces," *Diacritics* 16, no. 1 (Spring 1986): 22–27.

31. Maribel Casas-Cortes and Sebastian Cobarrubias, "Drawing Escape Tunnels through Borders: Cartographic Experiments by European Social Movements," in *Atlas of Radical Cartography*, ed. Alexis Bhagat and Lize Model (New York: Journal of Aesthetics and Protest, 2008), 51–68.

32. The Hebrew version of the database is available at http://www.zochrot.org/top/מקומות.

33. The Zochrot website includes Arabic and English versions of the Hebrew-language database, but they are less extensive.

34. See http://www.zochrot.org/en/content/remembering-al-ras-al-ahmar.

35. For "We're on the Map" instructions in Hebrew, see http://www.zochrot.org/content/אנחנו-על-המפה. Zochrot activists attempted to carry out this mapping action on Israeli Independence Day on April 25, 2012, but found their office building in the heart of Tel Aviv surrounded by police who kept them barricaded in the building for hours. The police also arrested some activists who began reading the names of destroyed villages. See http://www.haaretz.com/news/national/israeli-left-wing-activists-held-indoors-by-police-during-independence-day-event-1.426715.

36. Bronstein, *Studying the* Nakba, 11.

37. For links to the Hebrew curriculum, see http://www.zochrot.org/menu/זכרות/חינוך.

38. See, for example, http://www.zochrot.org/en/blog/דה-קולונייזר/learning-group-nakba-stopped-twice-continues-underground.

39. Eitan Bronstein and Malkit Shoshan, "Reinventing Lifta," *Monu* 4 (2006): 68. See also Bronstein, *Studying the* Nakba.

40. Zochrot concurs with Salman Abu-Sitta that the *nakba* names a deliberate process that continues without abatement today. Abu-Sitta, "Un Pays Aboli de la Carte," in *Le Droit au Retour: Le Problème des Réfugiés Palestiniens*, ed. Farouk Mardam-Bey and Elias Sanbar (Arles: Actes Sud, 2002), 101.

41. Ahmad Barclay, "Exile and Return to Miska," *Sedek: A Journal of the Ongoing Nakba* 6 (May 2011): 11–20.

42. Einat Manoff, "Counter Mapping Return," *Sedek: A Journal on the Ongoing Nakba* 6 (May 2011): 1–10.

43. Sandi Hilal, Alessandro Petti, Eyal Weizman, "Decolonizing Architecture," in *Solution 196–213: United States of Palestine-Israel*, ed. Joshua Simon (Berlin: Sternberg, 2011), 98. For additional discussions of decolonizing architecture in Israel-Palestine, see Ohad Meromi and Joshua Simon, "Repurposing the Kibbutz," in *Solution 196–213*, ed. Simon, 116–21.

44. See, for example, Ronit Lentin, *Co-Memory and Melancholia: Israelis Memorialising the Palestinian Nakba* (Manchester, UK: University of Manchester Press, 2010).

45. Quoted in Meera Shah, "'A Different Kind of Memory,'" 37.

46. Eitan Bronstein, "A Request from the Palestinian Refugees," May 2010. http://www.zochrot.org/en/content/israeli-nakba-day-'our-humanity-bound-your-right-return.

47. Zochrot program director Norma Musih bluntly states the implications of Palestinian refugee return: "Yes, it will be the end of Israel as we know it today, a racist state that is only for Jews." Quoted in Meera Shah, "'A Different Kind of Memory,'" 37. The dismantling of the colonial, discriminatory elements of the Zionist project, however, need not be the equivalent of eliminating the Jewish character of whatever state or states are present in Israel-Palestine, nor need it be the equivalent of denying Jewish attachment to the land. It simply means that Jewish return to and life in the land need not and should not be tied to Palestinian dispossession. Similarly, while Palestinian refugee return would undercut any supposed Israeli "right" to maintaining a Jewish demographic majority, it would not need to conflict with individual or communal rights of Israeli Jews. See Michael Kagan's analysis of how refugee return does not need to come into tension with authentic Israeli Jewish rights. See Kagan, *Do Israeli Rights Conflict with the Palestinian Right of*

Return? Working Paper no. 10 (Bethlehem: Badil Resource Center for Palestinian Residency and Refugee Rights, 2005).

48. My focus here on Zochrot's mapping performances in and around 'Imwas should not obscure the fact that Palestinians were active before Zochrot's establishment in commemorating the village and calling for the return of its refugees. See, for example, the appeal compiled by Sami Deeb, an exiled Palestinian Christian lawyer in Switzerland: *Reconstruct Emmaus: A Symbol of Peace and Justice* (St. Sulpice, Switzerland: Association for the Reconstruction of Emmaus, 1987).

49. Aron Shai, "The Fate of Abandoned Arab Villages in Israel, 1965–1969," *History and Memory* 18, no. 2 (Fall/Winter 2006): 86–106.

50. Noga Kadman, *Erased from Space and Consciousness: Depopulated Palestinian Villages in the Israeli-Zionist Discourse* [Hebrew] (Jerusalem: November Books, 2008) and Naama Meishar, "Fragile Guardians: Nature Reserves and Forests Facing Arab Villages," in *Constructing a Sense of Place: Architecture and the Zionist Discourse*, ed. Haim Yacobi (Aldershot, UK and Burlington, VT: Ashgate, 2004), 303–25.

51. Eitan Bronstein, *Restless Park: Zochrot and the Latrun Villages*, trans. Charles Kamen (Tel Aviv: Zochrot, 2007), 2.

52. Carol Bardenstein highlights the fictional return of a father and son to 'Imwas in the novel, *Road to the Sea*, by the Palestinian writer Faruq Wadi. A tree proves crucial to unlocking the father's memories of the village: "This was our new house! May God destroy them! I knew it from this China tree!" Quoted in Bardenstein, "Trees, Forests, and the Shaping of Palestinian and Israeli Collective Memory," in *Acts of Memory: Cultural Recall in the Present*, ed. Mieke Bal, Jonathan Crewe, and Leo Spitzer (Hanover, NH and London: University Press of New England, 1999), 157.

53. Bronstein, *Restless Park*, 18.

54. Ibid., 4.

55. Ibid.

56. Ibid., 7.

57. Ibid.

58. Ibid., 6.

59. Ibid.

60. Ibid., 14.

61. Ibid., 15.

62. Eitan Bronstein, *Studying the* Nakba, 9.

63. Ibid., 11.

64. Ilan Gur-Ze'ev, *Destroying the Other's Collective Memory* (New York: Peter Lang, 2003), 37. See also Ilan Gur-Ze'ev and Ilan Pappé, "Beyond the Destruction of the Other's Collective Memory: Blueprints for a Palestinian/Israeli Dialogue," *Theory Culture & Society* 20, no. 1 (2003): 93–108. While Gur-Ze'ev, Pappé, and Bronstein offer persuasive analyses of Israeli Jewish responses to the *nakba*, Yehouda Shenhav's caution—that the Israeli Jewish attitude toward the prospect of acknowledging the *nakba* is not uniform—is well taken. See Shenhav, *The Arab Jews: A Postcolonial Reading of Nationalism, Religion, and Ethnicity* (Stanford: Stanford University Press, 2006), 134–35.

65. Eitan Bronstein, "They Are Afraid: On the Relationship of Jews in Israel to the Palestinian Refugees," presentation at the Tel Aviv University Conference on "Zionism: Ideology vs. Reality" (May 31, 2005).

66. Bronstein, *Studying the* Nakba, 16.

67. Eitan Bronstein, "The Nakba—An Event That Did Not Occur (Although It Had to Occur)," December 14, 2005.

68. Dan Rabinowitz, *Overlooking Nazareth: The Ethnography of Exclusion in Galilee* (Cambridge: Cambridge University Press, 1997), 77.

69. Rabinowitz adds that these fears "are supplemented by an inherently orientalist outlook, so prevalent in Israel, which portrays the outpost, in fact the entire Zionist project including

hityashvut [settlement], as a singularly positive, if not redemptive element in an otherwise wild and primitive Middle East." Ibid., 81.

70. Bronstein, "They Are Afraid."

71. Eitan Bronstein, "'*Min wayn jaye inti?*' Where the Hell Do You Come From? Repression of the Nakba and Post-Trauma among Jews in Israel," lecture presented at IARPP Conference, Tel Aviv (June 2009).

72. Bronstein, "They Are Afraid."

73. Quoted in Meera Shah, "'A Different Kind of Memory,'" 37.

74. Edward Said, "Invention, Memory, and Place," *Critical Inquiry* 26, no. 2 (Winter 2000): 175–92.

75. Ilan Pappé, "The Exilic Homeland of Edward W. Said," *interventions* 81 (March 2006): 14.

76. See, for example, Shira Robinson, "Commemoration under Fire: Palestinian Responses to the 1956 Kafr Qasim Massacre," in *Memory and Violence in the Middle East and North Africa*, ed. Ussama Makdisi and Paul A. Silverstein (Bloomington and Indianapolis: Indiana University Press, 2006), 103–32.

77. Pappé stresses that reconciliation requires that "the past evil of transfer" be "rectified by the repatriation of those who were expelled." Pappé, "The Visible and Invisible in the Israeli-Palestinian Conflict," in *Exile and Return: Predicaments of Palestinians and Jews*, ed. Ann Lesch and Ian Lustick (Philadelphia: University of Pennsylvania Press, 2005), 295.

78. Kerwin Lee Klein, "On the Emergence of Memory in Historical Discourse," *Representations* 69 (Winter 2000): 145, 144.

79. Eitan Bronstein, "Position Paper on Posting Signs at the Sites of Demolished Palsetinian Villages," January 2002. Available at http://zochrot.org/en/content/position-paper-posting-signs-sites-demolished-palestinian-villages.

80. Vincent Lloyd, *The Problem with Grace* (Stanford: Stanford University Press, 2011), 120–21.

81. Ibid., 120.

82. Ibid., 110.

83. Ibid., 121, 111.

84. William T. Cavanaugh, *Torture and Eucharist: Theology, Politics, and the Body of Christ* (Oxford: Blackwell, 1998), 275.

85. Lloyd, *The Problem with Grace*, 111.

86. Ibid., 120.

87. Philip Sheldrake, *Spaces for the Sacred: Place, Memory, and Identity* (Baltimore: Johns Hopkins University Press, 2001), 77, 80, 87, 88.

88. Ibid., 86.

89. Lloyd, *The Problem with Grace*, 120.

90. Ibid., 121.

91. Jean-Yves Lacoste, *Experience and the Absolute: Disputed Questions on the Humanity of Man*, trans. Mark Raftery-Skehan (New York: Fordham University Press, 2004), 22.

92. Ibid., 9.

93. Ibid., 175, 25.

94. Ibid., 12.

95. Ibid., 98, 174.

96. Ibid., 37.

97. Ibid., 25.

98. Ibid.

99. For the distinction between "seeing" and "showing" Jesus, see Jean-Luc Marion, "'They Recognized Him; And He Became Invisible to Them,'" *Modern Theology* 18, no. 2 (April 2002): 151.

100. Ibid., 147.

101. For key texts in which Virilio develops his concept of dromocracy, see Paul Virilio, *Pure War* (Los Angeles: Semiotext(e), 1983) and *Speed and Politics* (Los Angeles: Semiotext(e), 2006). As Virilio explains, "the strategic value of the non-place of speed has definitively supplanted that of place, and the question of possession of Time has revived that of territorial appropriation." *Speed and Politics*, 149.

102. So, for example, Eyal Weizman, citing Virilio, underscores that "the checkpoints not only carve up space, but divide up time as well." Weizman, *Hollow Land: Israel's Architecture of Occupation* (London: Verso, 2007), 148. Julie Peteet describes how "time has thus become another commodity, like land and water, which Israel expropriates from the population in the occupied Palestinian territories." Peteet, "Stealing Time," *Middle East Report* no. 248 (Fall 2008): 14–15. Sharon Rotbard, meanwhile, analyzes how the traditional "wall and tower" (*homa umigdal*) construction of Zionist colonies was modeled according to principles of fortification and observation that "molded the entire landscape as a network of points, as an autonomous layer spread above the existing landscape, transforming the country by dividing it, not according to natural, territorial divisions, but according to dromological divisions, according to the speed of transportation and the lines of infrastructure." Rotbard, "Wall and Tower (Homa Umigdal): The Mold of Israeli Architecture," in *A Civilian Occupation: The Politics of Israeli Architecture*, ed. Rafi Segal and Eyal Weizman (London: Verso, 2003), 52. See also Peter Lagerquist, "In the Labyrinth of Solitude: Time, Violence, and the Eternal Frontier," *Middle East Report* no. 248 (Fall 2008): 24–32.

103. Virilio, *Pure War*, 59.

104. John Collins, "Dromocratic Palestine," *Middle East Report* no. 248 (Fall 2008): 8.

105. Ibid., 10.

106. Ibid., 13.

107. Virilio, *Speed and Politics*, 153.

108. For Yoder's understanding of patience as a moral/political stance, see Yoder's essay "'Patience' as Method in Moral Reasoning: Is an Ethic of Discipleship 'Absolute'?" in Yoder, *A Pacifist Way of Knowing: John Howard Yoder's Nonviolent Epistemology*, ed. Christian E. Early and Ted G. Grimsrud (Eugene, OR: Cascade, 2010), 113–32. For an analysis of Yoder's conception of patience in relation to Virilio on dromocracy, see Chris K. Huebner, "Patience, Witness, and the Scattered Body of Christ: Yoder and Virilio on Knowledge, Politics, and Speed," in *A Mind Patient and Untamed: Assessing John Howard Yoder's Contribution to Theology, Ethics, and Peacemaking*, ed. Ben C. Ollenburger and Gayle Gerber Koontz (Telford, PA: Cascadia, 2004), 56–74.

109. Edward Said, *Culture and Imperialism*, 402. See also Paul Virilio, *L'Insécurité du territoire* (Paris: Stock, 1976), 88ff.

110. Julie Peteet, "Cosmopolitanism and the Subversive Space of Protests," *Jerusalem Quarterly* 37 (Spring 2009): 95.

111. Azoulay, *From Palestine to Israel*, 16.

112. Walter Benjamin, "Theses on the Philosophy of History," in Benjamin, *Illuminations*, ed. Hannah Arendt and trans. Harry Zohn (New York: Schocken, 1968), 257, 263. It should come as no surprise that several of Zochrot's pamphlets have prominently displayed quotations from Benjamin's "Theses on the Philosophy of History": not only from the famous passage about the angel of history, but also from the description of the historian brushing "history against the grain" (257).

113. Building on Benjamin's conception of messianic time, Aloni asserts that "the binational reality (which is always already) is not merely compulsory; it is, fundamentally, the realization of a dream for both Jewish and Palestinian emancipation." Aloni, *What Does a Jew Want?*, 110. He continues that "it is binationalism that is already here, knocking on our door from both sides of the wall" (143).

114. Slyomovics, *The Object of Memory*, xxii.

115. Ibid., 117.

116. Jonathan Boyarin, "A Response from New York: Return of the Repressed?" in *Grasping Land*, ed. Ben-Ari and Bilu, 219.

117. Eviatar Zerubavel, *Time Maps: Collective Memory and the Social Shape of the Past* (Chicago and London: University of Chicago Press, 2003), 119.

118. Ibid., 110.

119. The discussion over the next several paragraphs will draw from the chapter "Beyond Human Rights" in Agamben, *Means without End: Notes on Politics*, trans. Vincenzo Binetti and Cesare Casarino (Minneapolis: University of Minnesota Press, 2000), chapter 2. This first English translation of this essay appeared as "We Refugees," trans. Michael Rocke, *Symposium* 49, no. 2 (Summer 1995): 114–19. I will follow Binetti and Casarino's translation except in one instance, for reasons discussed in note 126 below.

120. Agamben, *Means without End*, 16. Agamben refers to Arendt's essay, "We Refugees," most recently included in Arendt, *The Jewish Writings*, ed. Jerome Kohn and Ron H. Feldman (New York: Schocken, 2007), 264–74.

121. Agamben, *Means without End*, 21.

122. Ibid., 24. Julie Peteet echoes Agamben on this point, noting that because "the political logic of the modern state indicates a striving for symmetry among sovereignty, territory, and citizenship," refugees challenge the nation-state order. "In the modern order of nation-states, the refugee perpetually calls into question the nature of the state and society." Peteet, *Landscape of Hope and Despair: Palestinian Refugee Camps* (Philadelphia: University of Pennsylvania Press, 2005), 46.

123. See, for example, Agamben, *The Coming Community* (Minneapolis: University of Minnesota Press, 1993).

124. Agamben, *Means without End*, 24.

125. For analyses of contemporary realities in Israel-Palestine drawing on Agamben's notions of "bare life" and sovereignty as the "state of exception" in which the law is suspended, see Nurhan Abujidi, "The Palestinian States of Exception and Agamben," *Contemporary Arab Affairs* 2, no. 2 (April-June 2009): 272–91 and Yehouda Shenhav and Yael Berda, "The Colonial Foundations of the State of Exception: Juxtaposing the Israeli Occupation of the Palestinian Territories with Colonial Bureaucratic History," in *The Power of Inclusive Exclusion: Anatomy of Israeli Rule in the Occupied Palestinian Territories*, ed. Adi Ophir, Michal Givoni, and Sari Hanafi (New York: Zone Books, 2009), 337–73. Agamben develops his conceptions of bare life as existence subjected to the sovereign state of exception most fully in *Homo Sacer: Sovereign Power and Bare Life* (Stanford: Stanford University Press, 1998) and *State of Exception* (Chicago: University of Chicago Press, 2005).

126. Agamben, "We Refugees," 118. I have used Rocke's translation of this passage, given Binetti and Casarino's mistranslation of "in esodo l'una nell'altra" as "in a condition of exodus from each other" in *Means without End*, 24. The prepositional phrase "nell'altra" means *into* the other, not *from* the other. By translating this phrase the way they have, Binetti and Casarino have subverted the clear thrust of Agamben's text, which underscores the necessity of accepting the imbrication of Palestinians and Israeli Jews with one another, rather than calling for their separation or flight from one another. Rocke's translation, in addition to being grammatically correct, preserves Agamben's point that the two communities are heading out from a past of being bound to the circumscribed politics of the nation-state into a future of being mutually implicated with each other. For the original Italian, see Agamben, *Mezzi senza fine: Note sulla politica* (Torino: Bollati Boringhieri, 1996), 27. Many thanks to my late father, the talented linguist, Anthony Epp, for his counsel about this translation.

127. Agamben, *Means without End*, 25. Agamben's vision of reciprocal extraterritoriality and of Palestinians and Israeli Jews moving "in exodus one into the other" resonates with Doreen Massey's account of place. In contrast to nationalist portrayals of place as simple, static, and bounded, Massey advocates a complex and fluid "view of place" in which "localities can in a sense be present in one another, both inside and outside at the same time," an understanding of place

that "stresses the construction of specificity through interrelations rather than through the imposition of boundaries and the counterposition of one identity against another." Massey, *Space, Place, and Gender*, 7.

128. Agamben, *Means without End*, 25–26.

129. Building on Agamben's work, Maisaa Youssef asserts that the borders of the nation-state come apart in the figure of the refugee. In the case of Israel-Palestine, that means that taking seriously the materiality of Palestinian refugees upends the "statist logic" of peace processes tied to the nationalist presumptions of two-state solutions. Youssef, "Peace Material: Giorgio Agamben and the Israeli Palestinian Peace Accords," *New Formations* 62 (Autumn 2007): 109–10.

130. Maayan Amir, Ruti Sela, and Raji Bathish, "Exterritory Project," in *Solution 196–213*, ed. Simon, 86.

131. Ibid., 82.

132. Dan Rabinowitz, "Postnational Palestine/Israel? Globalization, Diaspora, Transnationalism, and the Israeli-Palestinian Conflict," *Critical Inquiry* 26, no. 4 (Summer 2000): 757–58.

133. Sari Hanafi, "New Model for Nation-State," in *Solution 196–213*, ed. Simon, 17–18. See also Hanafi, "Finding a Just Solution for the Palestinian Refugee Problem: Toward an Extra-Territorial Nation-State," in *Palestinian-Israeli Impasse: Exploring Alternative Solutions to the Palestine-Israel Conflict*, ed. Mahdi Abdul Hadi (Jerusalem: PASSIA, 2005), 187–204.

134. David Newman, "From National to Post-National Territorial Identities in Israel-Palestine," *GeoJournal* 53 (2001): 235.

135. See David Newman, "Shared Spaces-Separate Spaces: The Israel-Palestine Peace Process," *GeoJournal* 39, no. 4 (Autumn 1996): 363–75; Ammiel Alcalay, *After Jews and Arabs: Remaking Levantine Culture* (Minneapolis: University of Minnesota Press, 1993); and Gil Z. Hochberg, *In Spite of Partition: Jews, Arabs, and the Limits of Separatist Imagination* (Princeton: Princeton University Press, 2007). Such practices resonate with what Agamben calls profanation: "To profane," Agamben writes, "does not simply mean to abolish or erase separations but to make new uses of them." Agamben, *Profanations* (New York: Zone Books, 2007), 87.

136. Iris Marion Young, "Self-Determination as Non-Domination: Ideals Applied to Palestine/Israel," *Ethnicities* 5, no. 2 (2005): 139.

Conclusion

The two-state solution to the Palestinian-Israeli conflict, politicians warn, is in peril. Decisive action must be taken to preserve its viability. "If we do not make progress very soon, then the two-state solution could become impossible to achieve," cautioned British Foreign Secretary William Hague, in February 2013, sounding a common theme. Jordan's King Abdullah II anxiously wondered if "we're not too late," and underscored that "the two-state solution will only last as long as [U.S. President Barack] Obama's term."

The king's dire assessment would carry more weight if Jordanian officials hadn't been issuing declarations about the nearly terminal condition of the two-state solution for over a decade. The imminent demise of the two-state solution has been touted repeatedly since the signing of the Oslo Accords in the first half of the 1990s, almost always as an attempt to renew the perpetually on-again, off-again peace talks between the State of Israel and the PLO (at least the part of the PLO leadership that now resided in Ramallah while leading the Palestinian Authority). Palestinian academic and then-PLO official Sari Nusseibeh declared in 2001 that "[p]erhaps today is the last chance for a two-state solution." Five years later, PLO Representative to the United Kingdom Manuel Hassassian grimly repeated the same assessment. Newspaper and television analysts have in turn taken up the refrain, imploring the two sides to take action before the closing window on the two-state solution shuts for good.

As I write these lines, a new round of peace talks between the Israeli government led by Binyamin Netanyahu and the Mahmoud Abbas-led PLO/Palestinian Authority has just gotten underway after significant pressure from U.S. Secretary of State John Kerry. Once again, pundits have been raising the alarm that *this time*, this round of talks, is really, truly the final chance for the two-state solution. Yet even as politicians and pundits claim that the obituary for the two-state solution is about to be written, they also insist that the two-state solution is the only game in town. The two-state solution has been buried repeatedly, only to be revived time and again, maintaining a zombie-like existence through a never-ending (if occasionally suspended) peace process that has the effect not of resolving the Palestinian-Israeli conflict but rather of providing window dressing for the ongoing Israeli colonization of Occupied Territories. Any illusions to the contrary should have been dispelled when the

State of Israel announced plans for settlement expansion just as the most recent round of the never-ending peace process got underway in the summer of 2013.

The peace processes of the past two decades have been an expression of Zionism's national colonial theology, as Israel has sought to reinforce and extend landscapes of partition. Israeli politicians on the center-right—like Netanyahu, Ehud Olmert, and Ariel Sharon—joined Israeli politicians of the center-left (like Ehud Barak and Yair Lapid) in proclaiming themselves to be champions of a two-state solution, not because they became convinced that Palestinians have a just place in the land, but rather because the rhetorical embrace of the two-state solution now goes hand-in-hand with unilateral separation from the Palestinians (through walls, fences, checkpoints, and settlement construction) while helping to stave off criticisms that highlight the ethnocratic character of Israeli rule (and to fend off comparisons to apartheid-era South Africa). As Amnon Raz-Krakotzkin has explained, the peace process for Israelis has become an extension of the Zionist conceptual erasure of Palestinians through mappings of partition that would leave Palestinians confined to ever-smaller, discontiguous parcels of territory.[1]

Not surprisingly, few Palestinians hold out much hope that a just resolution will emerge from this newest round—or any future round—of the peace process, even as some worry that the Palestinian leadership is under tremendous pressure to accept an agreement in which the PLO trades refugee rights (including rights of return) for a mini-state in parts of the Occupied Territories. Such a resolution seems unlikely, for the Palestinian leadership has its own political restrictions and popular legitimacy to consider.

Yet if even a supposedly final agreement surprisingly issues from these latest negotiations, with Palestinian leaders relinquishing the refugee right of return for a state in limited parts of the West Bank and the Gaza Strip, thus "freeing" the State of Israel from the supposed demographic threat that Palestinian refugees and the Palestinians of the Occupied Territories represent, Zionism's national colonial theologies and cartographies will at a minimum continue to be challenged by internally displaced and other Palestinians within Israel who contest mappings of space that present the land's places as exclusively Jewish while erasing or obscuring the ongoing Palestinian presence. The percentage of the Palestinian population inside Israeli (i.e., excluding the Occupied Territories) is growing steadily, as are Israeli Jewish calls to limit that growth and to develop internal methods of separation to shield the Israeli Jewish polity from this alleged threat. So, for example, Bedouin and other Palestinians inside Israel are now mobilizing to oppose the Prawer Plan, the latest in a decades-long policy of uprooting, dispossessing, and territorially confining

Bedouin communities through ethnocratic land practices. Israeli politicians may insist, in negotiations with Palestinians, that Palestinians recognize Israel as a "Jewish state," but Palestinians inside Israel will insist, along with Elias Chacour, that they belong to the land, producing counter-cartographies that map the always already heterogeneous character of the land's places and thus rejecting Zionist mappings that would exclude them.

The peace process of the last two decades (including its current iteration) has proven to be a profound disappointment for those who long for a shared future of justice, peace, and mutuality in the land for Palestinians and Israeli Jews alike. For those looking for futures beyond zero-sum cartographic battles and nationalist mappings of space that are inevitably tied to practices of exclusion, hope will not, I suggest, likely be found at the negotiating tables of the current or the next round of the perpetual peace process, for that process is captive to and is designed to perpetuate a politics of partition. Political theologies (like mainstream forms of Zionism) that negate exile embrace this politics of partition, and in turn justify the violence and dispossession that partition perpetuates. Hope is instead to be found among the internally displaced of Kafr Bir'im and the Zochrot Association, among individuals and groups that are already now holding exilic vigils in the land and are thus through their actions mapping a shared landscape and outlining the contours of a coming community in which Palestinians and Israeli Jews find refuge in one another, recognizing one another as fellow exiles. May their numbers increase.

Notes

1. Amnon Raz-Krakotzkin, "A Peace without Arabs: The Discourse of Peace and the Limits of Israeli Consciousness," in *After Oslo: New Realities, Old Problems,* ed. George Giacaman and Dag Jørund Lønning (London: Pluto, 1998), 59–76.

Index of Names and Subjects

CPSIA information can be obtained at www.ICGtesting.com
Printed in the USA
LVOW12s1023111113

360816LV00005B/11/P